Antiques in Interior Design

ANTIQUES IN INTERIOR DESIGN

SOUTH BRUNSWICK • NEW YORK - A. S. BARNES AND COMPANY

BY HENRY LIONEL WILLIAMS AND OTTALIE K.WILLIAMS

LONDON - THOMAS YOSELOFF LTD

©1966 by Henry Lionel Williams and Ottalie K. Williams
Library of Congress Catalogue Card Number: 66-28022

A. S. Barnes and Co., Inc.
South Brunswick, New Jersey

Thomas Yoseloff Ltd
18 Charing Cross Road
London W. C. 2, England

6446
Printed in the United States of America

Authors' Note

This book is addressed to those who seek to acquire possessions with which to furnish their homes not as status symbols, but as repositories of the things they take delight in owning for their practical, artistic, or sentimental value. It is meant for those whose home interiors are designed — whether by themselves as amateurs or by professionals — for their own particular comfort and delight and not for mere display or simply to advertise their superior taste. It is for those possessed of the realization that objects collected with care and affection reveal not only the owner's discrimination, but his personality. The truth is that the world is sadly in need of those who strive for beauty and charm in their surroundings, who recognize these qualities when they see evidence of them; those who have little regard for passing fashion hate conformity for conformity's sake, and have as their guide a well-developed aesthetic sense.

These are not qualities one is born with (though one may have an inborn predilection toward them). These qualities must be acquired and cultivated by the study of practical examples, by learning to differentiate between the good and the shoddy, the noble and the pretentious, the beautiful and the banal.

The practical way of familiarizing oneself with interiors possessing the most desirable of these attributes is to observe and analyze and compare what has been done in homes of consequence, be they country house or city apartment, examining in particular the work of professional interior designers, examples of which are presented in these pages. Here, too, will be found a record of some of the artifacts and materials and furniture designs available, and a guide to the application of color and pattern and texture, the place of accessories as influencing the total décor, and the miracles that can be worked with them by the expert and, more rarely, by the talented tyro, who may lack the professional's skill, resources, and daring, yet achieve something satisfying, perhaps even enviable, that comes close to the heart's desire.

Interior Settings

Except for the actual interiors designed by decorators — or decorated by designers — many of these rooms illustrated are of settings and not of actual interiors, though they are the work of professionals and must be studied as such. Some of the pictures are not altogether practical, with furniture maneuvered to make the best picture or establish a point regardless of possible distortions. Nevertheless, despite these possible shortcomings from the reader's viewpoint, each picture has been selected because it does incorporate at least one basic idea, developed by an interior designer of standing, which can be adopted *in toto* or modified so as to become adaptable to some specific room or situation. The suggested arrangements can be changed in detail, substituting colors or furniture pieces, or used merely as a stimulus to the creative capacity in developing something entirely new. A picture designed to sell a rug, for instance, may actually become the basis of a grouping in which the principal feature is a floor entirely bare (or vice versa!), and so will have served a distinctly useful purpose.

Contents

Antiques in Interior Design

The Theme

These are the houses whose interiors smell of romance — anachronistic dwellings that gather to themselves the best of everything from everywhere — houses that have grown out of improvisation and began where the interior designer left off — more often than not out of some seed he has planted in the work he has done.—Anon.

The design and decoration of house interiors is a three-dimensional art involving color, texture, form, and the disposal of space. Like all arts, it calls for both knowledge of the elements involved and a cultivated taste to guide the creative instinct so that desirable combinations of beauty and utility will result and the interiors constitute both a practical and aesthetic success, and *one that is in keeping with the times*.

During the past half century or so, a quiet revolution in home furnishing has virtually abolished the so-called "period" room as an ideal for everyday living. At the same time there has been a notable increase in the popularity of antiques for contemporary interiors. Astonishing as this seeming paradox may appear, it is actually a part of a natural development based on a growing recognition of two important facts: 1) that houses furnished exclusively with period pieces provide little of the unusual or unexpected that modern living demands, and 2) that a greater variety of memorable interiors can be devised by mixing furniture styles than by adhering to any one design.

In putting this latter concept into practice, antiques of countries the world over as well as furniture pieces of a variety of dates and places of origin have played — and are playing — a vital role. Today, in the case of both old and new artifacts, it is the quality, design, character and, above all, the mutual affinity between the individual pieces that form the principal criteria by which their desirability is judged. The most notable result of all this has been the achievement of rooms — whether of antique, traditional, or contemporary style — possessing distinctive individualities and expressing a variety of moods unattainable in any other way.

In the beginning this transition was simply a matter of evolution, and almost universal. It was brought about quite naturally by the overlapping of furniture styles available to succeeding generations beginning in this country with the early eighteenth century when the Queen Anne was eclipsed by the Chippendale (and walnut by mahogany shortly thereafter).

In a little while, of course, Chippendale was to succumb to Sheraton and Hepplewhite (with a nod to Adam and his classical ensembles so suited to the Federal period); to Phyfe with his Grecian motifs from Herculaneum, plus McIntire and others who adapted English Regency, and French Directoire and Empire to the American taste. These culminated in the progressive and variegated Victorian styles and European period revivals representative of the materialistic industrial age, many of them for long scorned in our time as unworthy of

11

twentieth-century interiors and symbolic of things machine-made and mass produced in the name of profit to the neglect of art.

While there were those who seized upon the latest fashions in furniture throughout these passing decades, abandoning the old in favor of the new, most were apt to combine to some degree pieces of the various styles. This fact is largely attributed to heirlooms handed down through several generations, and the increasing availability of oriental rugs, Chinese export porcelains, lacquered screens, teak furniture and other foreign treasures which the clipper ships had brought from the Far East. Out of this practice arose the fashion of spicing the new with the old — or vice versa. Many, no doubt, were astonished, if not delighted to find that, regardless of their origins, a wide range of these assorted pieces looked very well together, while a touch of exotic enlivened many a sober setting. Eventually it was only the purists and those collectors needing a formally correct background for their treasures who continued to insist on strict separation of the pieces according to periods, styles, and origins, as they do to this day.

In our time, it would seem, this practice of furnishing with compatible pieces, both new and old, from all parts of the world, civilized or primitive, has been carried to its logical conclusion. It has also solved a lot of furnishing problems in the process, while giving the antiques a new authority and a new lease on life, even reconciling them to the astringent modern, adding a touch of warmth and romance to the otherwise bare and stark interiors which rely for their impact on contrast and rhythm.

What all of this amounts to, therefore, is that, despite the present preoccupation with eclecticism in furnishing (whose true nature so many still fail to realize), this is actually more than ever the age of the antique, in the broader meaning of the term. Furthermore, the mixing of old and new styles and backgrounds enables full use to be made of even the less endearing of Victorian pieces in evoking the past without actually reproducing the setting — or the clutter! Truly antique, handmade furniture pieces — and even antique accessories — have the further advantage of supplying a much-needed note otherwise unattainable, interjecting fragments of fossilized history that remind us of people and events of the past (whether of our own civilization or more ancient ones)

while adding a touch of continuity which implies a measure of immortality which we all like to dwell upon.

First of all, however, these antiques are, or should be, examples of original handcraftsmanship on which time has worked its magic, and which can never be duplicated in this hurried modern age. But we do not need to drown ourselves in a sea of such things to secure the effects we desire. Indeed, the modern approach is to select fewer examples with greater care so that we treasure them more. In doing so we give them added importance by setting them apart, and calling attention to their interest if not charm by displaying them against a background of fabrics, patterns, and colors that will best emphasize their contribution to the required mood and degree of formality of the total interior, something that was rarely thought of in the early days, and is sometimes overlooked even now.

This is one of the reasons why antiques today are used with far greater freedom than ever before. They contribute something that nothing else can do and in ways never before realized. However, in making a selection it is wise to remember that no one historical period, in America or elsewhere, can lay claim to the best of design, construction, decoration, and finish. On the contrary, one of the most important discoveries to be made in furnishing with antiques was that the very best of any period is likely to have an astonishing degree of compatibility with the best of almost any other, including the present, regardless of their sources — with one or two notable exceptions. Furthermore, any good period piece will not only look its best when grouped with equally fine examples that are distinctively different without being actually antagonistic, but will also most likely retain its individuality among equals, the group itself gaining in interest as a consequence.

From this discovery it is but a short step to the realization that other mixtures can be used and other contrasts devised by associating antique pieces with compatible designs of more recent vintage, and especially with copies or adaptations of antiques that would have been considered well made and impeccably finished even in their own day. And there are plenty of these to be had, many substituting happily for certain old originals which are now extremely rare or even unobtainable.

In these days therefore, when the antique does not have

12

to be the whole show, odd pieces can serve as a leavening that improves the total display by emphasizing classical design — a function that can also be assumed to a high degree by some modern reproductions so well designed, made, and finished that they are more likely to become the valued antiques of tomorrow.

One interesting development arising out of this current mode of furnishing is the growth in popularity of old-time foreign styles, especially those of the eighteenth- and early nineteenth-century French (Régence, Louis XV, and Empire in particular, which the newly revived Louis XIII of the early 1600's will have difficulty in overtaking), most of them diluted to good effect with American and other pieces instead of maintaining their strictly period integrity.

Still another notable fact that has come to be appreciated in recent times is that the triumph of the antique does not depend solely upon an historical setting of the kind in which it was originally staged. In other words, to our modern minds, a room full of first-class period furniture does not have to rely for its impressive effect upon a matching period background. Indeed, much of the old-time furniture seems to achieve new life and sparkle in a setting of rich, modern wallpapers, fabrics, and rugs regardless of a somber finish or unexciting design. And such discoveries are still to be made wherever new combinations are tried, perhaps, for example, with architectural type furniture removed from an environment of whitewashed walls into a setting of rich paneling — or vice versa — an experimental field in which highly decorative seventeenth- and eighteenth-century French pieces (especially those painted or gilded or richly inlaid) can produce some pleasant surprises.

In a less spectacular way, major antiquities as well as accessories, properly utilized, can help establish a note of individuality in any interior, often supplying an exotic touch that has little to do with age, especially if they should be unfamiliar objects, different in style or decoration from the rest, pieces whose origins and purposes are bound to arouse curiosity and comment. In some instances these differences in design and detail, if not actual purpose, make it possible to create a variety of distinctly different rooms within the same house or apartment. For example, one room may be made predominantly Chinese, another Scandinavian, and so on, utilizing prin-

cipal pieces sufficiently imposing to dominate the room, or smaller less-important ones strategically distributed so as to create an overall atmosphere of challenging mystery or merely endowing the familiar with a new and exotic air.

In general, therefore, the eclectic system allows for greater use of the imagination, a bolder experimentation, and there are few logical limits to what can be done without leading to a confusion of types and styles and purposes. These are some of the things to be demonstrated in the following pages, where differing solutions to the various decorating problems are shown by examples from the work of both amateur and professional designers in dealing with period, transitional, contemporary, and so-called modern interiors.

For purposes of comparison, the interiors shown here are grouped according to their purpose — living room, dining room, etc. — but the names of their designers are listed at the back of the book so that all rooms of the same house or apartment can be readily found.

In most of the houses it will be noticed that there is an over-riding motif or manner which ties together a variety of associated interiors that can express almost a mood, but never descends below a certain level of either freedom or formality. Totally unrelated groups of rooms are usually disconcerting. Here the backgrounds are as important as the contents, and the latter can be used in a variety of ways to create different impressions and set a different tone.

Some decorators carry this idea to its ultimate conclusion, using all sorts of objects to create an interior with what once would have been described as a Bohemian air — a type of interior useful for the small apartment where interest is paramount and style unimportant.

Normally, however, certain antique furniture pieces and accessories, or their modern counterparts, both domestic and foreign, play a variety of roles from pace-setter to nostalgic bibelot, and the uses of both the compatible and the antithetical in securing some desired effect are demonstrated. Some are notable for the taste displayed, others for cleverness, for the inspiration they reveal or the mere unusuality — a few of them admittedly to the point of absurdity — but all of them highly interesting if not amusing. What all of this suggests is that in every conceivable type of interior designed on today's prin-

1. Compatibility: From the stucco-ornamented ceiling of an all-white Greek-Revival room hangs a Waterford crystal chandelier beneath which a rose-red carpet is shared by an exquisite Venetian secretary in faded green, blue, and gold on parchment white; Italian Louis XV chairs in cream and gold with aqua and rose patterned chintz; a faux-marbre table in verde antico — a perfect example of compatibility plus the required mood that no unit could establish by itself.

ciples and under modern conditions, one has an exceedingly wide range of choice and ample opportunity for originality.

Whether any one of these rooms and groupings is the work of a professional designer, or a skilled amateur, each is photographed in such a manner as to simplify analysis of the elements involved and make it possible to evaluate the contribution of such elements to the total results. In making such an analysis it has to be kept in mind that any picture can only illustrate one particular aspect of the interior shown — and not always the most important one. Elsewhere, most of the background details such as floor and wall coverings, architectural features, lighting equipment, window treatment and so on, in a variety of styles for most rooms in any house are illustrated and analyzed, not only as an indication of what is available in the markets of the world, but also as a means of providing basic ideas (with possible exciting alternatives) from which novel and individual schemes of interior decoration can be developed.

It should be understood, however, that the solutions indicated to the various design and decorating problems are not based on any transient fashion or fad, nor are they dated. They will, therefore, be just as good tomorrow as yesterday because they are practical demonstrations of the modern concept of interior design through the subtle combination of old and new so as to secure the benefits of both in alloying comfort and convenience with charm and beauty — in creating surroundings that are timeless expressions of taste and individuality invested with the desired personality and mood in which the owner will feel mentally and physically at ease. These interiors are not meant to be copied, but they can profitably be analyzed. With the help of those materials and other adjuncts to furnishing which are shown and described, various other combinations of elements can be devised to produce different solutions to the same problems and original and striking answers to new ones, providing always that the basic principles of the eclectic system of interior design are fully understood and due attention is paid to the subject of compatibility and the liberties that can be taken with it in the search for special effects.

The majority of illustrations, therefore, should serve to display the varied and extensive possibilities inherent

14

in the eclectic system of furnishing, with special reference to the antique and the exotic, as applied to strictly American interiors plus American adaptations of European and oriental décors. They demonstrate ways in which the old can best be mixed with the familiar in developing interiors in many moods and periods from later medieval to modern. In these illustrations, the antiques employed may range from some small bibelot or a single oil painting to the major furniture pieces, in some cases serving as significant though relatively unimportant accents; in others establishing distinct period settings in which the old are perhaps indistinguishable from the new, while both exemplify the principle that though it is the total atmosphere that counts, even the smallest detail may influence the whole.

This eclectic system, then, is actually no more than a realistic attitude in adapting things of the past to the uses of the present, while taking advantage of the availability of objects of virtue from other parts of the world to extend the range of interest and, coincidentally, substituting the dynamic for the static so often inherent in the purely period room. In any event, it would be impossible to range through these beautiful examples of recently designed interiors by those who know most about such things without acquiring a new outlook — new ideas, new appreciations, new desires, and no doubt a sprinkling of new hates and aversions. Obviously no one interior can please everyone, or even interest some, but the ideas are there not merely to be copied but to be adapted to one's needs and purse — thanks to a clear understanding of the principles involved. And here it is the cultivated taste that must decide. As a certain English artist named Jackson was wont to advertise in the 1750's: "It is the choise (sic) not the price which discovers the true talent of the possessor!" — and never were truer words broadcast then or since!

PART ONE

Moods and Methods

It has long been recognized that furniture pieces of good design have much in common regardless of their styles, and that those with comparable characteristics can often be used together, with perhaps a contrasting piece dropped in for accent. This is one of the reasons rooms are no longer furnished with sets of anything, but with individual pieces selected for their compatibility. This mixing of designs is, in short, the eclectic method, and its chief merit is that it permits the use of an assortment of furniture styles regardless of their age or geographic origin, such objects being chosen because of their affinity, not their period.

Furnishing in the eclectic manner has the further advantage of offering greater diversity in matters of mood and character, and this is of particular consequence at a time when most people are possessed of an urge to get away from the commonplace and create for themselves an atmosphere reflecting something of their aims and ideals in a society where the lowest common denominator tends to set the pattern for living. To satisfy the average person of taste, this usually means that the interiors need to be not only interesting in a comfortable sort of way but satisfying aesthetically, reflecting a lively individuality in an age when all the social forces tend toward conformity, and that on a not particularly high level.

Happily, conditions in the decorating field are now more favorable in this respect than ever before. The choice of artifacts and materials is wider, and the range of styles and patterns of furniture and furnishings greater so that almost every conceivable mood can be captured and every nuance of taste and feeling expressed. It is for this reason that today the pursuit of perfection in strictly period décor has given away to that of investing a room with personality — the one thing that can spell the difference between two rooms of the same vintage — and even between rooms furnished with the same furniture and accessories by two separate designers.

All this, of course, does not mean that period interiors are altogether out of fashion. The ideal may remain but concessions must inevitably be made to modern living, to comfort and utility, so that it is but a small step to the admission of contemporary items and exotic bibelots from half a world away. At the other end of the scale, the most modern of houses may give shelter to interiors designed around antiques, while still others may rely for their distinctiveness on interiors that treat as antiques the art objects and furniture pieces of more recent periods not yet warranting the term antique.

Acceptance of these facts obviously does not diminish the importance of the antique in furnishing. Actually it extends that importance to rooms of any period or style, not excluding modern. And here, perhaps, it should be mentioned that modern antiquarians are tending to place less stock in dates in determining whether a certain piece is an antique or not. Within certain limits this is obviously all to the good, especially in dealing with pieces from the Far East, many of which show few signs of hoary age, particularly those made of hard woods such as teak. Such pieces naturally do not need to be very old to be interesting because of their exotic design and appearance.

The idea of mixing compatible pieces of various periods having been generally accepted, the era of eclectic furnishing may be said to have arrived. But since it has not noticeably contributed to the solution of shortages in the antiques field, still another door has been opened — that of providing a market for reproductions of the better-class antiques. Fortunately, some of the leading furniture manufacturers have, in recent times, found it possible to meet the demand for exceedingly well-made pieces that may be exact copies of the originals or modifications that often look more like old-time pieces than the antiques themselves. Where the processes of antiquing and mild distressing are omitted, the furniture undoubtedly looks as the antiques did before time and use had given them the patina and wear, the fading and unevenness of color that make them so precious to us today.

Actually some of these pieces are so well designed and made (despite the mechanical carving and machine work which may be a little too perfect unless hand-finished) that there is really no excuse for denying them equality with a true antique as many actually do. In any case, such pieces, whether accurate reproductions or

2. Perfection in Reproduction: a French commode of the Régence Period with the *pied-de-biche* foot. Photo 2a is an exact copy made in France which recaptures the delicate charm of the original.

20

adaptations of old originals, cannot logically be omitted from interiors planned in the eclectic manner in which, through judicious selection according to form, color and texture, certain units are combined with others of a different period or style with which they will be perfectly compatible. Furthermore, such odd pieces may be deliberately introduced in order to add spice to a grouping, or as accents in a room, even to the extent of establishing a focal point around which a complete ensemble can be arranged.

This is the reason that today we are not surprised to find rooms delightfully set out with single furniture items and accessories from England, France, Italy, or the Orient, some old, some new, but all representing the best that each country has to offer, interjected as accents or key pieces. Since this practice has been adopted in other civilized countries besides America, it may be concluded that the eclectic system of furnishing is international.

The value of furnishing according to this principle is that one is not restricted either to American antiques or American contemporary furniture. The whole world is opened up as a source of supply, multiplying a thousandfold the opportunities for adding elements of interest and surprise, the only limits being the extent of one's imagination — or the size of one's purse. At the same time the challenge to the decorator is greater because of the knowledge and organizational skill necessary to combine successfully certain contradictory, and possibly unfamiliar, elements.

A well-developed sense of form and color obviously is essential; an ability to contrive — to see the possibilities of something that the ordinary person would throw away, to detect the special in the otherwise commonplace, to possess a creative touch, especially in dealing with the rare and exotic from other lands with which one may not be familiar. Here, on occasion, a modicum of poetic inspiration may not come amiss. Fantasy, likewise, can be interesting — or outrageous — and while a touch of whimsey may not hurt, the shock treatment (which has its uses) may be less palatable to those who have to endure it for any length of time. On the other hand, nowhere are rules made to be broken more consistently than in interior decoration, though it takes an expert to know where to stop! This is the reason why more will be learned from studying what the experts do to get the effects they achieve than by trying to memorize a long list of do's and don'ts which fail to take notice of possible exceptions.

A general recognition of these things is largely responsible for the fact that today's decoration in private homes consists in no small measure of contriving relationships between mixed styles of furniture with an appropriate background to express character and induce a mood. Since the pieces themselves, together with the setting and accessories will vary with each interior, the individual rooms will naturally become invested with personalities of their own.

To be enjoyable, most up-to-date interiors need to be unselfconscious, paying small heed to convention, and preferably incorporating small elements of surprise — and therefore interest — which do not alter their basic character. Here the approach is important. A major problem is the avoidance of confusion of aim, of understanding the effect one is trying to achieve and being able to concentrate upon it.

It also has to be realized that there are usually many ways of accomplishing the same end. For instance, elegance can be combined with comfort by putting elegance first and adding comfort, or by making comfort the prime factor and elegance secondary — the result being a matter of emphasis. And while comfort may generally be equated with relaxation, it should combine the mental with the physical, the aesthetic aspects being taken care of by the elimination of disturbing and distracting features, leaving a residuum of quiet, uninsistent beauty that demands nothing beyond passive acceptance.

Besides providing for the use of contemporary interpretations of traditional styles, this new freedom no longer casts a disapproving look on the use of certain pieces for purposes for which they were never intended, such as reducing the height of antique cellarettes, drum and tea tables for use as coffee tables, adapting wine coolers, basin stands and dry sinks as planters, or even installing a *chaise percée* as a comfortable wing chair in the drawing room. Nevertheless, this tendency has to be watched with a critical eye, much depending upon the quality of the piece and its adaptability to the general décor, as distinguished from the intent to inject an element of surprise which, though permissible, and sometimes a welcome relief when not carried to extremes, would constitute bad decorating manners.

Except in the largest of mansions, the palazzos and chateaux, of which this country has some fascinating late nineteenth- and early twentieth-century examples still standing, the one thing to be avoided is an air of importance. The important room is necessarily possessive, and impressiveness is its least valuable element — except to those whose interiors are contrived as status symbols. These important rooms therefore often turn out to be less monuments to the ego than Frankenstein monsters which inevitably devour their creators, so that if a note of humor can occasionally be injected, so much the better.

These points need to be given particular emphasis in dealing with the unfamiliar — in furnishing with pieces, antique or otherwise, from foreign lands which introduce an exotic note and may easily deteriorate into an obvious affectation or suggest that the owner is a collector of the alien and strange.

Apart from this, it is definitely recognized that furniture groups comprised of pieces from a variety of countries throughout the world can be adapted to almost any type of setting, depending upon the effect desired. This serves to emphasize the fact that any worthwhile work of art or craftsmanship is timeless, and that backgrounds can be devised from the multiplicity of materials and techniques available to invest such a piece or grouping with almost any desired degree of significance. In other words, the background mood may be manipulated so that a room of almost any style can be made to appear elegant rather than imposing, the commonplace endowed with an air of romance, and an air of gayety be imposed upon the otherwise austere. Not that austerity is something to be avoided. It is, as a matter of fact, the latest thing in decorating as exemplified by the style of furniture and interior architecture of the Louis XIII period. This juxtaposes ruggedly monumental furniture and whitewashed stucco walls, a background which, incidentally, also brings out the best in both Early American furniture pieces and modern art. Such austerity, however, should not be confused with aridity into which it can easily degenerate in the hands of the inexpert, usually through lack of interesting touches. In strictly period rooms or

others lacking focus, a dominating accent such as a striking Cambodian figure, a twelfth-century Chinese goddess in stone, a white Cycladic idol or black African mask will add an exotic touch to a whole décor and lift it out of the commonplace. Similarly, a larger piece such as a single seventeenth-century Chinese lacquered armchair or a Ming rosewood coffer can bring to life a white-walled room whose furniture is of the starkest modern design.

When one enters a room one can sometimes decide at once whether it is appealing or not. But ordinarily first impressions are not reliable, and it is necessary to see it from more than one viewpoint, to analyze it before coming to any firm conclusion. Here, the placing of individual furniture pieces in relation to the points from which they will most frequenttly be seen is of the greatest importance and secondary only to the characteristics of the objects themselves. This is why two designers using the same material can create two entirely different interiors, and the colors they use are only part of the reason.

Relationships are of first importance in furnishing in the eclectic manner because everything that bears an interesting or exciting degree of affinity to another immediately establishes a mood which can influence the feel of an interior. If that combination relates well to the rest of the interior, the parts of which it is composed are unimportant. One most interesting bedroom had a pair of old iron hayracks flanking the bed, each with a polished semicircular board on top to serve as a lamp table. This small but imaginative touch tied in that end of the room with the opposite end which was occupied by an antique Spanish table with decorative iron braces supporting the legs. In this way the whole interior was given a certain unity, though no two pieces, except the hayracks, were alike.

For many decades it has been recognized that, with few exceptions, the best of antique furniture of the late seventeenth, eighteenth and early nineteenth century may be wholly compatible with the finest of modern classical designs, and even with some that have nothing in common beyond a pleasing wood grain. Nevertheless, this whole matter of compatibility more often than not calls for individual judgment regarding any particular piece from among the tremendous variety of styles available from which to choose.

In associating two different styles of furniture, however, it may be necessary on occasion to slightly modify one or the other to achieve the desired degree of compatibility. For example, if it is proposed to use Louis XV chairs alongside modern ones, such as Mies's Barcelona type, the mixture will be much more palatable if the French pieces are upholstered in leather of some telling color such as red. Properly carried out, this will not seriously detract from the appearance of the antique chairs which often are upholstered in heavy monochrome silk with the same dull luster as leather. On the other hand, reversing the process and covering the steel chairs with old-time fabric probably would not be so successful. In either case, the rest of the pieces would obviously have to be taken into consideration since both the eighteenth- and twentieth-century chairs would have to harmonize with them also. In passing, it should also be noted that this process has nothing in common with that of replacing horsehair in a wholly Victorian interior with a gayer fabric as is so often done. In such a case the pieces are presumably compatible to begin with. And, as the chintzes and other patterned fabrics were popular in the later Victorian era, there is no reason why they should not be used today.

This leads to consideration of fabrics generally in the eclectic interior, a major point being that many old-time woven materials are still reproduced in a wide variety of weaves and patterns and colors so that duplication is rarely a problem. In the eclectic interiors, however, where the new can mingle with the old as a matter of course, there is no reason why modern upholstery materials cannot be used on old pieces any more than new drapery fabrics and wall hangings to secure some special effect. As was noted earlier, the only yardstick is the degree of compatibility, the unifying quality that takes no stock of age, though the maintenance of an established degree of excellence among the furniture and furnishings may be a *sine qua non*.

In studying groupings for various rooms and purposes,

it will be observed that much of the American furniture consists of modern adaptations of early designs — our present valued antiques — from many countries, often in the newer furniture woods such as Polynesian koa, pecan, Carpathian elm, wild-grained teak, and so on, making use of their striking grain formations in place of inlays. These new styles and new finishes make possible variations in effects which cannot be captured by any other means.

These designs and the effects they produce — depending largely on the amount of carving, inlay, grain matching, and so on — must not be judged by comparison with the familiar traditional furniture of any period or provenance, but solely for what they contribute to any room, and the degree of taste they represent. Today many of the newer designs, apart from those of Scandinavian influence which display a notable economy of line and material, are loosely classed as Far Eastern or Mediterranean, though among the latter the influence of any one of these countries from Italy to Greece may occasionally be hard to detect in the court cabriole legs, the baroque curves, and the incised panel work, though Moorish lattice and arches can hardly be mistaken.

The natural course in the development of traditional designs in recent times seems to be in the direction of elaboration. Few such baroque innovations, however, appear to be wholly successful and need careful study before being adopted to distinguish between changes that improve and those that cheapen. The determining factor in such cases must then be quality, i.e., excellence of construction and manufacture, the amount of hand-finishing involved (often obvious only to the expert), and the quality of the finish whether rubbed or painted. Over-elaboration in either design or decoration is usually a warning sign!

These are all things to be seriously considered, for in the study of interior design one needs, above all things, to know furniture, its most important element.

The Drawing Room

The drawing room, or best parlor as it is sometimes called (a distinction based more on geography than means), is normally the most formal room in any home. Formality, therefore, should be the keynote of its interior design, the grouping general, the air patrician, representing the best that can be achieved in the style selected. Probably the sanctuary of the home's best antiques and most treasured furniture pieces, it should be the most meticulously designed of all interiors, expressing a quiet, unpretentious perfection. That is the ideal, admittedly rarely achieved, but nevertheless representing a goal to be aimed for in a room whose only raison d'etre is to provide a background for ceremonious occasions — the room in which important visitors are formally entertained and to which the feminine members of the family and the wives and daughters of guests are supposed to retire for the post-prandial coffee and liqueurs. This is, in short, one room in which formality takes precedence over comfort and quality over convenience. This is the showpiece of the home which (theoretically, at any rate) sets the pace for the rest of the interiors and, like a Sunday suit or party dress, reveals the social aspirations of the owners as well as their fundamental taste. Since taste, according to the old adage, is something that cannot be argued about, its manifestations vary tremendously, and, in the matter of drawing room interior design more often than not calls for professional help and guidance if unfortunate mistakes, admissible elsewhere, are to be avoided.

Elegant good taste, therefore, is the ideal, based on sincerity and the avoidance of pretense and sham. Luckily, however, this in no way limits the choice of style of treatment as the varied specimens presented here will attest.

The ideal drawing room for a house of a certain quality is represented by illustration 3. Its most obvious characteristic is formality in the background as well as the furniture. It will be observed that this particular drawing room has considerable architectural merit, not only as a result of its wide cornice and molded baseboard, its classical paneled and pilastered doorway, and its Adam mantel, but also because of its proportions — actual and visual — which together endow it with a basic dignity concomitant with its function.

Though this is not a particularly large room, the most is made of its dimensions by emphasizing the width of the chimney breast and similar expanses of clear, flat wall which are finished in a cool turquoise with off-white trim. Even the sash windows, reaching almost from floor to ceiling, are given a measure of stateliness by the geometrical precision of the pelmets which top off the floor-length draperies of while silk with turquoise fringes.

The rich overall carpeting and a large hearth rug of the same tone which has sculptured Greek-key border add to this atmosphere of sleek perfection in which each piece of furniture is of the best, its quality self-evident, with no suggestion of flamboyancy. The fireplace unit

3.

also meets these standards from its gilt-framed over-mantel mirror with an églomisé panel, and a limited, un-crowded, and balanced shelf garniture consisting of a pair each of fine porcelain vases and figurines, and an exquisitely modeled small clock. The fireplace itself is likewise dignified but simple with an antique mantel of pickled pine, and tall, slender andirons that are works of art behind a finely modeled fender of black diamond mesh and brass trim.

On either side of the fireplace are pembroke tables of inlaid mahogany, supporting silk-shaded lamps of bronze and marble. Next to them are richly upholstered love seats in quilted English chintz whose gay pattern of white magnolias and turquoise leaves is repeated on an arm-chair, in each case meticulously centered. The small tables, differing in size and shape, have beautifully de-signed pierced galleries. The rest of the furniture has the same rich appearance of well-preserved antiquity — the spider-legged table in the corner and the elaborate bracket above it, the Chippendale chair and Regency caned armchair in gilt and black enamel, with a seat cushion in coral satin, all properly spaced for effect as well as convenience.

Quite different but equal to the foregoing in its re-strained elegance is the room shown in illustration 4, which interprets the tasteful formality of a French eighteenth-century interior as applied to a Philadelphia penthouse. Dominated by the sweeping curves of dec-orative festoons and Roman-arched ceiling-high windows and wide doorways, this drawing room represents a tri-umph of balance and symmetry characteristic of the period. Far more reminiscent of France than the United States, it also reveals, on careful analysis, the surprising amount of ingenuity and resourcefulness that went into its transformation from a run-of-the-mill apartment in-terior.

In the remodeling of this room the three conventional French windows in one outside wall were masked by an inner facing pierced by three Roman arches which con-verted them into the more acceptable round-topped style favored in the Louis XVI period — a concession to the few pieces of this, the earliest style involved. Arches and walls were then decorated with Louis XV *boiserie* in off-white on a puce ground of glazed canvas. Though

4.

not antiques themselves, these decorative swags and pendants, and the masks that join them, were cast in antique European molds by an old-world craftsman who also applied them.

In the window openings are pleated and swagged puce draperies bordered in rose-pink and red, and, underneath them, incredibly rich-looking Austrian shades in laven-der silk, fringed and tasseled in off-white. Another dec-

26

orative triumph is represented by the heavily impressive mantelpiece designed around a pair of almost life-size white-marble caryatids acquired by the owners on one of their Mediterranean trips. Over it is a ceiling-high mirror crowned by the same off-white *boiserie* as that of the arches.

In two walls are other wide archways, one of them fitted with doors whose lavender-tinted panels are set off with gilded moldings. The other open archway connects the drawing room with the dining room, both rooms being floored with large vinyl tiles which have all the appearance of white marble slabs with black cabochons, like rows of punctuation marks, receding into infinity. In this fabulous setting the furniture, which consists mostly of antiques of several periods and points of origin (some of them quite important) are equally at home, the wealth of detail minimizing any suggestion of severity. The rug, for example, is an antique Aubusson in the flambeau pattern, its colors soft rose, blue-green, and pale gold. It marks the floor center in a line with the fireplace, and serves a dual purpose by interrupting the wide sweep of formal floor tile which might easily become overwhelming, besides tying the furniture groupings together around its colorful oasis. Nearby is a gold-ormolu mounted *bureau plat*, a Louis XV piece in red lacquer with a black leather top. Centered in the windows is an original Louis XVI *lit-de-repos* (long enough to form a window seat) upholstered in French rose moiré and at either end of it is a painted and gilded Louis XVI fauteuil in its original tapestry covering.

In the left rear corner of the room stands a comparatively plain Louis XV bombé commode whose beauty lies in its exquisite marquetry. This is balanced on the other side of the archway by an eighteenth-century slate-topped table made by some skilled if not eminent menuisier. Probably the only eyebrow-raising piece in this ensemble is the little coffee-table — a marble-topped creation from Venice, possessing an apron upholstered in white silk damask, and extravagantly decorated legs in a form reminiscent of Louis XIV "*chimère*."

As might be expected, this room assumes quite a different aspect when viewed in the opposite direction (illustration 5), and through the archway which connects it to the dining room. The same white tile flooring continued through the archway extends the vista to the dining room windows (which duplicate those of the drawing room) thereby enlarging the visual space tremendously. Flanking the archway is an interesting pair of screens made by framing in wide molding a pair of Zuber, antique French, wallpaper panels which depict tropical landscapes. These not only add a touch of the exotic but also liven the corners and soften the impact of the architectural elements.

Behind the Venetian coffee table, and barely visible in the first picture, is a large sofa — a *canapé* in fruitwood and white-silk damask. Alongside it, with its back to the screen, is another Louis XVI painted armchair. Between the *bureau plat* and the other screen stands an elaborately carved and pierced armchair with scroll feet serving as a *fauteuil de bureau*.

Though nothing so far has been said about the accessories, these are the details that give the room that essential lived-in look which distinguishes it from a museum setting. They constitute accents that emphasize important features while offering intriguing items of interest in themselves — collector's pieces such as Chinese figurines in biscuit, decorative lamps made from silver, crystal candelabra, decorated pottery planter bases, bouillotte-style shades, plus a simple mantel garniture of white porcelain vases planted with creepers flanking a gilt bust of some Roman emperor on its ormolu-mounted pedestal. On the floor an oriental jardiniere with a sprouting bamboo plant strikes a homelike note. On the red *bureau plat* a pair of azure pottery cats as bookends provides a spot of lively interest, and so on — nothing massive, nothing to induce an air of clutter yet constituting grace notes that lighten the overall air of formal dignity. As for the walls, the delicate paneling eliminates any need for paintings, and the arches with their tinted fabrics provide all the color and texture the background needs while accenting the architectural details that help make the room memorable for its striking individuality and charm.

Entirely different moods are expressed by the series of drawing rooms to be considered next, though only basic groupings are shown. These are sufficient to indicate the variations in atmosphere that can be effected by slight changes in décor and grouping, with traditional pieces of the same quality and importance in rooms that

5.

are both sophisticated and refined.

Undoubtedly the most richly decorative is that of the room shown in illustration 6, whose wallpaper pattern matches that of the fabric used for the chairs, sofa, and draperies. There is also a definite affinity between this pattern and the extravagantly baroque design of the mirror frame, as well as that of the elaborate chandelier. The painted chair frames likewise incorporate a wealth of curves, as does the sofa.

Against this background so full of life and movement, to which the colors add still another dimension, the plane surfaces of the lamp shades and monochrome rug provide the necessary contrast. Even the three tables in their smooth rigidity provide a further restful note which the handsome urn and pedestal bases of the lamps do not. In a room such as this, which is basically so busy and excitingly rich, much of the visual effect depends upon the colors. These preferably should be soft tans, pale yellows, light browns and greens, so that the overall impact is reduced to a comfortable level.

In the next of these (illustration 7), most noticeable is the atmosphere of gracious formality that is achieved without the slightest trace of aggressiveness, the feeling being reduced to one of calm acceptance instead of challenge, the background receding rather than dominant.

The sofa is not only deep and ultra-comfortable, but upholstered in colorful flower-patterned fabric, puff-quilted so that the design has a three-dimensional, sculptured look. Such richness obviously calls for background that is utterly plain and relatively colorless — preferably off-white — with no competition from a chair upholstered in the same material. Contrast is the key — plain floor covering in monotone, plain furniture and window fabrics, straight lines, and very little carving on the furniture pieces. On the other hand, it does need some positive associations such as architectural detail in the major furniture pieces, though an accessory such as a lamp can be decorative in a formal manner, adding perhaps a touch of whimsey or an exotic note in the wall decorations and odd bibelots to relieve the tension.

In illustration 8 is shown the same dynamically colorful type of sofa fabric adapted to a room designed to express a quite different mood — more casual and less overpowering. Admittedly, the size of this sofa — one

6.

third larger than the other — and the smaller decorative pattern which shows much more light-colored background, may have some effect on the result, but that would be difficult to assess. In any event, the setting is more open and free, and the comparisons between the sofa and the surrounding pieces — not to mention the pictures — are more vividly apparent. Here is the same

29

7.

solid back wall, but the other vertical surface, presumably covering windows, is now light-colored drapery instead of dark wood sheathing. The floor covering is similar but the furniture pieces are less pretentious, with simple lines, and the easy chair seemingly almost an intruder with its light color and slick, leather texture, bold lines, and slim bandy legs, not to mention a towering height that dwarfs everything else.

Actually it seems that the relaxed air of the interior, in spite of the busy upholstery pattern, is due mostly to the large informal painting of a somewhat soothing subject, and the still less formal small ones alongside it, the tall sconces above them tending to hold the group together. The end tables, being reproductions, are duplicates, in excellent proportion to the long sofa, and solid enough in appearance to form substantial bases for the tall lamps. At the same time they are static enough to counterbalance the restless impression created by the sofa fabric, a reaction which a few larger cushions in monochrome would augment to good effect. As it is, it represents a neat and not at all forbidding arrangement.

In the next view (illustration 9), the most notable feature is the balanced distribution of the tables, each one of which is large and solid enough to serve its partic-

8.

9.

ular purpose regardless of the size of the upholstered piece it is designed to complement. For full appreciation, however, it needs to be seen in color. The principal pieces consist of a cabinet commode two feet square, an octagonal corner unit with bookshelves designated simply as a lamp table, a 20- by 20-inch commode at the other end of the sofa, and the center piece which is a large cocktail table over three feet in diameter. These all exhibit the warm brown tones of antique wood, and in life they are less starkly outlined against the gold of the carpet which, in turn, has a strong affinity for the pale greens of the wall and the left-hand easy chair, as well as the glossy yellow-white of the sofa covering. The draperies are off-white with pale green stripes, a fitting background for the gold-embroidered white chair which is the outstanding accent repeated to a minor degree by the white silk lampshade. The three floor cushions are, from the top down, purple, brown, and copper, and designed to serve as a pouf for floor sitters — a symbol of the informal atmosphere which this setting is supposed to characterize in spite of the luxurious lamp bases and the tall tour-de-force in glass on the corner table. The pictures and their frames are the only antiques.

A corner conversation group that is given importance by a tall cabinet is the subject of the next picture (illustration 10), which shows a section of a much larger drawing room-style apartment. It forms a self-contained unit that delights the eye from every angle. The two-piece cabinet, enframed by voluminous draperies at the windows, has a Regency air with its gold-wire mesh and pagoda top, while the little round table suggests a younger Empire piece despite an inset marble top and off-white finish which makes it a natural companion to the upholstered tub chair.

This chair actually has a swivel base, and rocks, a hush-hush gesture toward modernity which would never be suspected from casual inspection. The table lamp, modeled on an ancient torchère, is finished in white with gilt details, and crowned by a parchment shade in gold. The most obvious feature of the large oval coffee table is its huge marble top whose color and markings tie it in unusually well with the small-figured cane-backed sofa, and both have much in common with the sculptured rug which constitutes an interesting accent in itself. Rein-

10.

forced by the black-lacquered and gold-trimmed sconces, the old print on the wall, in its decisive black frame with a gold fillet, is of a height calculated to balance nicely the lamp and cabinet. The polished parquet floor adds a touch of gentility to the whole, doubtless setting the pattern for the rest of the room.

While it contains the usual mixture of periods, the drawing room shown in illustration 11, of which one gets but a glimpse through an open door, serves principally to show how much atmosphere can be created by very little. In this room the fireplace is in the left-hand corner, typically eighteenth century with its pierced-brass fender and painted wooden mantel. The furniture therefore is disposed so that the most can be made of it, taking into consideration the awkward placing of the doorway which is itself a work of art with its paneled reveals and soffit.

The background carries out the architectural theme of the entrance, with formal floor-length draperies of silk damask under box-type embroidered and fringed pelmets of the same material. Though the walls are not paneled,

A Living Room, the ultimate in stateliness, reveals informal details

In this modern setting both antique and contemporary furniture pieces are compatible

Illustrating the textural and color values of tiles in kitchen

Window shade, sofa, and chair share the same pattern

A deeply dramatic Persian
style striped fabric

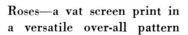

Roses—a vat screen print in
a versatile over-all pattern

A modern studio with a sixteenth-century background

The Mediterranean influence
combines elegant simplicity
with coolness

A bathroom with basic
French Provincial features

Showing the use of complementary colors of counter
and floor

A formal eighteenth-century
New England fireplace

A modern substitute for the
old-time dining room suite

Rich fabrics, textures and colors can turn a room into a jewel box

Here the apparent wall height is reduced by an ornamented ceiling and border

A modern multilevel rug of this type has universal appeal because of its intriguing pattern

This custom-designed rug would be perfect for an interior having an Oriental flavor

This exquisite living room has a crystal chandelier with emerald drops complementing the delicate floral wall panels

A favorite Adam mantel by Wedgewood

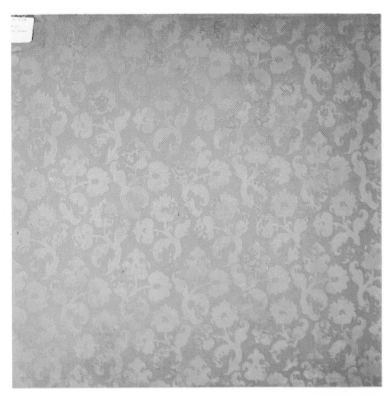

Another over-all pattern with a freehand air reflecting the dappled appearance of some vinyls

A pleasing pattern for English, French or Italian fine furniture

This reproduction in vinyl captures the color and character of delft tiles

Here a carpet defines the limits of a dining area

Flap corners permit this being used on footless beds

This exotic Florentine bedroom is a riot of form and color

A Library-cum-bar wood
sheathed in faux bois and
paneled in fabric

Antique and modern with
cherry-paneled walls

An eighteenth-century French Provincial pattern

Color compatibility ties together walls, draperies and furniture

Files can be an attractive part
of the study interior

Eighteenth—century French
and Victorian pieces in a
setting of red, blue and black

In this small foyer a feeling of depth is contrived by opening it into a solarium several steps higher

This foyer is made interesting by opening into a long passageway

11.

12.

they do have a molded chair rail, painted the same light color as the walls. In contrast, the dark-stained plank flooring is almost entirely hidden under a fitted carpet with a deep looped pile. This helps to accentuate the shapes of the white-painted Louis XV chairs which are upholstered in plain red silk.

The comfortable-looking tufted love seat, with its back to the wall, is located as close to the fireplace as possible, and just about centered in the doorway, attention being called to the whiteness of its self-striped material by a pair of round, red cushions trimmed in white. In front of this is a very low black-lacquered coffee table of Chinese design calculated not to intercept the firelight. On the wall above the love seat is an exceedingly delicate Adam-style oval mirror of unusual design despite the familiar ribbon and bell-flower husks which Adam shared with Hepplewhite. This mirror emphasizes the center of the grouping, giving a semblance of balance to what is totally unsymmetrical.

The only other pieces are a mahogany serpentine table with a galleried shelf and its accompanying porcelain-based lamp which latter provides illumination for occupants of the sofa and nearby chair; and, in the window corner, a tall, mahogany basket-type plant stand with slender, curved and tapering legs, its bouquet filling with a mass of color and form what would otherwise be a blank, uninteresting spot as a background for the chair.

On occasion the designer's problem will be aggravated by that of creating an interior around a client's existing furniture, as happened in the room shown in illustration 12, further complicated by the necessity of incorporating certain collector's items as part of the décor. In this drawing room the collection comprised a number of oriental export porcelains, some Staffordshire pieces, and a few pictures. The solution was a bold one, utilizing a colorful rug of almost overpowering design to fuse the many disparate elements into one. The colors of the rug, which was made in Hong Kong, were dictated by those of the porcelains and pictures, and everything else was subordinated to this.

A gold-plated steel coffee table with a plate-glass top was used over the rug so as not to hide its pattern or the splendor of its coloring. The porcelain collection was given pride of place in a wall recess balancing a lavishly draped window beyond the fireplace. The walls, naturally, were kept plain, as was the upholstery of two of the three sofas, and the floor darkened, with what admirable results the picture makes clear.

While the display of unusual objects of art is one way of introducing an exotic note into the décor of any interior, there are others equally effective, such as a leavening of unfamiliar furniture styles. A mild but noteworthy example is represented by illustrations 13, 14, and 15, which show a desirable drawing room, warm and inviting, and eminently adapted for entertaining in a pleasantly formal manner. Separate groupings cater to either small or large parties.

Four countries are represented (if one includes Venice as a city-state) by the antique furniture pieces. The key unit is, of course, the beautiful and quite large bombé cabinet (13) whose highly decorative upper section is nearly all glass. This is an early eighteenth-century Venetian piece, and its importance in the present setting has been emphasized by placing it against an eggplant colored section of the wall, flanked by figured silk window draperies. The fine porcelains and lovely old book bindings which the cabinet displays confirm it as the room's focal point with which the facing fireplace can scarcely compete.

The whiteness of the glistening, translucent curtains is picked up by the Greek "Astrakhan" rug which seems radiant against the dark parquet floor, and the Venetian and French furniture pieces which are upholstered in white silk damask (14). Some of the seated pieces are covered in Wedgwood-blue velvet to establish a lively contrast and, at the far end of the room — in another corner grouping — a velvet-draped round table is surrounded by armchairs in the Italian Empire style.

The only vivid accents here are supplied by a pair of odd-shaped, brightly colored lamps beside which a group of modern paintings in comparatively subdued tones are almost neutral. Contrast is also to be found in the straight lines of the modern sofa and the curves of the antique chairs, the spidery chandelier of bronze and crystal, and the velvet table cover beneath it.

Contrasts of a different kind appear in the group (15) at the other side of the fireplace where the room opens into the foyer. The atmosphere here is slightly more for-

13.

mal because of the types of furniture pieces and accessories used. The sofa sacrifices a little of comfort to formality, exposing the wood of the back, sides, arms, apron, and legs and enframing the definitely rich nubby textured fabric, front and rear. The porcelain lamps also express quality and have none of the saucy air of the other pair. The matching marble-topped lamp tables are of course French Empire. The coffee table, on the other hand, is a modern piece with a glass top and metal base, and gracefully curving stretchers. The remaining pieces are a Louis XV bergère in silk damask and a cane-back fauteuil. The latter differs from those in illustration 14 in having no cross-stretcher, and its plain cushion adds somewhat to its simple dignity. Here as elsewhere the wall's solid color throws into high relief the whole ensemble including the impressionistic painting above the sofa.

14.

15.

37

16.

Fireplace Groupings

The natural focal point of any drawing room is the fireplace, and as a rule this fact serves to simplify the furniture arrangement. Where there is no fireplace a massive or otherwise important piece of furniture may be called upon to take its place. The formal drawing rooms shown here do have fireplaces, and the furniture placement in relation to them normally sets the pattern for the rest of the room. The fireplace groupings are therefore worthy of close study and analysis.

Beginning with illustration 16, this is a twentieth-century room with a large one-piece overmantel mirror and wall-to-wall carpeting. The mantelpiece, however, is of classical design set with a plaque and ornaments depicting romping cupids and grape baskets respectively, in low relief, reminiscent of Wedgwood decorations, plus fluted pilasters and a white marble hearthstone. An eighteenth-century brass fender, bowed and pierced, and brass acorn andirons in period, complete the ensemble. On either side, shelves reach from dado to cornice, displaying Oriental Lowestoft and other porcelain rarities, while on the mantel itself are ceramic figurines and crystal candlesticks with hurricane globes.

This combination of old and new, therefore, sets the stage for an equally gracious mixture of antique and modern furniture. The twin sofas are obviously recent, but at the fireplace end they are supplemented by a pair of eighteenth-century mahogany pembroke tables. In contrast, the outer ends sport a pair of round-topped, square-footed pedestal tables, also in mahogany, possibly dating no earlier than 1820. These introduce a welcome note of symmetry not often found in traditional fireside groupings.

Another rather striking focal point has been created in the wall space between windows. This eye-catching group is composed of a fine English bracket clock (circa 1700) with ball feet, perched on a tall trifid carved bracket which tapers down between four ivory miniatures, terminating a foot or so above a Sheraton swell-front chest. This mahogany piece has three drawers, and on its top are displayed twin porcelain candlesticks and a Lowestoft platter.

In one window corner is a modern two-manual electronic organ in mahogany which appears to be much older than it is, and a Chippendale wing chair upholstered in the same gaily patterned chintz as the fireside sofa cushions. Opposite the fireplace is still another sofa upholstered in the same material — an exciting triple play on a theme which distributes this colorful patch of design around the room thereby breaking up the monotony of the plain carpet and the fabrics of the fireside sofas plus the floor-length window draperies. The draperies, it will be noticed, are skillfully tied back — one side high, one low — so as to draw the eye in a sweeping curve from the low furniture pieces in the corners to the clock high in the center, emphasizing the already striking symmetry of the balanced wall arrangement so that interest is sustained in all directions.

In illustration 17, a somewhat similar room to the foregoing is more formal, with even greater accent on the antique, though not blatantly so. This particular mantel is also of a classical design, all in white including the decorative plaque. In place of an overmantel mirror, however, there is a large eighteenth-century style eared panel with dentils. This architectural accent offers space for a work of art, in this case an early nineteenth-century genre painting. Weight is given to the whole assembly by the black marble hearth and the bold sweep of a curved brass fender around a pair of flame-finial andirons. Much of the impact of this chimney breast is reduced by a pair of highly ornamental two-candle wall sconces in the side panels. These are as tall as the overmantel panel and set somewhat higher so that their ribbon-patterned metal tops are in line with the architrave. These sceptre-like fixtures in a bird-and-arrow motif are finished in silver and black. Strongly suggesting Regency period design, they pair exceedingly well with the black and silver vase-type lamps beneath them. Of these two lamps one stands upon a mahogany table with tapered legs, the other on the glass top of a delicately turned whatnot, and both are accompanied by martial figurines in ceramic.

Other pieces of furniture visible in the picture consist of an antique mahogany cabriole-legged gaming table with a silver candlestick on one corner, an occasional table with drop-leaves on which stands a rosewood-based Chinese lamp of white porcelain, with a white silk shade

17.

40

18.

An imaginative variation of the above is seen in illustration 18, the principal change consisting of filling the entire overmantel frame with canvas. In the illustration this is seen to be an early eighteenth-century landscape with ruins which seem to have been painted to fit that exact spot. The two wall sconces beside the picture match it perfectly as to period, and the black basalt urns — forming, with the little casket, the complete mantel garniture — also are in keeping, the coleus leaves in the arrrangements supplying a touch of the exotic. In this instance the ceramic-display shelves have been enclosed in gilt wire mesh foreshadowing the Regency period which was to become the rage well before the turn of the nineteenth century.

Going a step further with the fireplace theme, it is well recognized that not every hearth is the heart of the house. In the small drawing room or parlor in illustration 19, glimpsed through a half-open door, enough is seen to indicate a possible alternative. Here the fireplace is reduced somewhat, both in size and importance. The mantel is smaller and more delicate in design than usual, and its garniture dainty rather than forceful, consisting of two small urns of flowers, a tea caddy, and a pair of Chinese cups. In place of a significant and moody painting is a charming portrait of a young girl which suggests an informal approach. This delicate touch is repeated in the adjoining shell-cupboard on whose open shelves is displayed a collection of Lowestoft porcelains. Ordinarily this would suggest furniture covered in flowery prints instead of which formal quality is the keynote of a grouping ranged along the side wall instead of in front of the fireplace.

The few pieces here are businesslike and practical, comprising a long sofa in apple green antique satin, its lamp table (there is another at the opposite end, both of the Chippendale pedestal style with piecrust tops), and accompanying chairs, one of them an open-arm style chair in gold antique satin, and a coffee table, the latter in the Chinese mood. Equally important with the sofa is the gilt-framed oil painting above it — a large atmospheric landscape with bucolic overtones. This is the eye-catcher in the room, and therefore the center of interest which determines the arrangement of the rest of the pieces

19.

duplicating those of the fireside lamps. In the far corner a glimpse is afforded of what must be a tall mahogany secretary-bookcase of eighteenth-century vintage. Altogether this grouping constitutes an object lesson in how much can be done with so little so long as that little is good.

in a room that combines intimacy with a certain formality and is certainly not designed solely to impress.

Where there are two fireplaces in a room, the problem of establishing the main centers of interest is automatically solved by relating separate seating groups to each, as was done in the oval, Adam-style drawing room of illustration 20. This makes it possible to use only one fire for family occasions, reserving the second for larger groups.

The first thing to be noticed here is that the major seating is away from the walls, and that self-sufficient, curving love-seats are used in place of the usual square-ended ones which crave something to rest against, if only a library table and a pair of lamp stands to hide their uncompromising ends.

This is really a gracious room with soft colors and ample lighting — twin crystal chandeliers to dispel the gloom at both ends, table lamps for intimate illumination. The Chinese wall panels set the mood with their pale greens and yellows, while the oval rug in deep greens and greenish grays with orange accents on a beige ground establishes the limits for the conversational groups where oval coffee tables are fitting mates for the *canapé á corbeille*-style loveseats with their coral copper velvet cushions matching those of the Louis XV cane-back armchairs. Within those limits the loveseats can obviously be rearranged in a variety of positions to accommodate a larger single group as the occasion demands. The lamp and game tables and their separate chairs are confined to the perimeter of the room beyong the rug. The whole aggregation achieves an air of refinement and grace, a touch of dignity being supplied by the formal draperies in ivory satin lined with green, which occupy a large proportion of the wall space, setting off the splendid ceiling-high triple sash windows to perfection.

20.

Living Rooms

Living rooms being everyday rooms for all occasions that do not demand formality, their hallmark should be livability regardless of the type of home or the quality of the furnishings. They are rooms that suggest relaxation, and they are usually equipped to provide for reading or writing, for indulgence in the quieter, more civilized pastimes such as cards or chess, or listening to music. Above all, they need to have facilities for entertaining intimate friends or other members of the family informally.

The atmosphere that the ideal living room demands, therefore, is one of quiet cosiness and comfort without inducements to boredom, perhaps with books at hand, and certainly plenty of occasional tables, with ample lighting wherever it is likely to be required, and a scattering of everyday objects that will serve to induce a lived-in feeling. The details will of course be determined by compromise between the masculine and feminine members of the family.

Ideas as to comfort naturally differ according to the temperament and experience of the individual, but perfection of style will always be of comparatively little account where atmosphere is of prime importance. In designing such interiors, therefore, the principal concern needs to be with mood, as most of the rooms to be reviewed in this section will indicate. A good start can be made with rooms that incorporate fireplaces since their principal focal point is thereby already established.

Illustration 21 represents a living room suited to the settled and perhaps studious types with an appreciation of things beautiful and a leaning toward the traditional, with its period furnishings and the inevitable open fireplace which seems to strike an evocative note with most people whether of modern or traditional preference.

The overall tone is one of luxurious living, the furniture and furnishings being of the finest quality and happily chosen. The room itself is well ordered for a variety of the more cultural activities. A Georgian air is imposed upon it by the neat fireplace with its bold moldings, the deep cornices unadorned, and the unit bookcases flanking the chimney breast well-made but simple, with all woodwork painted a delicate gray. The mood is restrained, even the minor objects of art speaking of quality with a total absence of flamboyance or shoddy craftsmanship. The overmantel painting is in sober tones — a lush eighteenth-century landscape with tall, spreading trees, almost enveloping a castle perched high above a smoothly flowing river, moody and provocative.

On the mantel shelf below is a colorful three-piece garniture, in the center a boat-shaped vase of fine porcelain at the moment a riot of seasonal blooms — yellow, coral, and white — with ferns; the rest a remarkable pair of ceramic mopheaded fowl, almost lifesize, marvels of anatomical precision in brown, green, yellow and white. The wide fireplace mantel with a surround and hearth of

21.

22.

black slate, sports a tall brass-bound wire fender, enclosing massive andirons, and the usual accessories. The gleam of all this polished brass is repeated in the bail-handles and wire screening of the ceiling-high bookcase doors, and also in the ball-type chandelier whose round dozen, gracefully curving arms and offset drip cups hold high the slender tapers.

Beyond the bookcases with their masses of leather-bound, gold-stamped volumes are the tall windows with their colored venetian blinds and floor-length tasseled draperies in beige under smooth box-pelmets with scalloped and fringed lower edges. Other masses of color are supplied by the shaggy beige rug of almost room size, and the upholstered easy chairs in their rich-looking, hand-blocked damask in floral stripes of coral, brown, green and white. Into this background of architectural integrity, of variegated color and pattern, some static, some full of vitality, the antique furniture is totally absorbed, each piece an inevitable part of a satisfying whole, contributing its quota as an accent of texture and form.

Two major pieces are the Queen Anne side tables, either side the fireplace, whose principal function is to support a pair of canister-based lamps. At the other side of the easy chairs are two contrasting small square tables of oriental design, and in a corner of the room by a window is a larger piece common to many living rooms — a large, flat-topped desk displaying curios and objets d'art, and lighted by a table lamp of its own.

Even this small section of a completely furnished living room is sufficient to convey the atmosphere of the whole where emphasis is on the comfortable elegance of an earlier day, conservatively expressed.

In comparison with this, the living room in illustration 22 strikes a somewhat less formal note despite the classical architectural detail and dignified setting of precisely organized draperies, the twinkling crystal girandoles, the Louis XVI mantel and urn-based lamps. For the most part the differences are subtle but definite, the dividing line being established by such details as the charmingly informal portrait over the mantel, the casual stool in front of the fireplace which has much in common with the sturdy end tables, the lack of a formally patterned hearth rug, the games-table grouping in the corner, with its

casual, odd-sized paintings, and even more decisively by the round cocktail table, its accessories, and attendant Régence armchairs (with tangerine leather cushions) which emphasize roomy comfort rather than formal placing and straight-backed dignity in a room where even the curved end of a fringed rug in spice-gold suggests a more relaxed mood where conviviality and individual enjoyment are the order of the day.

A still different interpretation of the theme expressed in illustration 22 is represented by 23 and 24. Here there is the same note of relaxation due in no small measure to the more modern touches, such as the metal-bound black opaline fireplace enframed in a huge sectional mirror, the formal sofa with its magazine-laden étagère end-tables, and the fringed hearthrug with its padded bench. Actually this is an interior in the Anglo-American manner, its setting smooth walls, raised door panels and chair rail, and the simplest of cornice moldings, all painted a delicate gray called doeskin. The ceiling is white, and the dark-painted wood floor almost entirely hidden beneath a velvety doeskin-colored carpet. Three sash-type, small-paned windows reach up to the cornice where they are crowned by straight-edged, boxlike pelmets whose severity is softened by a tasseled fringe following the scalloped and swagged contours of its irregular hem. The floor-length draperies themselves are of heavy doeskin silk, minus the tassels, hanging in loose but regular folds.

In this comfortable but astringent atmosphere, the brown English chintz of the fireside easy chairs with its clumps of pinky-white mountain laurel and leaves of a rich and shining blue-green against a neutral ground of soft gray adds a note of gayety that contrasts interestingly with the blue-green textured fabric of a sofa and the antique wing chair in the background. With this aura of bright tones and spirited accent, the dark reflective glow of the mahogany pieces is heightened; the warm wood tones seem to come to life, and the contrasts resolve into harmonies, converting each assemblage of unlike pieces into a unified group.

Along the rear wall of the room extends a very fine eighteenth-century English Chippendale cabinet with an unusual style of broken pediment. In it is displayed a collection of Dr. Wall Worcester porcelains. Before it

23.

stands a folding service table temporarily decorated with a pair of silver bon-bon dishes and a lacquered silver biscuit canister. Since much of the wall is taken up by double doors, the remaining space is left clear to afford passing room between the cabinet and the cabriole-legged Chippendale wing chair whose accompanying spider-legged occasional table adds another casual note. Between the windows stands a baby-grand piano, also in mahogany, the group being completed by a massive flat-topped desk inset with tooled leather, acting as a sofa table in the center of the room. The sofa with a Chippendale ladder-back armchair at each end, together with the

24.

fireside easy chairs and a hearth stool, forms the principal conversation group.

Lamp tables — one oblong, one oval — flank the fireplace, supporting duplicate lamps of a highly formal pattern with urn and pedestal bases, and drum-type leather shades banded with gilded brass. Over these are bronze and crystal wall sconces which, unlike the rest of the wall fixtures, are converted for electricity. The others are of a gilt-bronze ribbon type holding twin tapers, one hanging above the piano, another over a Chippendale lowboy ornamented with a small bracket clock and a pair of exquisite porcelain covered vases.

25.

A merely casual examination of this interior shows that even with the rigid lines of mirrors, fireplace surround, and window tops dominating the background, the antique pieces can not only look attractive in themselves but contribute a certain warmth and charm to the whole décor, and this despite the close proximity of cumbersome upholstered pieces, and a luxuriant but undeniably modern floor covering with its uncompromising lack of color and pattern. Furthermore, with proper arrangement, the formal and informal pieces may be unified; neither dominates the other, a result that any competent designer would applaud — and possibly envy.

In vivid contrast to all the foregoing is a living room in summer dress (illustrations 25 and 26). Its basic design is distinctly modern with antique accents, backed up by the use of certain elements in classical style but contemporary form.

Since two photographs were necessary to show the entire room, each can be analyzed separately — a fortunate circumstance because of the contrasting nature of the groupings. The color view shows the dramatic impact that can be generated by adapting antique artifacts to contemporary decoration. In this room the architectural overmantel panel becomes a plain tombstone-shaped backboard for a composition of almost overwhelming intensity. The unit is assembled from a simple Pompeiian urn, or amphora-shaped wall fountain of dark blue-gray tôle with gilded ring handles and paterae, mounted above a semi-circular basin or lavabo. It is, however, not used as a wall fountain; instead it serves as an unusual and impressive receptacle for a flower (or foliage) arrangement which actually dominates this section of the room.

Alongside the projecting chimney breast is another striking novelty — a vine molded in stucco climbing the wall. Its eight branches terminate in flat-topped clumps of leaves, bunches of grapes, or bird's nests which act as shelves for porcelain figurines, small plates, and other collector's items. The base of the vine is a pyramid of tangled roots arranged so that it appears to rise out of a white-painted, dado-high cabinet. The cabinet itself provides display space for a pair of silver candlesticks and an antique green-bronze flower bowl.

The other antique furnishings include two tables flanking the fireplace, one a pedestal type with a bronze guilloche-patterned gallery holding the round marble

In the window recess by the fireplace wall a mahogany pembroke table supports a pottery cachepot with a somewhat overpowering cut-leaf philodendron. Scattered about the room are colorful accessories such as china bowls, huge mugs used as flower holders, tiny bronze busts on marble pedestals, exquisite ceramic horses, a brass-mounted rosewood cigar box, and a tall cubical wine cooler in mahogany that doubles as an end table by one of the fireside chairs.

50

26.

27.

top, the other a trestle-style double-deck magazine table, brass mounted and with a Regency air. On this a tôle canister-base lamp, its opposite number being a pillar-and plinth type in black and gold. Finally, there is, in the hearth, an antique semi-circular pierced-brass fender with a pair of ball-finial brass andirons, all of which together make quite a brave show.

The next picture (26) shows the other side of the room, which incorporates a huge curved bay composed of five ceiling-high glass panels and an adjoining wall of sliding glass doors. All of these overlook the gardens so that the room acquires a series of sylvan murals that change with the seasons. In this view the fireplace is actually located between the chair and ottoman in the foreground and the sofa at the other side of the rug, as observed in the previous view. The pink rug therefore extends lengthwise from the fireplace to the center of the room. In this position it serves to tie the fireplace grouping together visually. These three upholstered pieces — the chair, ottoman, and sofa — are given added prominence by being covered in off-white material patterned with huge clusters of coral and beige roses and green leaves — a design well scaled to the size of the room. These masses of color, counterbalanced by the white, supply cheerful accents while adding little warmth to a room whose present décor is planned for summer weather.

Dividing the floor of the room into large squares of black and white terrazzo tiles adds to its importance but also tends to reduce its apparent overall size while adding to the spacious, airy feel of the room. Small tiles used here would obviously have resulted in an overbusy, frustrating pattern with little character. The long, curving sofa filling the bay is deeply tufted in keeping with the other pieces and contributes its quota of sumptuousness. It is of a pleasant shaded green that shows up well against the white draperies, and adds a feeling of stability to the overall décor without drawing attention to itself in a room which already is possessed of all the bright gaiety it can stand without becoming frivolous. A touch of classical dignity is added by the painted American Sheraton chairs (four of which surround the card table), by the large circular table with an oriental flavor, and the Japanese willow-pattern screens either side of the bow window, whose delicacy contrasts charmingly with the boldness of their surroundings.

Room size has of course a definite bearing on design possibilities especially in the case of living rooms which normally demand ample space for traffic as well as for individual activities in which several people may simultaneously be engaged. Naturally, much depends upon the extent (and ages) of the family and the normal number of visitors expected to use the room at any one time. In the room represented in illustration 27 this aspect has well been taken care of, the activity and relaxation areas being well defined and amply spaced. It has the further advantage of admitting plenty of daylight and, at the same time, ensuring the availability of artificial lighting in all areas. Not only are there wall sconces and table lamps sufficient for ordinary purposes, but sunken ceiling lights also are provided at strategic points. This ensures that the furniture can be moved around and rearranged as desired.

Another important facility is the provision of adequate seating accommodation in the area of the large bow window in the form of a continuous sofa in brown leather. On the other hand, the principal conversation center is that provided by the grouping around the fireplace where a sofa, a cockfight chair in red leather, side chairs, and occasional tables are assembled. Adjacent to this area are the fireside bookcases. A separate area for reading or games is established in a corner by a window, and served by separate bookcases. A third relaxation area consists of a round tray table with armchairs and a view through both windows — an excellent spot for light refreshments. From the picture it is obvious that the traffic lanes are amply wide, and the floor covered with a tobacco-brown fitted carpet so that there are no throw rugs to be tripped over whatever the haste!

In the furnishing of this traditional room the old combines with the new to create an aura of quiet comfort. The walls are sheathed in pickled pine, and together with ceiling-high bookcases, raised panels, and heavy cornices provide an interesting architectural setting. This goes well with leather seating enlivened by the blue-green crewel work of the high-backed chairs and the needlepoint decorated cushions (which fail to detract from what is definitely a masculine room). Some of the chairs

53

and small tables are antiques, and the tall, scepter-like bronze wall sconces with their riband and wheatear embellishments look as though they were every bit as old.

Another interesting living room and one which probably approaches the ultimate in stateliness is the subject of illustration 28. It might indeed be taken for a drawing room were it not for the informality of a floor cushion and other small but significant details. In any case, it is not a room to romp in. Of chief interest are the colors, the pale green of the walls having been successfully blended with various tints of blue represented by the rug, the sofa, the window drapery, and, bluest of all, the pyramid which forms part of the mantel garniture.

Vying for interest with the greens and blues is the gorgeous yellow of the chair upholstery, decorated with trapunto as is the pale-blue sofa. This rich yellow is reflected palely in the tall portrait over the sofa which outclasses the white-marble fireplace mantel as the room's main center of attraction.

The only antiques here are the folding fan-type firescreen, and the copper lavabo over the mantel which makes such an effective decorative feature when filled with ferns. The furniture is modern, the chairs and one table featuring brass trim, the other tables having sufficient eye-appeal in their classical design and the walnut veneers with burl accents of which they are made.

Quite often the smaller, or bachelor apartment living room may offer the designer more problems than the spacious penthouse or mansion, and illustration 29 shows a fair example. This situation is due to the fact that the foyer opens into the living room through a wide archway and at a considerable angle, leaving but a fragmentary section of wall in a corner next to the only area available for the principal seating.

In arranging this group, therefore, the opening is not only ignored but the line of demarcation between the two spaces is emphasized by using a fringed rug in the living room, and leaving a gap of a foot or more between it and the fitted carpet of the foyer, though both of them are of the same oatmeal color. This gap is further accented by a black line worked into the carpet a few inches from the edge.

Another detail which calls attention to the difference between the two areas is the fact that, though the living room has neither baseboard nor cornice, the foyer has both — painted in black on the wall with the moldings shaded in. Furthermore, a chair rail is added in the same manner, and though the foyer wall is covered with faux-bois paper to imitate vertical sheathing, the living room walls are of plaster painted buttermilk white, in deep contrast to the dark parquet floor.

The principal group, then, consists of a sofa upholstered in a print of regimental red, charcoal, and ochre on oatmeal linen. On it are pillows in red English corduroy. The easy chair with its back to the foyer is covered with wool hopsacking in the same red. In front of this sofa stands a sturdy turned coffee table of waxed wormy chestnut, with a three-quarter-inch plate-glass top, a remarkable combination of old and new!

At one side of the sofa is the usual end table with a brass-based lamp; at the other end a desk is substituted. This desk is a substantial piece, made of ash with twisted legs and plain stretchers of square-section black iron. The drawers in the table face away from the sofa so that it can be used as a writing table. It holds the telephone in addition to the urn-based pottery lamp with a bouillotte-style shallow shade. The desk chair is a slender, geometrical affair of black iron, with arms and a tall back, its seat and cushions covered with red vinyl imitation leather.

This group is completed by a large plate-glass mirror in a wooden frame, and in it can be seen the reflection, not only of the red tôle hanging lamp in the ceiling's center, but also the games table in the opposite corner with its four chairs of teak-colored bamboo with red vinyl back-cushions and seats. Above them a colorful print is seen hanging with a tall, leafy plant in the corner beside it.

Contrasting strangely with both groups are the glass shelves on the narrower side of the archway with their random collection of modern miscellanea which add nothing to the décor but at least indicate that the owner is in residence!

A dished ceiling, light-colored walls, a floor of pink vinyl tile, and a wall-high fireplace panel of rosewood veneer whose veining forms an abstract design, all combine, as illustrations 30 and 31 indicate, to create a variegated background of light and shadow against which an intimate mixture of antique French and modern Ameri-

28.

can pieces melts into a contrasting but unified whole.

Decoration is applied in the form of silk draperies depending from classically styled braided pelmets over tall French windows that reveal an intimate country landscape dotted with garden statuary. After dark, with the pale curtains drawn, the light of floor and table lamps reflects warmly from the bare and shining floor, bringing into prominence details that the daylight wrapped in shadow or merely silhouetted.

There is no cornice or ceiling molding, and the walls are plain, comprising what is essentially a modern setting softened somewhat by the scalloped pelmets and the rosewood grain. The interior therefore relies for its color and pattern almost altogether on the well-polished furni-

29.

ture in general, and the eighteenth-century French pieces in particular with their vibrant areas of decorative fabric.

The setting itself provides the straight line, both vertical and horizontal, the chairs and tables contributing the complementary curves. The old and the new furniture, as a matter of fact, offer a mixture of fluid surfaces — the rounded backs and saber legs of the modern chairs, the cabriole legs of the reproduction gaming table, and the exaggerated sweep of the legs and scroll-like stretchers of the metal, glass-topped one. There are curves and flowing lines also in the upholstered fireside sofa, and the arms of the cane-backed chair, all of which tend to increase their compatibility with the French pieces — the Louis XV fauteuils, and the Consulat-Empire bergères. The former are of the Boulard type, upholstered in heavy brocade spectacularly patterned on a white ground. The fabric-covered bergère, on the other hand, has no pattern at all, and both contrast most pleasantly with the room's largest piece of furniture, the modern upholstered sofa in black felt. This is a piece designed for fireside comfort, so that it has little in common with the bare-backed settee of classical lines that occupies the center of the long window as the focal point of its own immediate group. Because of this situation, the one has little effect on the other while harmonizing with its neighbors. In spite of the number of pieces, this separation into groups leaves ample space in the center of the floor, with access lanes thereto effectively separating the fireplace grouping from the games-table unit, and both from that of the window assembly. Tall, potted plants and a round, glass-topped table fill the odd corners.

An interesting feature of this room is the fact that the background — the walls and floor and ceiling — is a thing apart, sufficient unto itself. The furnishings, in other words, are something separate made up of three units without even the usual rug to tie them together visually. The only fixed point of contact between the two is effected by the fireplace sheathing which establishes complete rapport with the fireplace grouping. Far less complete is the relation between the window grouping and its background of glass and curtains. Actually, there is a third point of contact where the living room connects with the adjoining room via one step up to a wide opening. This step is formed of stained and polished wood,

30.

wide enough to accommodate a pad-style cushion at its center without interfering with access from one to the other, and serves to tie the third grouping into its surroundings. Thus all the islands become peninsulas demanding no connecting links yet unifying the whole interior.

Two problem rooms are represented in illustrations 32,

57

31.

33, and 34, each of them a living room which appears to be an extension of a foyer, and both comparatively narrow taking into consideration the traffic areas connecting them with adjoining space through very wide openings.

In the first of these (32), there is a deep recess in which most of the furniture was required to be located. The walls of textured plaster and the exposed timbers in the recess invest it with an air of primitive simplicity which needed to be counteracted somewhat because of the formal character of the interior. Furthermore, the furniture arrangement had, of necessity, to be adapted to the low, sloping ceiling inside the recess, and the limits of each floor area defined in separating the adjoining spaces.

58

32.

These problems were solved by covering the living room area floor in parquet, and relying on the larger furniture pieces to establish the character of the recessed wall space — a scheme obviously successful in reducing the effect of a simple rusticity to meaningful proportions. In the recessed area, the large picture on the rear wall acts as a focal point while serving to balance the sofa with the tall cabinet. In turn, the two massive end tables and their lamps, together with the coffee tables, emphasize the symmetry of the arrangement which is unified by the large rug extending under them. This rug actually projects the effective area of the group farther into the open room so that the writing-table group becomes a part of it instead of being isolated around the corner. Like-

33.

wise, a pair of tub chairs (only one of which is visible) set limits to the space this double grouping is intended to occupy, and define the traffic lane behind them.

While the furniture pieces shown are modern interpretations of a classical design, the pictures, the lamp bases, the books, the various bibelots, and the bouillotte lamp converted for hanging, are all worthwhile antiques adding to the overall flavor of authenticity without accenting period.

In contrast with the foregoing, the second room (33 and 34), which also is characterized by exposed timbers and white walls, and opens into both a foyer and a dining room, has an entirely different atmosphere induced by skillfully mixing contemporary designs with definitely

34.

exotic pieces, plus a couple of antique lamp bases — one crystal, one pottery — and various objects of ancient art such as a small Cycladic idol, Chinese cups and casket, and an iron and crystal chandelier. The Louis XVI chest is actually a reproduction in chestnut, housing a bar under its divided top which opens by sliding to right and left without displacing the items displayed on it.

The floor of this room is entirely covered with short-pile carpeting in a luscious bronze-yellow, and at each end of the room is a modern sofa in bronze-gold silk with lacquer red and leopard pillows, with a brass-and-fabric framed mirror over it. Against the window wall is a pair of lounge chairs in white canvas with lacquer red, tête de négre, and black stripes, and in front of the fireplace an ottoman in felt of the same pungent red with striped canvas edging.

Around the marble-topped games table is a set of four bamboo-style chairs dated around 1802 which have Gothic quatrefoil frets in the back rails. These, too, are painted in the lacquer red and have seats of simulated leopard skin. The whole room therefore is extremely colorful, and it is this color that ties the furniture pieces together so well.

Two other contrasting rooms (35 and 36) also mix the old and the new to secure strikingly different effects. The first of these is an L-shaped room of considerable size with five smooth walls and one so ornate as to compensate for the comparative bareness of the rest. This decorative wall, which probably has never been duplicated, has three openings for two double doors and a large window. Almost in its center is a sizable fireplace enframed in black marble. Around this is a huge bolection molding of white marble whose central decorative keystone supports a massive marble urn with a flame finial.

From the molding to the insignificant cornice is a great glass mirror bounded by strips of marble which also form a double ogee pediment across the glass. On either side, from floor to ceiling, are other mirrored areas, interrupted only by the doorways and window, the former having overdoors decorated with other marble devices, the latter shrouded in figured yellow Fortuny draperies. The doors have oversized decorative brass knobs centered under their tall glass panels shaped in French provincial style.

This tremendous tour-de-force in marble and glass naturally dominates the room which has yellow walls and off-white ceiling, the undecorated, monochrome surfaces heightening the contrast. The larger of the two walls facing the mirrored expanse incorporates a deep sunburst-topped niche, and, next to it, a large window. Depending from the ceiling in this area is a crystal-and-bronze, six-light chandelier, the rest of the illumination being effected by table lamps of various sizes and shapes, most of them having bases in the form of porcelain vases and amphorae.

In this highly original setting, which boasts a thick, white, long-pile carpet, the furniture comprises a variety of styles and periods from a modern grand piano to an eighteenth-century brass-bound wine cooler. There is a Louis XVI round-backed, painted fauteuil, a transitional Queen Anne Chippendale side chair, and a pair of Adam open-arm chairs in antique green and gilt, upholstered in white brocade with spring-green and primrose-yellow flowers. Between them is a rare Chippendale tripod table and, to one side, a love seat in primrose-yellow strie silk. There is also a Sheraton inlaid kidney table and a papier-mâché tray-table, while in front of the fireplace stands a Hepplewhite bench. The large bookcase-secretary is of the Sheraton style, and next to it a sofa in a yellow print and two tufted chairs in yellow silk add a spot of color.

All of these pieces are arranged in convenient groups with ample space for circulation, resulting in a comfortable but gay room, in some respects decidedly impressive, the varied tints of yellow combining to induce a sunny glow on the dullest days.

In spite of the mirror-and-marble wall, and the many important antique pieces, this room is not overly formal, particularly when compared with a living room such as that pictured in illustration 36, which at one time was an open porch. Today its wall and dado sheathing of Parana pine is finished in a soft tobacco brown, its elaborate cornice is complete with dentils and mutules, and it boasts of floor-length pleated draperies of silk. The French windows with their semi-circular fanlights fully exposed are architecturally correct, and overlook a boxwood garden with the mountains beyond. Each furniture piece is meticulously placed. On the floor is a heavy woven cotton rug in three sections, light in color to reflect the illumination from an eight-branch ball-type bronze chandelier, the tall table lamps, and desk candles.

The sofa and easy chairs are upholstered in a gay chintz having a beige background, with patterns in red, gold, and green. The coffee table is a galleried type made from an old black-lacquered tray with bronze handles. The arm and side chairs are in simulated bamboo, Gothic in design, with pad seats. Two of the armchairs are drawn up to an antique folding games table, while a side chair serves the eighteenth-century English slant-top desk which is unusual in that it has brass candlesticks fitted into its top.

Above this desk hangs a tall trumeau of unusually

35.

simple design, with small antique portraits to one side, and tall plants on the other growing out of a lacquered planter redolent of the Orient. Between two of the windows is a painted Regency bookcase with gold-meshed doors and a scagliola top, and on it is perched a 30-inch tall lamp with an hexagonal leather shade. There are masses of foliage by the French windows, tying the room to the gardens. Small objects of art (dustcatchers?) have been reduced to a minimum, the principal ones being a brass-mounted, mahogany tea caddy, a tinted bust of Washington on a marble base, and a highly polished brass-and-copper tea kettle — all things of interest and not merely useless trivia.

36.

Victorian living rooms, so long anathema to decorators, are gradually coming into their own again and are as cautiously being accepted, thanks to imaginative interpretations which carefully avoid the clutter and make use of modified designs in everything from wallpaper to bric-a-brac, introducing here and there a classical note and replacing many of the earlier fabrics with bright and modern creations. Victorian, in short, is back, but the horsehair is a thing of the past!

The modern version of the interior of the nineties is the subject of illustrations 37 and 38 and constitutes an excellent example of the manner in which the romantic late Victorian atmosphere can be recaptured while adapting the interior to modern living without loss of either dignity or charm. Backgrounds are, of course, of first importance in creating such an interior; the warmth of rich coloring, the softness given to the walls by the velvety looking, all-over pattern reminiscent of a day when cosiness was a prime consideration and the bleak togetherness of the open plan had not been conceived.

The warmth and cosiness is evident in the two pictures in which the all-important coloring must be imagined. The wallpaper actually is red on red; the thick carpet also is red, but there is no sense of oppressiveness thanks to the wide window trim in off-white overlaid with a border in rose-arbor design. The handsome Austrian shades, also in off-white, successfully break up the dense pattern, substituting panels of soft fabric in delicate stringy swags calculated to disperse any suggestion of gloom.

Though it may seem daring to introduce still more solid pattern into the room, this has been successfully accomplished by covering the love-seat in an avocado-on-white rendering of an eighteenth-century fabric design. This contrast between the red of the wall and floor, and the avocado of the fabric plus the white background causes the pieces to stand out dramatically against both of them, emphasizing its exquisite — and quite unusual — lines. Two other upholstered pieces — the pull-up chairs flanking the octagonal lamp base — are covered in antique-white damask. Between these chairs and the love-seat is a large, round cocktail table of Polynesian koa having scroll-shaped iron legs and cross-base, and behind the love-seat is a lightly-scaled writing desk (reminiscent of the once-popular sofa-table) with beautiful scroll-shaped pedestal legs, together with its rush-seated chair which has a touch of sophistication in its carved top-rail. Besides being highly functional, these give balance to the room.

Between two of the windows has been placed a console of classical lines with eared panels to its four doors. This is painted the avocado color used in the fabrics but softly antiqued. On it have been placed a pair of porcelain items — a small bust of a young girl, and one of those surprisingly delicate-looking pieces of Victorian ceramic modeling that have somehow survived — a leafy bush growing out of a stemmed vase shaped like an old-time sugar bowl, lifelike in coloring and far less fragile than it seems.

These two pieces successfully bridge the gap between the console and the atmospheric Eastern painting above it— Arabs on the steps of a mosque rendered in watercolor in an almost impressionistic style. Tying in with this picture very nicely is an eighteenth-century Moroccan hanging lantern of figured brass suspended by a fine chain from the ceiling. Each of its glass sides is pressed into the form of 22 circular disks like miniature bull's-eyes — a pattern reflected in the cresting of the desk chair and echoed in the scalloped top of the table-lamp shade. It is, as a matter of fact, the repetition of such graceful curves — those of the lantern, the desk legs, sofa back, the table, the shades, and the extravagant sweep of the chair backs, that gives this room its look of delightful homogeneity, emphasizing the factor of compatibility to a degree rarely encountered — a feature skillfully punctuated by the rigid lines of the console and window trim.

Quaint Victorian details are introduced here and there, such as a gold cupid and a pair of oval-framed modeled and painted flowers on the wall, china figurines of children somersaulting, and so forth, but the whole assembly seems to bridge successfully the inevitable gap between Victorian and contemporary taste.

How wide that gap can actually become is demonstrated by the modern living room which is the subject of the next photograph (39). Space and light seem to be its most prominent characteristics, at least by day. Con-

65

37.

38.

tributing to this are the ample windows and the large glass area of the entrance door. It is, however, the manner in which these light sources are handled that constitutes the decorator's contribution. This treatment consists of stretching net curtains over the glass areas, and, in the case of the windows, of hanging shades of white

felt which are trimmed with applied bands in oriental pink.

To make the most of the transmitted light, the interior walls and the fitted carpet are of a buttermilk white. Furthermore, the extra-long sofa is upholstered in white French rep, while the Empire-style cabinets at each end are both painted white and fitted with white *faux marbre* tops. Also white are the Louis XV-style cocktail table bases whose tops are black slate with beveled edges.

Despite this concentration on light and reflectivity, the room does have ample areas of color in addition to that provided by the large impressionistic painting. The lounge chairs flanking the sofa are covered in oriental pink silk, and the ottomans are upholstered in an oriental-pink and white hound's-tooth check. Other spots of color and pattern are provided by the sofa pillows, two of which are in oriental pink, the other pair in black-and-white zebra stripes. The long side table under which the ottomans are temporarily stored is a reproduction of a Louis XVI piece enameled in black.

Artificial light is supplied by a tall pair of antique

French crystal column lamps with short, and very wide white silk shades reminiscent of those used on bouillotte lamps.

This furniture arrangement is of course highly symmetrical, with straight lines predominating, except for the legs and stretchers of the coffee tables. Much therefore depends on the accessories for the overall effect. The most impressive of these is the fine Louis XVI mantel clock on the side table which it shares with a piece of African sculpture. By the entrance door the spiny leaves of a spindling palm form an intriguing silhouette against the white plaster, filling the otherwise empty space and creating another center of interest. On the cabinet nearby, the eye is taken by a brass-bound box, and a bronze

39.

whippet on a marble base. On one coffee table a bronze tripod upholds a glass bonbon dish, which, together with the vase of flowers on the next one, assuredly betrays a feminine touch.

An interesting modification of the same type of interior is supplied by illustration 40, this time applied to a suburban apartment. This is particularly useful in showing the variation in atmosphere that can be achieved by even minor changes that scarcely affect the mood. It also bears out the dictum that in rooms sparsely furnished the individual pieces should be of exceptional quality.

In this room a certain formality is suggested by the ceiling-high draperies of charcoal and white striped ticking over net curtains, which extend across the terrace

40.

doors. These draperies serve to control the daylight reflected from the buttermilk-white walls, in which task they are aided by the absorptive capacities of a grass-green carpet, and the charcoal-gray silk upholstery of the two chaises longues, and the ottoman, not to mention the black slate top of the coffee table. This still leaves an ample total of white surface in the long table between the sofas, in the bamboo-pattern bases of the latter, and the cocktail table, plus the marble top of a Louis XV table in the corner.

Pattern, and some color accents, are supplied by the sofa which is upholstered in gray and white striped ticking embroidered with grass-green and oriental-red flower sprays. This same material is used on the pillows of the chaises longues. The white walls, incidentally, form an excellent background against which such things as the bronze lamps are silhouetted thereby emphasizing the details of their modeling. The whole constitutes an intriguing, though somewhat ascetic, setting for modern living which allows for expansion in almost any direction.

One of the beauties of the eclectic system of furnishing is that many antique pieces can be made to seem quite at home in almost any surroundings. Perhaps the greatest test is to apply them to the modern interiors where they are to be seen against the starkest of backgrounds — the flat white or tinted ceilings and walls, and often characterless floors. The astonishing thing is that in a carefully planned room of this nature, many old pieces will not only look their best but actually bring the room to life, even to the extent of transmitting some of their warmth to the contemporary pieces with which they are mingled. An example of such a modern room is reproduced here in illustrations 41 and 42, which serve to demonstrate how utterly compatible antique and contemporary can be, both with one another and their comparatively stark surroundings.

The house itself is one of the most advanced of its type. Glass walls surrounded by a wall of brick arches, plus an interior glass-walled shrub-and-creeper-filled atrium so that light enters the room from two sides, or more, this being an open-plan design with most of the rooms opening into one another. An important feature of all these room areas is the ample wall space available for the placing of furniture and the hanging of pictures.

This can be seen quite clearly in the spacious living room which is divided into "conversation" areas by furniture groupings. In all rooms there are triple-section windows, each with its sliding door. On either side of these windows is a wall space equal to the glass area. In the living room these spaces serve to accommodate a piano, a tall secretary, and paintings. At the far end there is a free-standing fireplace wall separating it from the dining room. Each of the two group areas is unified by a large Aubusson rug, and both employ two sofas facing one another, with auxiliary chairs and tables arranged around them.

It is in this area that the delightful results obtainable by mixing antique and modern furniture pieces can be seen. The off-white curtains, the pale tints of the rugs, the light walls and ceiling that match the curtains, all provide a faintly contrasting — and receding — background for the sofa upholstery and the cool white of the damask chair backs and seats, the satin seat pads and the parchment lamp shades. In the fireplace area, stronger accents are provided by the rose tint of the chair backs and seats.

In both these groupings the happy marriage of old and new furniture is obvious, the antique spider-leg tables offsetting the solid mass of the sofas; the coromandel screens provide both dark areas of black enamel and delicate tracery as a counterpoint to the light colors and gay paint of the Adam and Louis XVI chairs, and so on. Add to these the colors and textures of the Sheraton chairs in black lacquer and the tripod tables, plus the dark tooled leather of the fine antique Hepplewhite secretary, and interest is supplied wherever the eye ranges.

A variation of this system of making antiques the principal feature of contemporary settings is to use one exotic piece as the center of attraction of either the room itself or its principal furniture grouping. An excellent example of this is the subject of illustration 43. To anyone entering this room the inescapable focal point is the large octagonal coffee table occupying the center of the floor — a spectacular piece that would catch any eye because of its unusual design, its total beauty, and the exotic aura of the Orient which it exudes. This is a teak and bamboo piece hailing from Hong Kong, lacquered black, and filled with interest from its four framed legs to its deeply dished top.

69

41.

42.

43.

Probably the most remarkable thing about this table, however, is its affinity for its setting which is composed largely of heavy upholstered pieces of western design in monochrome, framed in drapery fabric of deep color and all-over pattern against a long, bow window and paneled walls. Part of this compatibility of course lies in the presence of other pieces of Chinese flavor including not only the small tables but the huge lacquered antique tea canisters in black and gold that form the bases of two table lamps. On the other hand, the mahogany drop-leaf tables seem to have something in common with the small teak tables, while the shaggy tufted rug in pale beige emphasizes the luxury of its design and finish from which the tweed-covered easy chairs with their printed cushions detract not one whit.

The next step forward in the scheme of injecting oriental touches is of course to add more such pieces. Whether this will be successful or not will depend upon the designer and the effect he is trying to achieve. At any rate, illustration 44 represents one solution to the problem of designing a preponderantly Asiatic interior incorporating a few western pieces, mostly antiques. These intruders are represented by the painted Louis XVI *bureau plat*, the upholstered modern sofa, the hurricane lamps, the shaggy rugs, and the mirror. The Chinese furniture includes reed armchairs of two types — one large with seat and back cushions, and a small rounded-back type with cushions only on the seats. There is also a three-cushion sofa of the same type, barely visible by the mirror. These reed pieces are of a soft honey color in their natural state, which looks well with a wide variety of western furniture woods from apple to walnut. They can, however, be dyed or lacquered almost any color.

Interspersed with the reed chairs are antique Chinese garden seats, both of carved teak and of pottery decorated in relief. Splashes of color are provided by the huge floor bowls, the brilliant lacquer-red of the porcelain lamp bases, and the wall painting on canvas, the yellow rugs contributing mildly colorful areas on the dark stained wood of the floor. Altogether this is a gay and flavorful room which can either be muted or made more exciting through simple color changes.

Equally fascinating in a less exuberant manner is the room pictured in illustration 45. This has the same reed

44.

45.

46.

47.

furniture, now including a pair of sofas which can also be used as beds. In the corner is a table made in the same manner as the beds. Over this hangs a set of one large and four smaller globular lanterns of pierced brass.

The room wall, it will be noticed, is covered in a Chinese style paper, patterned so that it looks almost like damask. Against this wall is a drop-front desk with drawers, and on it a display cabinet used principally for porcelains and Chinese flower arrangements. These two pieces have moldings formed of split reed which also is used for the drawer handles. The rest of the furnishings consist of a pair of teak stands, one of them forming the base for a round porcelain planter which stands on a circular coffee table between the two armchairs. These chairs are upholstered in a nubby tweed which goes extremely well with the large floor rug sculptured in strips of varying widths.

The multiple window shutters behind the shantung curtains also add their quota to the oriental atmosphere in a large, airy room eminently suitable for subtropical climates such as that of our own deep South.

Reverting to the more familiar eighteenth-century American interior, the large living room illustrated in 46 and 47 was designed around a fine, hand-made rug of a grayish white with widely spaced white moss roses having pink buds and dark green leaves. The interior, as might be expected, leans toward the formal though obviously intended to be lived in by an active family, and it is this rug that dominates the setting, adding to the feeling of spaciousness while contributing enough beauty of color and pattern to eliminate the need for crowded walls or massive furniture pieces. These would obviously have detracted from the architectural interest provided by the projecting chimney breast and its delicately unobtrusive mantel, the smooth plastering over corner posts, girts, and ceiling beams, the latter trimmed with plain cove molding to form room-wide panels which add tremendous character.

To counterbalance these features the large windows are encased in damask draperies of pale gold, with valances formed of swags and cascades in the Georgian manner, all weighted with a beaded fringe in gold and black. This dark outline endows the curtains with a positive decorative accent instead of allowing them to melt gracefully into the background.

The furniture is a mixture of bamboo-pattern arm chairs (painted antique red), upholstered-back side chairs with a Directoire air in green with seat and back panels outlined in white, plus modern upholstered easy chairs in pale gold silk damask.

The sofa, opposite the fireplace, and the loveseat in front of the large window are modern but everything else is antique in style if not in fact, including the butler's-tray table in front of the sofa, and the tray table assigned to the loveseat, the inlaid cabinets alongside the projecting chimney breast, the galleried cabinet in one corner, the Chippendale secretary with its display of export porcelains, and so forth.

The pillar-type table lamps with their gold-trimmed dark green columns and white shades are quite conservative in contrast with the delicate crystal chandelier and the smaller lamps which have Chinese porcelain bases and teak stands. The fireplace cabinets are adorned with elaborate crystal candelabra, and the mantel sports a pair of glass nosegays under bell jars. The pictures are few but important to the décor — a sizeable painting of a horse over the sofa, a pair of eighteenth-century prints of George III and Queen Charlotte, and a large ancestral portrait over the mantel. There is also one piece of export porcelain at a strategic point on the wall.

The important points to note here are the background details, including the floor covering — the plain white walls and the pale gold draperies which are somewhat lighter in color than the rug, and the rich upholstery material, accented by pillows in red and black, and the dark green of the side chairs. It is altogether bright, homelike and commodious, amply furnished yet far from overcrowded thanks to the light scale and open design of the chairs and tables.

There are few simpler ways of endowing an interior with a feminine air than by the lavish use of delicate fabrics, plenty of color contrast and decorative detail, with a scattering of mementoes and family portraits. Such an interior is well exemplified by illustrations 48, 49, and 50, where the crimson walls, pale pink ceiling, the

moire-topped pouffs in red and white with gold accents, the sofa upholstered in a flowery design of red, pink, and black, chairs in black with gold trim and red seats, all on a white rug, offer convincing evidence that this is no room for a man, despite the prevalence of hunters and hounds in pictures and porcelains.

This room is entered from a tiny foyer where the apartment door is gray with borders of green and gold, and the wallpaper vertically striped in red, gray, and gold. This paper is carried across the under-surface of the flat-topped archway separating the hall from the room which suddenly becomes an uncompromising red. The velvety carpet is white, invested with a pale pinky tinge from the walls, and extends to the far end of the room which is nearly all window. This window is draped in white silk with a border of jet-black embroidery where the two curtains meet. This curtain, together with the other light-colored fabrics including the white, flower-splashed chintz of a sofa big enough to double as a bed, white-painted chairs, and white-sided pouffs, provide an intensely contrasting background for the lovely inlaid, banded, and carved secretary in fruitwood, the sofa ends in the same tone, the end or occasional tables in faded mahogany, black, or white paint. All stand out strongly in a room that is far less light-absorbent than one might expect.

There is no fireplace so the huge, plump sofa occupies the center of one long wall. Opposite is an antique dresser of inlaid fruitwood surmounted by a Regency mirror with flanking pillars, painted white and gold, and trimmed with a swan cresting and egg finials. On the wall facing the windows is the tall secretary with its medallions and decorative bronze hardware in the French manner. The floor space is organized to ensure an open traffic lane from one end of the room to the other, between the chest group and the sofa group. The latter includes a white-painted chair at each end of a shelved coffee table topped with black glass and having decorative bronze legs, and the pouffs alongside which take up less space than chairs. Along the far wall, lyre-back chairs in black and gold and upholstered in white are disposed either side of the chest, each standing below a three-tier display shelf with its quota of porcelain figurines, cups, and saucers. These shelves are painted black with gold trim. In one corner

48.

50.

49.

is a three-stage whatnot displaying a glass-enclosed épergne in ivory and silver, and on the chest stands a large bust of Othello. The center of the window area is occupied by a round table covered with a white quilted fabric and black border, and in the corner by the sofa is a writing table in faded mahogany with a red leather top which serves as a lamp table, laden with bibelots and pictures. The lamp, matching one at the other end of the sofa, is a columnar type in black with gold trim and a gold shade. The other end table is an oval urn table with a brass gallery and a pair of candle slides on which bronze figurines hold the tapers.

One of the most prominent features of the room is the collection of pictures over the sofa, ranging from a large oil painting by Chapman of a hunting scene to small color prints all framed in gold, and flanked by a pair of decorative gilt ornaments that tie them nicely together. Judging by the number of family portraits displayed, by the bibelots and pictures, this represents a very satisfying room for a lady with deep family interests, a liking for life in the saddle, and gracious living in general. Few interiors could capture that essence so well.

The single end of a living room represented by illustration 51 is included to show how the library-cocktail room of illustration 148a is tied in with it, decoratively speaking. Both have the same black-and-white cane blinds which set off the gold on white draperies so successfully, and combine so well with the white walls.

The sofa, with its seat and back deeply tufted, is covered in oatmeal linen, the upholstered chair in a light tan, while the Sheraton armchairs have white cushions. The rug and the lamp shades also are white. The principal accents are provided by the black lacquer of the cane-seated armchairs and the black seats of the simulated bamboo chairs grouped around the games table in one corner. These bamboo chairs are actually brown antiqued with black so that they are very dark as are all the tables.

An orange tint is introduced in a lacquered tray on the circular coffee table, in the sofa cushions, and in a lacquered box on one of the lamp tables, a color theme apparently adapted from the picture over the games table which is black and orange-red. The large portrait over the sofa is, except for the skin and hair tones of the sitters, almost entirely in a lovely gray-green which the gold-rubbed frame sets off to perfection. The two table lamps are accents in themselves, one of them eighteenth-century French in its ormolu modeling with a gunmetal column, the other equally striking with its molded silver stem and gilt-bronze mounts, topped by a gleaming bowl of golden glass.

Gracious interiors, befitting a small country home — the parsonage rather than the mansion — often have a calm and comfortable air of their own that is unmistakable. There is probably nothing exciting about them, but the furnishings are good and there is no striving after effect.

Such an interior, with its fine antiques, is the living room of illustrations 52 and 53. The house is old, except for the over-sized window that floods it with light (there being no merit in gloom) and providing a view over the garden.

The walls have their old paneling, painted a soft gray, or tan, or blue, with a fitted carpet that adds an air of luxury while hiding a replacement floor with nothing to

51.

52.

53.

In illustration 53 the other side of the room reveals a neat mantel with dentils, paterae, fluted pilasters, and a band of fine reeding around the opening. The hearth gleams with the polished brass of a pierced fender, fire-screen, and antique andirons. Over the mantel, black metal sconces with globes occupy two small panels, the larger center one being reserved for a painting in a gold and black frame. To one side is a modern loveseat, at the other a tilt-top tripod table with a silk-shaded lamp made from a Chinese porcelain vase. This stands along-side a pad-footed Queen Anne wing chair with flame-stitch upholstery fabric. Two Queen Anne, Dutch-foot vase-back chairs are against the wall, with Chinese pictures in gold frames above them, sandwiching a tall bracket-footed secretary between them, its upper section serving, with obvious modesty, as both a bookcase and a china cabinet.

It will be noted that between the window and fireplace groupings there is ample space for traffic, the skillful placing of the furniture creating an illusion of light and air in a room which is quite adequately equipped for family use and normal entertainment on a modest scale.

The somewhat exotic living room shown in illustration 54 achieves a touch of distinction in its interpretation of an oriental interior, and it is the pattern and texture of the major surfaces that do most to create that atmosphere. The walls are sheathed in elm, the floors are of oak, both treated with transparent finishes to emphasize the grain while retaining the natural look which goes so well with the stone of the hearth and the brick chimney wall. The black beams and white ceiling are all a part of this pattern.

In place of shojis or other oriental partitions, sliding glass panels are used behind large adjustable translucent shades in white with a velvety flocked leaf design. Sil-houetted against one of these, the young bamboo is a vivid reminder of the delicate traceries of bamboo and willow in those murals that supply the background of so many chinoiserie interiors in this country.

Because of this setting, the handsome old Chinese rug in blue and gold looks its lovely best, and quite at home with the bronze-accented teak chest, and the low table of Chinese inspiration in black lacquer on which yellow cushions have been placed so that it may double as a seat. Another oriental piece is the small table whose top frames

recommend it. The ceiling doubtless is white, the window sash likewise, its little square bay spanned by a quietly elegant fabric pelmet delicately embroidered at center and ends with star-like flowers. The matching draperies, which cover the ends of the bay when not drawn, are possibly plum colored (and certainly plain) to set off the sofa in the window recess, clad in its richly patterned chintz of pinks and greens on white that looks like crewel work, matching that of the two eighteenth-century-style armchairs grouped with it.

Two different styles of lamp tables are used — one a round tilting top pedestal style, the other a square, tray-topped piece with a shelf, and both supporting tall, un-pretentious lamps with spindle turnings and drum-shaped silk shades in white. Before the sofa stands an interesting tea-table with candle slides, Dutch cabriole legs and slipper feet, and nearby is a miniature three-drawer chest serving as a table. Behind this is a ma-hogany console table displaying a small twin-candle stick and other bric-a-brac, with an early framed print above.

78

this house, one might feel impelled to remove one's shoes!

Exotic for far different reasons than the foregoing is the room shown in illustration 55. This is a living room designed to take advantage of a view, whether of back garden, solarium, or terrace, through its rear wall of glass. Set into the wall are three glazed panels, swinging on their centers, each fitted with a venetian blind, the end ones yellow, the center one white. This window arrangement ensures perfect control of the quantity and quality of the interior lighting, as well as ventilation, and the yellow units can flood the interior with the mellow glow of sunshine while reflecting the heat. This is the detail responsible for the room's tropical air on a sunny day, and the reason behind its chromatic scheme. The flooring is in alternate yellow and white tiles; the brick fireplace wall is white, the papered area red with a beige pattern.

Contributing to the room's unusual atmosphere is the fact that French, Spanish, and American pieces are combined with an Italian wall fountain and a large abstract painting which dominates the papered wall. The foun-

54.

a square of white marble. This shares the rug with a modern sofa in orange linen.

To the left of the picture can be seen one corner of an illuminated shelf on which oriental porcelains and curios are displayed, but even more effective is the lighted case on the end wall above the chest, with its painting and porcelains. Bathed in its glow is a modern ceramic horse which, to the uninitiate, might well have come from some T'ang Dynasty tomb, another reason why, on entering

55.

79

tain, which is mostly of glass, hangs over the fireplace and acts as a fruit bowl, being within easy reach. The fireplace brickwork is extended to form a bookcase recess facing one end of the sofa. This piece is upholstered in red of a darker shade than the red of the wallpaper, and before it stands the Spanish coffee table which has a red-tinged marble top and iron-braced scroll legs.

Closer to the window where it receives full benefit from the available light is an antique French country table of the circular, bulbous-pedestal type, made of apple wood. Set up to it are two handsome antique French ladder-back chairs, with heavy tasseled seat pads in a red and white print duplicating the wallpaper pattern, and above hangs a ring-type tôle chandelier with six lights and a large diameter concave reflecting shade. A Spanish bent-iron stool with a seat in yellow drill, and a copper rooster, a refugee from a wind vane, complete the inventory except for a floor lamp and a few other odds and ends, of a furnishing scheme that could be adapted to a less enviable setting, but doubtless would lose much of its originality and charm in the move.

The fundamentals of any living room are few but important. These fundamentals set the stage for those extra items dictated by the special needs and interests of those who use the room. The entertainment features usually have to be incorporated as unobtrusively as possible in order to maintain a reasonably high level of charm and comfort, and dignity.

One good skeleton outline of such a room is conveyed by illustration 56, which endows furnishings of obvious quality with a mood of relaxed gaiety against a background of cheerful color. Even the creamy floor covering has a splattering of unobtrusive colorful spots so that it forms a non-committal background for the room's predominant red and white accented by chocolate brown.

In the picture the window wall is of a medium brown, much of it hidden by the widely draped curtains which are white with a large stylized flower pattern in red and dark green. This pattern is repeated in the paper of the adjoining wall which has a chair rail and white-painted dado to reduce its apparent height. The sofa, which has a loose-pillow back, is placed against the window, its most notable feature the extraordinarily wide stripes in its upholstery material. This effect was secured by sew-

ing together two strips of fabric of differing colors — one light red and the other chrome orange.

The three chairs shown are low-seated, and each is in a different color (or colorless!), the low-backed, black-lacquered chair with casters being upholstered in white, while the high-backed upholstered chair is unashamedly red. The third one, which has an exposed pecan frame, is covered in a large houndstooth check of red and black.

56.

The wooden pieces include a striking octagonal table with a heavy pedestal base, and a novel removable centerpiece. There are two end-tables to the sofa, one with legs, the other cabinet-style which supports a heavy, octagonal-based lamp. There are also two side tables, one round and inlaid, the other rectangular with boldly carved legs, and a wall cabinet designed to act either as a disguise for a television set, recorder, or radio, or to house the family library.

On one of the tables is a reproduction in brass of an unusual antique candlestick; on another is a twin-candle student's lamp with tôle shades. This whole group is tied

57.

together by a short-piled bordered rug in beige. Ideally, of course, a ceiling fixture should be used in addition to the lamps to provide basic illumination for the whole area in which so many and varied activities are likely to take place.

One of the most difficult effects to secure in almost any room is a fusion of restrained elegance combined with informality, though this is not so much a contradiction in terms as might be supposed. The living room represented in illustration 57, for example, is elegantly furnished yet pains have been taken to ensure that an air of distinction does not diminish its invitingly casual comfort. For this reason the arrangement of the furniture is deliberately unsymmetrical, and the background

58.

59.

of floor and walls is designed more for lively contrast than to constitute an impressive backdrop in itself.

There are no architectural elements in the room to give it character, and no massive strictly period pieces, yet the furniture, inspired by traditional patterns, is beautifully designed and obviously well made. The vinyl flooring, however, represents red brick-shaped tiles which, registering a taste for simplicity, are the essence of informality, as is the shaggy rug which is hardly designed for pacing up and down upon. On the other hand, the sofa is decidedly handsome with its trapunto paneled cushions of amber velvet. The wooden pieces add notes of architectural grace with their pillared construction enlivened by beautifully veined veneers. Adding to the air of casual elegance is the games table beyond the sofa, its unusual top gracefully curved inward to accommodate players and outward to keep glasses and ashtrays away from careless elbows.

In contrast, the easy chairs are built for comfort, and upholstered in a dramatic print having a pattern of tropical flowers in yellow, orange, red, and dark green. These gay bouquets are well distributed around the room, nicely calculated to afford ease of conversation without formal grouping.

In a little country cottage the problem of conversation groupings rarely arises even though the living room is usually the center of all activities except for preparation and eating of meals which is the proper function of the old-time kitchen. An interesting exception is the one huge kitchen-dining-living room of the rural hideaway, devised for her own use, by a prominent New York designer. The kitchen-dining section is shown in the kitchens chapter. Judging from the two views (illustrations 58 and 59), its living room is the anthithesis of everything she is associated with in a normal working week.

The cottage is old and tiny, but modernized, the shabby plaster walls hidden beneath weather-worn siding gray with age, the interior doors constructed of the same material to which old-time hardware has been applied. The modern oak flooring in narrow tongue-and-groove strips has been appropriately darkened so that it is barely noticeable; the single, small-paned windows have been made into twins both to admit light and permit of a wider view over the gardens and woods, with little detriment to the bucolic atmosphere evident even without furniture.

It is the furnishing, of course, that spells the difference in all these old-time interiors so many of which cling to the same old eighteenth-century country pieces that are more decorative than useful. This living room area, however, is interesting because it is both practical and different, its furniture ranging in age and style from the late seventeenth century to the early twentieth century, and tending more to comfort than elegance, as it should.

The oldest, and most fascinating piece is the press cupboard, far too beautifully carved and detailed to have been a country piece, boasting linen-fold panels, cocks-head hinges, and strapwork carving. The rest of the furniture consists of New England ladder-back chairs (tall four-backs, and scalloped splats with splint seats at that), a dry-sink doubling as a modest bar, and a fireside bench as a cocktail table. Tall, opaline-shaded lamps with decorated tôle bases in antique yellow occupy the old-time end tables (one oval, one square), alongside the modern sofa upholstered in hard-wearing tweed. At either end of the cocktail table are mid-Victorian wicker armchairs, real works of art with thick pad seats.

In the center of the antique woven rug is a colorful but plain massively solid round table made from a Victorian mahogany top and a country-designed base, 20 inches high, and painted for use with a group of round-back wicker occasional chairs. An antique three-legged stool serves as a telephone table.

Color is supplied by the floor-length curtains of checked gingham in brown and white hung over bamboo "roll-up" shades, by the orange and yellow sofa cushions, the rust rug, and gay oil paintings on the walls. With this background the whole room comes to life when the wire basket containers on the two tables are filled with fresh flowers, supplying a fragrance to match that of the garden in the morning sun.

The Dining Room

In the not-too-distant past, when the "open plan" was all the rage and walls gave way to "room dividers" or nothing at all, the dining room became the dining area, an ill-defined space between the kitchen (often equipped with an open serving counter) and the so-called living area. With the open plan now passé, the living-dining room is out of fashion except in circumstances of limited space which occurs more often in town apartments than in houses. Such an arrangement therefore does not need to be considered here, except to note that the dining room with its separate small table for family meals, and the kitchen with its breakfast "nook," both of which are discussed in detail, contain ideas which can be adapted to the dining area.

In the matter of the standard dining room, an important difference between the furnishing of the living room and that of the dining room is that in the latter comfort is secondary. Apart from this, the furnishing of the dining room offers great variety, depending upon the period (if any) to be emphasized, the class of interior, and the degree of formality required. As a rule, however, the room does not need to be as spectacular or so full of interest as the others, since it presumably will be used only for meals when the dining table will be the focal point instead of the fireplace.

Plain walls with but few or no pictures seem to be favored, except perhaps for the country house, or cottage simulating an early American or other simple décor,

though murals picturing the outdoors (and incidentally pushing back the walls) are preferred by some. Certainly a feeling of spaciousness is to be desired in addition to the extra room that always should be provided in the area of the table. Such details however are largely matters of personal preference, and may be governed somewhat by the overall size of the room and the number of furniture pieces considered necessary or desirable.

In all instances therefore, the largest amount of floor space will have to be devoted to the table and its chairs, including room on all sides for service and general traffic. In the smaller rooms this may have to be secured through the use of auxiliary furniture built to a smaller scale, or the elimination of certain pieces altogether. The table naturally should be adjustable as to length to accommodate both the maximum and the minimum numbers of guests comfortably — the maximum being determined by the available space, and the minimum by the smallest number of persons who can comfortably use it without being seated too far apart for coziness. The shape of the room may also determine whether the table is round or oblong. In addition to the regular dining table it is often a good idea wherever space permits to have a separate small table for intimate meals and dining á deux.

On the other hand, there are many extensible table designs which lend themselves well to this Jekyll-Hyde existence so that the only problem is that of arranging the interior to avoid major adjustments in switching over

84

from one to the other. This volte-face is simplified if one large rug or overall carpet is used, and if the table can be centered in one place. This is doubly important if a single chandelier is to be relied upon in place of candelabra.

As far as the auxiliary pieces are concerned, their number and functions will be governed by the arrangements available for storage of china, silverware, and linen. The range of possibilities is enormous, but ordinarily the table and chairs will have to be supplemented by a sideboard or good, solid serving table for carving or the opening of wine bottles, or the placing of viands after carving or in readiness for serving, and those removed from the table. In some cases there will have to be available storage drawers for flat silver and napery, and cupboards or shelves for the hollow ware and china not kept with the everyday stuff in the kitchen. The whole thing however is so flexible that the only way to develop specific ideas is through the study of a wide variety of solutions to individual problems as encountered by interior designers in houses both large and small. One can then mentally strip them of their furnishings and use the bare bones to stimulate the creative capacity in adapting them to one's own taste.

Beginning with the larger and better — which are of course not synonymous — there is in the room shown in illustration 60 an antique English triple-pedestal table in mahogany and four reproduction chairs made in Italy, which are covered in a soft coral antique satin. The rest of the pieces are English antiques. In one corner of the room is a large semi-circular console table with a pair of three-light candelabra, a couple of antique plates on display, plus two decanters and a silver tureen. Elsewhere against the same wall is a mahogany five-drawer chest, with silver candlesticks, and a pair of mahogany knife boxes. Above this hangs a cupboard with a scroll top and open shelves displaying rare porcelains. A brass-bound mahogany wine cooler stands in a window recess not far from the head of the table, while a service table and sideboard occupy the adjoining wall. Under the table and chairs (and allowing space for a chair to be pushed back), is a large, off-white rug which leaves a foot or so of the dark-stained floor showing all around it.

The room itself is definitely formal, the walls colored a soft turquoise, with floor-length striped draperies of turquoise silk over the tall windows, topped by deep scalloped pelmets of the same material plus an off-white fringe. The double doors opening from the drawing room are in a paneled recess set off with reeded and mitered trim painted off-white, and flanked by a flat dado whose molding is embellished with old-time gouge work. The room end facing the windows incorporates a fireplace with an overmantel mirror in gold, and, on one side, the door to the kitchen.

Centered over the dining table hangs a gilt-bronze and crystal chandelier of a delicate openwork type in keeping with the character of the room. The only pictures on the walls are a series of three old prints — two large, one small — over the console. It will be noted that the walls, draperies, chair upholstery, and rug are all perfectly plain and in muted colors so that the total effect is opulent, in quiet but perfect taste.

Bearing a close relationship to the foregoing but quite different as to total effect is the room shown in illustration 61. In this the room has the same architectural quality, amplified by the discreet draperies of white antique satin in a large bow window and over a small sash to one side. Both overlook a charming garden, but at dinner time, with the curtains drawn and the lamps lit, both the interest and the feeling of added space is supplied by two large Chinese panels of birds and boughs, and a gold-framed mirror over a sideboard.

Under one of the panels is a console with globe-shaped candlesticks, and from the ceiling's center depends another of those bronze chandeliers with its looping strings of lozenge-shaped crystals. At each end of the bay is a gold-wire and crystal-drop sconce, while in the window's center stands a folding service tray equipped with a globular silver urn and a silver tray with tea cups of elegant porcelain. On this floor also is a plain rug, this one fringed, with two corners trimmed to lessen the contrast with the curved window. This dining table has only two pedestals, and the chairs of both arm and side types are of beech painted and carved to represent bamboo in the Regency manner, with coral velvet backs and seats tufted in white.

The third of this series (62) is shown in color with the table laid for dinner, its centerpiece a silver épergne

60.

61.

62.

Chinese scenic wallpaper of white boughs and blossoms under a blue sky dotted with gay birds and butterflies. In the same corner the paneled areas of door and wall and dado give way to a heavily molded fireplace, all of them painted off-white. Over the mantel is a gilt convex mirror, the mantel itself adorned with a pair of Chinese blue-and-white lidded vases flanking a bouquet of flowers in a silver bowl. At dado height, under the blue Chinese panel is a side table displaying a pair of porcelain plates, a silver urn and a silver tray laden with porcelain cups and saucers, the whole an exquisite composition of color, texture and form — the acme of formality.

Turning from the classic antique to the classic modern, illustration 63 shows the dramatic effect that can be secured with some of the new woods applied to current furniture styles. These pieces are truly eclectic in origin, the chairs being adaptations of a Spanish comb-back, the sideboard of Jacobean inspiration, the dining table with a carved gothic base. The handsome two-section cabinet has iron scrolls in the lower doors, lined with scarlet fabric which establishes the keynote color duplicated in the rug and the table mats, and, somewhat lighter, in the chair upholstery which is of a pattern reminiscent of the Hungarian point or flame stitch.

The interior of the cabinet's vitrine top uses orange as a background for various display pieces in blue, black, white, and gold. The black is picked up in the draperies and the narrow, wall-high shutters closing the entrance archway. The chandelier is an antique replica, the delicately curved iron branches attached to the central wood turning being painted red. A handsome brass pair of scales on the sideboard, and the life-size chinaware hare on a charger are authentic antiques which lose nothing from a background of walls in simulated stone blocks and a floor of wood slabs that look older than either.

Another essay in up-to-date design which lends itself equally well to association with certain antiques, particularly furniture pieces in walnut or the fruit woods that are not too rigid in line, is provided by example 64. This is based on an Eastern design which suggested the so-called "Persian trumpet" table leg, the sideboard embodying Eastern architectural motifs, and the hardware said to be Saracenic. The cabinet interior, incidentally, is fitted for the storage of linen, china, and silver. The

of luscious fruits. The general lighting is supplied by wall sconces and candlesticks on sideboard and serving table, the board itself illuminated by six tall tapers in antique silver candelabra. Drawn up to the table are six of the later Dutch-style Queen Anne chairs with pale-blue striped seats, all on a shaggy white rug.

This island of gleaming crystal, shining silver, and sparkling white napery is set against a background of

88

63.

64.

90

double-decked serving table with its built-in cupboards is also strikingly oriental in design, and lends itself well to the display of exotic antiquities, as the bronze Buddha and the foliated sconce may suggest.

In the previous chapter an apartment living room (40) was shown which had a grass-green carpet and butter-milk-white walls. In illustration 65 is seen the dining room of that apartment with the same floor covering and wall color. This dining room also reveals the same simplicity in its furnishing, including a brass and black slate wall shelf which serves to hold the table lamps along-side the black-and-brass framed mirror enlivened by a band of gray and white ticking.

The principal source of light is of course the central chandelier hanging over the dining room table. This chandelier is an importation made of pewter hung with "charcoal" crystals. Its suspension chain is encased in red oriental silk, and the candle shades are of laminated embroidered ticking.

The dining table has a marbleized lacquer top and an antique green pedestal base banded in white. Around it are reproductions of Louis XVI cane-backed and seated chairs equipped with down-filled cushions of a medium red color. Along the wall to the right is an adaptation from a French country-style bookcase, with slides, drawers, and cupboards, all in an antique gray-white crackle finish, with pewter hardware, and curtains of green silk stretched behind the door panels of pewter aviary wire.

With the green carpet, the red chair seats, and the green curtains, this little room is far more colorful and attractive than the monochrome of it can begin to reveal.

A quite different atmosphere to any of these is sup-plied by the room shown in 66, which has a touch of the seventeenth century in the cabinet with its linenfold carving, the upper section being reminiscent of the later livery cupboards with perforated tin panels though it does not have any of its own. To these might be added a soupçon of Spanish in the iron chandelier and the brass urn. Nevertheless, the group, whatever its inspiration, represents something quite different with its extraordinary mixture of formal and informal detail.

The sturdy traditional chairs with their embroidered seats, and the round, inlaid pedestal table are undoubted-ly coupled with the café curtains and a round chenille

65.

66.

rug to indicate their adaptability to an informal setting in the breakfast window corner. The cabinet, with its carved and painted embellishments, further accentuates the informal despite the impressive niche within which it is installed, while the dignity of the sideboard is somewhat impaired by the antique yet crude tôle tray in which the handsome breakfast cups nestle. Quite obviously all these pieces could be used in either a formal or informal setting and look well in both, which is quite an achievement in itself.

67.

Another breakfast corner — this one with a modern flavor — is suggested by 67. Actually it could serve as a dining room for four in a small country house or even in a town apartment where the casual air would not seem out of place. Seen in black and white, the rigid lines of the corner cabinet seem to dominate the setting. This impression is modified by the fact that the cabinet is in light-finished mahogany, set against walls whose paper simulates linen, closely matching in color the natural

cane of the cabinet's sliding-door panels. A touch of warmth is added by the paintings, and even more by the copper of the country-style chandelier. The octagonal rug contributes pale tones of red, tan, and blue which set off the mahogany and cane of the chairs with their seats of light-blue linen, as well as the mahogany table with its travertine marble top.

Touches of the antique are provided by the copper tea-kettle, the molded glass cake dish, and the display of pewter mugs and tankards in the cabinet. The tall window of tinted glass is curtained only to dado height in sheer white wool, beyond which the wall becomes brick-red, setting a visual limit to the dining corner.

Where the dining room area is limited it is sometimes possible to increase its apparent size by replacing a connecting doorway with a wider, ceiling-high opening so that there is no break in the line of vision somewhat in the manner of 68, though this is actually no remodeling. This dining room, as will be observed, opens directly off the adjoining room, sharing a common ceiling as well as the carpeting which continues uninterrupted from one side to the other. This junction of the two rooms is made all the more indistinct by an offset wall angle at one side, and advantage is taken of this to accentuate the dining room entrance by attaching to the wall a large antique French panel extending upward to the ceiling. Against this panel is set a small serving table with its appropriate candlesticks, decanters, etc., and mounted on the panel is a wall sconce set off by a couple of silhouette portraits. Both the table and panel extend part way into the next room and actually serve to tie the two rooms together while adding to the visual dimensions of both.

Inside the dining room several informal touches are added, such as the use of a tall open-shelved satinwood dresser as sideboard, and mounting above it, an antique carved and gilded French barometer, together with the use of astral lamps in place of candlesticks on the table, and standing a huge colorful plant in the corner. The furniture likewise is reduced in formality somewhat by being painted white, while the adjustable table top in parquetry injects a modern note with its tapered sides and sharp corners. A striped Roman shade of white linen with turquoise braid is used on the single window. Above the table hangs a chandelier of crystal and bronze doré,

92

a final touch of elegance in an unusual room.

It is pretty much of a truism in design circles that a background should be just that — a setting for the furniture and accessories and not a dominant feature of the room. The clever designer, however, will often find a means of defying a rule and turning the transgression into a triumph.

68.

Something of the sort seems to have happened in the case of illustration 69, where the traditional dining room interior has been invested with an air of fantasy by covering the walls with frescoes in trompe-l'oeil scenes of an Italian landscape replete with mountains, palaces, statuary, and Ionic columns swathed in colorful draperies sweeping down below the dado which becomes a marble balustrade.

All the architectural features are depicted in gray and black, the landscapes, houses, flowers and fruits in natural colors, the draperies a deep green. In happy counterpoint, the distinctly architectural door and window trim, the fireplace surround and mantel, are all a pale gray with the panels and ogee curves of the friezes outlined in black, so that they stand out strongly. The floor covering is a muted tan, the furniture painted white, including the twin-pedestal table, though the seats of the gold-accented eighteenth-century Italian chairs are covered in watermelon-pink brocade.

Thanks to the variations in coloring, and the three-dimensional effect of the landscapes depicted therein, the fresco is far less overwhelming than it may appear in the illustration and in the light of the dinner candles becomes excitingly ethereal. On the other hand it is something that none but the highly trained artist should ever attempt.

In providing a touch of the exotic nothing can equal furniture pieces from the Far East, particularly those made from rattan which do not suffer by comparison with the earlier domestic bamboo innovations or that imitation bamboo made from solid, turned wood which became so popular in Regency times. Rattan, cut from the stem of a climbing palm, is today the aristocrat among natural fibers, rugged, beautiful, and long-lasting.

In illustration 70, side and arm chairs are shown with a table made in Hong Kong to suit the American taste. Though heavy appearing these pieces are light in weight and terrifically strong, and in their dark honey colored finish quite handsome with that little extra of an exotic air that only these products of the Far East can suggest.

The chairs are upholstered in red silk which contrasts nicely with the shaggy rug of a somewhat darker hue. In the background is a pair of tall, shelved cabinets in teak with split-bamboo trim. These serve for the storage of dining equipment, but, as the following picture shows,

93

69.

94

other types of pieces can be substituted, even modern or traditional sideboards in either natural or painted woods.

Next is 71, which presents an idea for a breakfast or supper grouping in a small room or alcove that is almost wholly oriental in its décor. The table and seats are of the same rattan in different designs, the armchairs in particular having a somewhat familiar look, though the loose back cushions may strike an odd note. These chairs have thick seat cushions and are so comfortable that they can also serve as pull-up occasional seats for after-dinner conversation over coffee and liqueurs.

The table, strangely enough, is extensible, being provided with two 15-inch leaves which give it a maximum length of 75 inches. The screen mounted on the wall is typically Chinese in the modern manner.

The only antiques in this area are the Han dynasty horse, and some artifacts in the vitrine atop a Chinese-made teak cabinet which has oversize ring handles and escutcheons in bronze adorning the unusually deep drawers and the cupboards. On the floor is a short-pile white rug, but obviously a variety of decorative rugs, fiber mats, or even polished wood could be substituted without loss of oriental flavor.

An even more attractive group of rattan furniture pieces is the subject of illustration 72. This includes a small table suitable for any one of a variety of purposes except formal dining. The pieces are quite substantial, and the chairs are fitted with casters. This view is particularly interesting because it shows a typical oriental dresser in a black-and-white lacquer finish, together with grass shades and scroll paintings which constitute splendidly authentic background material for such a room. This dresser, incidentally, would have been a desirable addition to the groups in illustrations 61 and 67, and especially in the latter with its white-topped table.

There is also something faintly oriental about the American-made furniture group of illustration 73, which might well be a view of the family corner of a large dining room. This tenuous exotic air may be a result of the fascinating and unusual shape of the table legs and stretchers, complemented by the equally interesting chairs with their fan-shaped backs of woven cane accented by frames in black lacquer and the gold of the seat cushions. These chairs are somewhat reminiscent of the Seignouret

70.

71.

95

72.

73.

chairs of early nineteenth-century Louisiana, especially as regards the arms. However, all are quite modern, and serve to demonstrate the compatibility that can be achieved between pieces so varied as to color and so full of contrast as to shape as well as material. Between the black and the gold — the occasional chairs being close cousins in a deep yellow — the off-white of the walls,

and the blue of the painting, and the streaky-white of the floor, the blue-green rug does a marvelous job of reconciling them all.

Still another grouping which has a faint and entirely illogical flavor of the exotic is shown in 74, which has no seductive curve to betray it, unless it is those of the cabinet's embryo pediment. The cabinet, however, is

96

74.

75.

finished in black relieved with gold, including the highly decorative grilles. The display of porcelains adds to the illusion which is also heightened by the simulated Chinese characters in black on the white rug.

While this is shown as a breakfast group, the table actually may have its four-foot length extended to eight feet so that it becomes a regular dining table. The rug,

which appears to be round, is really oval, and long enough to accommodate the table fully extended, with ample room for the chairs. All of this of course involves moving the table bodily over whenever extra guests are expected or the meal is to be formidably formal.

A somewhat similar arrangement to the foregoing is represented by 75, which may be considered as a break-

76.

77.

fast unit in a small room having a chandelier at its center, or a large room with two chandeliers. This arrangement is not quite so impressive since the large cabinet has been replaced by a six-foot sideboard. The formality also is somewhat reduced with the china display abolished in favor of three framed prints.

The table in this case has a heavy, open base with four brass-bound black columns as legs, and the rug beneath it really is circular, with a textured weave and a fringe — a plain, hard-wearing type in keeping with the sturdy furniture pieces centered upon it. The chairs are modern with Italian overtones, having cane backs and seats upholstered in nubby silk, all eminently suited to a dining room used every day of the year.

More distinctively Italian in inspiration is 76, in a room where white-painted brick hobnobs with wallpaper in a damask pattern of antique reds. It is the rug, however, which establishes the true character of the setting with its bold stripes in reds, blues, yellows, and blacks. It is largely this background color and pattern, centered on a floor of white vinyl terrazzo that softens the severity of the bold and dignified furniture pieces and reduces their architectural character to manageable proportions.

The room is small, its triple cabinets with their bold carving overpowering. The chairs are tall and graceful in rich damask, the back cushions tufted; the table almost monumental in feeling with heavy, tapered legs and carved and shaped apron painted a light gray to emphasize the distinctiveness of the polished, paneled top with its splendid grain; the massive sideboard sitting solidly on a seemingly marble floor, the whole reduced to order by the detail of a metal chandelier and fireman's speaking trumpets masquerading as lamp bases, all capped by red-velvet shades like so many Turkish fezzes. Such is the novel and interesting note which summarizes the total impression created by this mélange of patterns and colors gracefully punctuated by the gleaming white accents of china and porcelain.

To those long familiar with traditional eighteenth-century pieces, the room in illustration 77 will doubtless prove nostalgic even though there are certain unfamiliar innovations. This represents the work of present-day designers seeking to preserve the best of Chippendale and Queen Anne while taking advantage of the wood grains and finishes in the modern manner. Such designs are apt to influence the mood of the room, in whatever manner they are handled, because of these vestigial traditional features. On the other hand, with the proper grouping and background, they contribute a certain freshness and élan to the otherwise everyday interior.

One outstanding piece here is the oval dining table with its sweeping lines and stunning proportions, with its deep bracketed apron and carefully modified Queen Anne legs with the slipper foot. It is these curves that make the table so compatible with the upholstered side chairs which successfully combine elements of Louis XV with the cabriole leg. In comparison, the armchairs are almost pure Chippendale of 1760-65, with added interest in the form of a couple of decorative quirks. These chairs contrast somewhat with the Queen Anne cabinet which in turn has influenced the design of the sideboard where arched, or tombstone, panels are combined with a decorative bracket foot and brass H-hinges. The cabinet is noteworthy for the raised panels and the retention of the Queen Anne arch both in wood and glass.

As arranged in this interior, the pieces undoubtedly look their best without much help from the backgrounds, though the framed heraldic devices, the silver candlesticks, and the footed planter are quite in keeping. Only the reproduction portrait and the candelabra flanking it cheapen an admirable "variation on a theme."

Much more elaborate is 78, which reveals touches of Louis XV and French provincial combined with pure inspiration. The rug is an Aubusson in keeping with the elegance of the furniture, just as the archway suggests the architectural quality of the interior of which this dining room is a part.

The most attractive pieces are the armchairs which represent a pleasing exercise in curves, the covering in antique white leather a stroke of genius, serving to link them with the dining table whose beautifully carved legs terminate in scrolled feet. These and the apron match the white of the chairs, with the addition of a gold-stripe edging which follows the contours of the apron. The side chairs have damask-covered seats, and backs of fine-mesh woven material which is semi-transparent. The twin cabinet owes almost as much to the matching grain of its panels, the light carving, and the antiqued brass of its

78.

79.

99

hinges, lever-handles, and escutcheons as it does to the basic design. The chandelier is a late pattern in gilt-bronze which looks as though it was made for this particular setting. The walls are light tan, the archway a pinkish stone color, the one a perfect foil for the other, and both adding a touch of warmth to the total décor.

In the realm of modern furnishings nothing could be simpler than 79, which has furniture pieces of deceptively simple design posed against a background of fantastically grained veneer with plain white walls on either side to add to the contrast, and a large modern painting providing dramatic impact. The wood grain of the furniture amplifies their decorative appearance, though the chairs and table gain both in grace and character from their very definite curves.

The two side pieces shown are quite angular and present extensive flat areas of polished wood. The dresser, for example, has five doors, three of which are adorned with ring handles and angular escutcheons. Above this box-like unit is an attached shelf which displays one of the few antiques in the room — a Chinese porcelain vase in celadon. Other pieces are displayed in the vitrine which has shelves and sliding doors of glass. The table with its double rounded corners and bowed edges, and its deeply grooved and tapered legs is almost Chinese in feel, as is the chair design which incorporates a wide, vertical back splat bowed to conform to the human spine in the style of the so-called mandarin chairs. This would seem to justify the lively oriental rug whose gay and delicate pattern adds so much to the room.

In contrast with the static case pieces, the curves of the chairs' rear legs and stiles give them a dynamic appearance which is responsible for much of their charm, and really bring the room to life.

A somewhat similar formal dining room (illustration 80) using contemporary furniture has a setting matching the good taste and restraint of the pieces. The china-cabinet — a breakfront with a triangular pediment — is set against a wall featuring a paneled dado with scenic wallpaper above it, and flanked by bronze wall sconces with globes.

The dado which continues around the room, together with the door trim, a lovely shell cabinet, and a fireplace with a paneled overmantel with fluted pilasters, create a

80.

fine architectural interior in which a marble fireplace surround and parquet floor complete the rather formal picture.

All the woodwork is painted a sparkling white whose liveliness is reflected in the light background of the oriental rug occupying the center of the floor. On this stand a dining table and chairs of impressive design with Italian overtones. The chairs have tall curving backs with small shell carvings in the cresting, and their back panels and seats are covered in silk. The table has twin octagonal pedestals nicely carved and molded above their tripod feet, while the oval top is inlaid with matching veneers.

Lively touches are supplied by colorful porcelains in the open-shelved cupboard, and by the china, glass, and silver ware behind glass in the cabinet. The total effect induced by the tinted receding wallpaper, plus the large areas of decorative woodwork in white which envelop the smooth and shapely furniture pieces of dark, polished woods is suggestive of softly glowing treasures in a sparkling casket. If one can imagine the normal ad-

100

81.

it including the entire bay, was painted white. From the darker ceiling down to the lighter dado, the wall was papered in a striking and unusual pattern with vertical bands of alternating design and color. In this way emphasis was placed where it was needed — on the dado area — without changing the interior's apparent proportions to any significant degree, despite the paper's accent on the vertical.

The floor, including the bay area, was covered with linoleum in a spatterdash pattern of reds, yellows, browns, and blues on gray. Much of this, however, was blotted out when a comparatively dark, ten-foot circular braided rug was centered on the floor. In this rug the dominant colors are dark and medium reds, gray, blue, and black, with a lighter patch at the center. This marks the focal area of the room, its center occupied by a pine-legged, cherry-topped round gateleg table. Above it hangs a bronze, three-light chandelier.

The chairs used at this table are of a specially interesting type — an English country style of the late eighteenth century, with twin spindle backs, a turned front stretcher with a central boss, and turned front legs with pad feet, with seats of rush beneath thin pads of checked gingham, in reds on a natural ground. At some time the chairs had been painted black, and with much of this now worn off, the original antique air is pretty well restored. A somewhat similar pattern of gingham to that of the chair pads is used for the sill-length draperies which are confined to the side windows thus ensuring a maximum of daylight when the venetian blinds are not in use. The Welsh dresser, an early eighteenth-century piece, is country-made of oak, with iron hooks under the cornice and in the front edge of the top shelf. As the photograph indicates, these hooks serve as hangers for pewter measures and drinking vessels. On the wall at either side the dresser hangs a large platter in sgraffito ware, the dresser shelves displaying smaller specimens of pottery, porcelain, and pewter.

With this small number of furniture pieces occupying the limited space available, the diners should experience no lack of comfort, nor those serving the meal any inconvenience, both points of importance in a room where free circulation is essential.

An equally interesting dining room in a more formal

ditions of sideboard and extra chairs ranged against the unseen walls, and soft window draperies adding a splash of color for warmth against the wide areas of reflective white, the picture of an unusually inviting yet dignified interior would be complete.

Dark wooden furniture is best seen in pale surroundings for contrast interest, which is one reason why antique pieces so often look even more attractive in a contemporary setting. This fact apparently was recognized when the small, square dining room in illustration 81 was planned around a variety of English pieces in dark oak, cherry, and black-painted pine and elm. The room itself, though basically square, offered difficulties, having a shallow "octagonal" bay — one side and two half-sides of an octagon — with narrow jogs in the wall at each end, an awkward shape best dealt with by ignoring it.

The room also was high — a useful feature where a chandelier is involved — but visually lowered by making the ceiling a shade darker than usual. A chair rail was added to the walls and that, together with the area below

style, that comes as near today's expression of the traditional of 150 years ago as it is possible to make it, is represented by 82. This room does not owe its appeal solely to the fact that it is furnished entirely with antiques — or even to the beautiful modern portrait which lends so intimate and personal a touch. Much is due to the

82.

selection of the individual pieces, and the details of the background and choice of colors, all of which reflect the highest taste.

Mahogany is king here, from the huge three-part reproduction Empire table to the delicate Hepplewhite mirror with its wheatears, urn and flowers, and the perky, almost vertical scrolls. The chairs are a 1780 English, Hepplewhite design with shapely top rails and the urn outline in the pierced splats. Their seats are covered in two-tone rust silk, brass-nailed. The sideboard is pure 1790 Hepplewhite, the doors and drawers banded or inlaid, or both, the mahogany faded to a mellow brown. On it stands a pair of exquisite eighteenth-century can-

delabra and a Chinese export tureen competing with an equally antique footed silver tureen on the table doubling as a flower bowl — or épergne. Not appearing in the picture is an English mahogany breakfront of 1780.

The fireplace mantel is severely architectural, the pilasters delicately reeded, the whole thing painted white to match the rest of the woodwork, and contrast faintly with the pale pink of the walls. Its garniture is restricted to a pair of decorated, flower-filled vases flanking the above-mentioned portrait. Over the table hangs an English six-light crystal chandelier with glass branches from which hang festoons of diamond-cut crystals and pear-shaped drops.

The french window — the only window in the room — is hung with pink silk over a box pelmet, with one central, rust-lined swag, and cascades that reach down to a few inches below the dado molding. The Oushak rug is of a strong rust color with touches of turquoise. In spite of its limited size, this is a stately room, adequately yet simply furnished and free from meaningless decoration and objets de virtu that have no purpose other than to impress or fill a vacant spot.

Dining rooms featuring wrought-iron chairs are a comparative rarity but they can be extremely attractive if the interior is competently designed around them, as illustration 83 shows. The chairs, however, must be elegantly designed and made thoroughly comfortable thanks to substantial upholstery.

Originally this room lacked even architectural interest, though it had both stone and plaster walls. The designer featured the stone, painting all walls and the ceiling white.

The architectural character was then supplied by painting in some ceiling beams and a cornice in celadon-green *faux bois*. The floor was then transformed with vinyl tiles of the same color, in a pattern of large octagons and small squares, emphasized by grouting the joints in white. Along the window wall was hung a series of Roman blinds in lacquer-red felt with dyed tête-de-nègre trim.

Featured against one of the long walls is a large breakfront cabinet with a carved pediment. This is finished in antique celadon-green with white striping, the upper doors being paneled with pewter aviary wire

102

83.

behind which are stretched lacquer-red silk curtains. The huge dining table top is of dark-stained ash, solidly perched on a handsome pair of pedestals in polished steel and brass. Over it is suspended an old three-foot-diameter Spanish chandelier in black wrought iron.

The table seats eight, and the custom-made chairs of black iron with brass feet are heavily lacquered, the seats and backs being covered in a black and red wool plaid.

In the window is a delicate, beautifully painted serving table with a shelf, ogee-curved apron, and slender cabriole legs reminiscent of the Queen Anne style. This has its own lighting device in the shape of an antique triple-candle bouillotte lamp in bronze with tôle shades in dark green, a fittingly tasteful finishing touch to an interior so thoroughly planned.

Dual-Purpose Rooms

Whatever the size of the home, whether house or apartment, it often happens that a single room must be adapted to two or more purposes. Living rooms need to find space for informal dining; the comparatively little used dining room may have some corner preempted for special activities involving the introduction of a desk or games table, or a bedroom called upon to double as a study whether of books or archaeological artifacts, and so on. Perhaps more often, difficulties arise in finding space for collections of all sorts but more particularly of art displays where wall space is at a premium, or porcelains which can have an upsetting effect on the general décor when overdone. Still other problems arise when bulky collections have to be stored in suitable cabinets, or the composer's music room must, on occasion, be given over to a variety of quite different purposes.

The decorating problem in such cases will usually be subservient to the overall design, function being more important than mood, much depending upon the degree to which the interior can be unified and the multiple functions made to contribute to an agreeable whole.

Commonest among decorating problems in these dual-purpose rooms is that of stealing space for dining in what is properly the living room without involving too much shuffling of furniture pieces prior to each meal, or necessitating total rearrangement for larger or more formal functions. Much will depend upon the total footage available, and the sizes of the respective furni-

ture pieces — always remembering that one large unit may be more efficient than two smaller ones. Also to be considered are the possibilities for separating the two areas. In confined spaces neither partitions, tall furniture pieces, nor folding screens can ordinarily be considered because of the factor of limited view, not to mention the incidence of claustrophobia.

In many small apartments where separate dining areas are impractical, the maintenance of an open view throughout the combined living and dining areas is essential as adding to the feel of space in both. Quite often this also involves the continuation of one floor area into the other without any line of demarcation such as terminating the floor covering at the boundary.

When all of the furniture in the room is visible at one time, every piece, obviously, should be more or less compatible. In the city apartment, which is the subject of illustration 84, the two groupings are not only harmonious but of the same high quality so that the whole room is equally attractive whether the dining table is set for a meal or not.

The basic arrangement of this somewhat small apartment living room is controlled by the hooded fireplace. Maximum seating is afforded, with the least waste of space, by placing a long sofa on each side the fireplace and at right-angles to it, with one large circular coffee table between them. These three pieces then form a group which is complemented by two upholstered chairs,

84.

which have their own table and lamp, beyond the fire-place traffic lane. One of these chairs is a low-backed lounge type which does not interfere with the view throughout the room, the other a decorative tall-backed occasional chair set slightly farther back.

Against the far wall, to one side of a recessed window, is a tall armoire, a distinctly decorative storage piece carved in relief and with curtains of a rich fabric behind the brass grilles of the doors. In the window recess is a paneled commode which could very well accommodate chinaware.

The dining group, behind the nearest sofa, consists of a four-legged table with a stunning inlaid top, and one deep leaf, together with two Venetian fan-back chairs — one of the most beautiful chair designs ever conceived. Elsewhere in the apartment more of these are available for intimate social occasions when the table is moved back, away from the sofa, and its leaf raised — the whole thing a lesson in practicability combined with lovely surroundings in a limited space.

It should also be noted that in the event of larger gatherings, where no seated dinner is to be served, the table can be moved back still further, against the wall where it could, if necessary, be used for buffet refreshment. The adjoining sofa could then be moved in the same direction to allow of a larger conversation area before the fireplace.

Quite a different set of circumstances exists in the small room shown in the next illustration (85). This could readily function either as a living-dining room or a simple living room with a "writing corner." In either case it is much more formal but not nearly so rich, yet reveals a passion for both elegant comfort and curiosities that are antique works of art.

The room is divided into two areas by painting one side and half of each end wall and papering the rest. One of the papered corners is occupied by a large harvest table set at 45 degrees across the angle. This has but a single drop-leaf which, together with the top, is ornamented by a dramatic inlay of butternut veneers set into the walnut, the surrounding grain suggesting expensive banding. Its tapered octagonal legs terminate in carved tulips and brass pads.

This corner has two windows, one in each wall, with plain silk curtains draped under elaborate pelmets with decorative borders. These stand out against the damask-type wallpaper which has a large stylized floral pattern in silver over alternating light and dark vertical bands. The whole papered area contrasts prettily with the pale mauve of the painted wall sections, and their relationship is accentuated by running the floor's large terrazzo-patterned vinyl squares across the room cornerwise. This helps to make the corner space behind the table seem a perfectly natural location for a chair — an illusion emphasized by one edge of the octagonal rug which parallels the tiles.

Two other sides of the rug are in line with the sofas, which are arranged at right-angles for easy conversation. These pieces are covered in textured linen fabric with a jumbo-sized check, and in front of each is a double-decked coffee table on casters, the lower shelves laden with books. In the angle between the adjacent sofa ends

85.

is an iron-legged table supporting a tall lamp whose turned-wood base actually forms a six-branch candelabra.

Against the dark area of the end wall is a tall bookcase-cabinet in butternut and walnut veneers with brass hardware. On its top rests an antique lion carved in the round. The cupboard section displays antique porcelains and leather bindings which are equally handsome. Two accent pieces which stand out against either background are the twin, tall-backed lounge chairs upholstered in sheer white, their strikingly unusual shapes adding glamor to drama not surpassed even by the tall statue of some female "Neptune" with a candle impaled on a somewhat modified "trident" in another corner of the room.

Exotic interiors are not confined to the hot countries, as illustration 86 demonstrates. This interior was designed to incorporate furnishings and artifacts from Japan into a small house in Maine, with the addition of certain pieces made in America. This part of the house consists of a bedroom and a living room separated by a

107

86.

ceiling-high screen of linen which is the color of sesame seeds — equivalent to the color known here as less romantic "putty."

The whole floor is in parquet and the walls are covered in putty — or sesame — linen as is the low modern sofa. In the bedroom section two low daybeds are formed of black wooden plinths with mattresses of foam rubber covered in Ming-blue and brown printed linen. There is also a low, square modern table with a bronze base and smoked-glass top. In the living room beautifully carved screens of sandalwood from India form a sliding wall that gives access to a tiny, white-pebbled garden planted with dwarf trees. This garden is enclosed by wall-high windows.

Inside the room Ming-blue is the predominant color. Not only is the area rug dyed in that hue, but the rush-seated Spanish side chairs are painted to match. In contrast, the long, modern oriental dining table is made of oiled walnut with a slate top. There is also a low cocktail table of a Chinese pattern which has a black and white marble top, and an equally low-seated copy of a mandarin chair in walnut. All of these look exceedingly well against the blue.

At the back of the room a pair of reproduction cam-

87.

paign chests in walnut with brass fittings blend nicely with the Far Eastern pieces, and should be quite at home with the painting of an ancient fortified town in what was later British India. All throughout this room are smaller pieces of oriental artistry that add tremendously to its alien flavor, such as the copper hanging lamp and the water jug, the bronze fishes, a metal hibachi, a hang-ing tea kettle on a bamboo pole, and an exquisite piece of translucent white porcelain.

An equally nostalgic collection of Spanish, Italian, and English pieces transformed the barn shown in illus-tration 87 into a comfortable though somewhat casual country hideaway. The picture actually shows only what was the combination living and eating room (the word dining here would undoubtedly conjure up a more luxurious and tidy setting!), a place prepared for occupancy by covering the floor with loosely laid rough wood blocks in parquetry fashion, and staining them a dark red. The ceiling was plastered between the beams to eliminate the danger of sifting dust, and an enormous fireplace installed on a raised platform, with a wide metal hood and chimney and brick hearth.

A row of three wide windows occupies part of one wall, each with its shade of striped cloth. Underneath, the wide sill serves to carry a tobacco jar, an antique table lamp, and a bowl of ferns with a hanging lantern of wood suspended just above it. Backed against this sill is a large modern sofa covered in coarse red wool. Against the opposite wall is a tall, wide, and handsome Spanish hutch cupboard (armario) with latticed doors, the whole thing painted antique red.

Nearby is another major piece — an oval, pedestal-type Spanish dining table of the same color, flanked by a pair of Spanish turned dining chairs enamelled antique black with tie-on cushions over the reed seats. Between these and the wall is a wooden spindle-backed settee, painted to match the chairs.

In the middle of the floor stand two massive armchairs, also from Spain, painted the same black and fitted with cushions in fuschia-colored felt. The only floor covering is an area rug of paisley design in a brilliant ruby red, and on this stands one of a pair of old English campaign chests, with a Cromwellian-looking stool from Italy nearby. The rest of the room is actually littered with items of antiquarian or utilitarian interest — a painted Spanish chest, an Italian gilt-wood candlestick, a metal wine-storage bin (probably the most useful of all!), intriguing looking pieces of copper and brass — an ideal bachelor's retreat such as more often "just happens" than is designed when once the colors are decided upon and the basic pieces acquired, all the rest being atmosphere — and from this one can learn a lot.

A quite ambitious example of a dual-purpose room is the subject of 88. This has fireside sofas in place of the less commodious loveseats. A grill occupies one end of the fireplace opening, a regular fire grate the rest, and beyond that is a large enclosed storage space for logs, with an antique leather fire bucket a decorative feature

of the raised hearth. Behind each sofa is a table, and beyond them a complete dining area equipped with table, chairs, and sideboard, illumination being provided by a double-decker chandelier with castellations in black and gold, plus a pair of three-bracket candelabra.

The fireplace wall is of brick extending to the dining area where it gives way to the louvered doors of storage spaces which actually are deep enough to accommodate a Pullman kitchen. The end wall is of vertical barn siding adorned with four excellent prints of wild ducks in full color.

The entire floor of this room is covered with white vinyl tile, using no rugs for obvious reasons. Some of the furniture is Early American in pine, the dining chairs being Hitchcock pieces in black, decorated in gold. One of the cocktail tables is a country piece in pine, another consists of an antique drum. There is also an early eighteenth-century oval gateleg table, and the table lamps have bases made from old-fashioned lacquered canisters.

One wing chair and one sofa are upholstered in heavy sailcloth in a checkered pattern of reds and blues with white squares. The other sofa has a pattern of birds and flowers on a background of gray and white stripes. On the sideboard and tables are china figurines and a porcelain piece or two, with gaily colored old-English pottery groups on the mantel sporting a decorated tin tray in the middle — all evidence of the excellent taste that inspired the whole décor.

Even in the larger houses it is sometimes more convenient to combine the living room and the library, especially if the bookshelves are comparatively little used. Furthermore, if the room is fairly large, one activity need not interfere with another since a variety of independent furniture groupings can be arranged with ample space between them.

Illustrations 89 and 90 show one such living room-library, the shelves being confined to bookcases flanking the window on each side of the fireplace. One end of the room provides space for the large English Chippendale mahogany secretary which has a lot of drawer and shelf storage space besides the fall-front writing area. This piece is given a little added importance by the oil paintings of horses, one on each side of it, and by the

110

88.

89.

90.

beige grass cloth-covered wall against which the mahogany stands out strongly. Along the adjoining paneled wall, a large English Chippendale sofa commands the services of two sizable end tables which hold much more than the tall lamps. In front of the sofa is an oversized oval table in walnut. At either end is a comfortable seat, a 1780 English Hepplewhite wing chair opposite a Raeburn chair of the same period. The whole group is graciously presided over by a large English hunt picture in period.

The facing long wall is taken up by a large fireplace, the recesses on either side being occupied by the bookcases and a window. Nearby is placed a Queen Anne walnut open-arm chair with a flame-stitch seat, and an American, four-drawer, bracket-footed birch chest with an ox-bow front, and between them a stunning Herez rug in shades of beige, rust, soft pinks and faded blues. In this inviting room the paneling is of birch, the draperies linen and silk in tones of rust, the ceiling white for maximum reflection and embellished with an early eighteenth-century, eight-branch, ball type chandelier in bronze. Each painting is separately illuminated, and rust-color tiles add their warmth to this pleasing example.

Although 91 shows only a corner of an artist's apartment, it serves to illustrate the fact that pictures in a large variety of shapes and sizes — and frames — can be displayed in a neat and orderly manner regardless of the subjects, the technique, or the style of the framing. All that is needed is an eye for balance and proportion, taking into account the intensity or visual impact of the subject portrayed and the massiveness of the frame.

Artists are, of course, a class apart, and many collectors who take their avocation seriously have similar ideas as to the manner in which their home interiors should be designed. Quite often the demand is for one or more rooms to be devoted to the display of art objects, sculpture, paintings, archeological artifacts, and so on, sometimes to a point where comfort, if not convenience, is decidedly secondary. This attitude can present the interior designer with problems.

Plain white walls undoubtedly form the best background for works of art that require contemplation because there is no distracting note—providing the space is adequate — and no clash of color or pattern to distract the eye. On the other hand, plain interiors do not necessarily have to be at all severe; on the contrary some simple interpretations of early rooms can be quite lively, with exposed timbers, decorative dadoes, paneled areas (especially around fireplaces) and so on. There are also situations in which the displays can be largely absorbed into the decoration, as some of the examples presented may suggest.

In illustrations 92, 93, and 94 all walls are white; in 92, which shows the opposite end of the room to 94, the damask-covered wall is acid-green. The upholstered pieces likewise are either white or acid-green. The carpet is white, and the draperies white with crewel-work embroidery.

With this room predominantly white, the daylight from one very large and one smaller window is usually more than ample, and the distribution fairly even. After dark, when impressions are usually more important than detail, the illumination is taken care of by a number of large table lamps with translucent shades so that the light is partially diffused and partly reflected, and thus more evenly distributed and softer.

In 92 it is interesting to note that the entrance to the apartment is via a short hall with damask-covered walls and parquet floor. The large room into which it opens is divided into a small dining area and the equivalent of a living room, the junction being emphasized by the parquet giving way to a large white rug extending to the window at the other end. A sofa and an end table mark the limits of the dining area which does, however, contain some of the display objects, though these are actually secondary to the major groupings of artifacts and paintings.

This dining section is furnished with Louis XV-style cane-back chairs, having damask-covered seats and a table to match. There is also a marble-topped side table surmounted by a marble and ormolu flower vase. A second table, behind the sofa, supports a large vitrine in which is displayed a brass sculpture of Max Bill. Beside it, on the window sill, is a terracotta seated figure by Henri Laurens, and on the wall is a couple of pictures forming part of the major collection whose emphasis is on twentieth-century German expressionist art.

In the living room area the displays begin at the sofa

91.

92.

113

93.

114

convenience in viewing the displays. There is, nevertheless, a small conversation group by the terrace window in addition to those afforded by the two sofas and their satellite pieces.

This type of interior obviously represents a logical solution to a situation in which art takes the precedence over mere decoration, so that the tendency is toward functional simplicity. Fortunately it is a simplicity that can provide a window for the soul!

The arrangement in illustration 95 was designed to meet the needs of a rare-book collector and a connoisseur of ancient literature. Here display is a secondary consideration and storage space all-important. Straight lines and plane surfaces are emphasized to secure a basic effect of architectural integrity into which life and color are injected by a pair of mahogany framed scoop-backed chairs in patterned scarlet fabric, and an equally vivid scarlet rug which defines the furnished area as an island in a sea of oak parquet.

94.

with a pre-Colombian pottery figurine from Jalisco on the end table. On a low, oval tray-table in front of the sofa is a sixteenth-century Japanese pottery jar and a collection of bronze cows by E. Mataré. The rest of the art collection is spread over the walls. This consists of drawings and watercolors by Pissarro, Heckel, Schiele, and Feininger, not omitting a ceramic plate by Picasso.

On the floor, at wall center, stands a Mirko copper column and, in the corner, a gilt bronze figure by G. Franklin. There are also small figurines on the triangular table together with a collection of Ashanti gold weights. This brings one to the great window and a glass door to the terrace on which is a large bronze group by Marianne Pineda. Inside the room, silhouetted by the window, is another bronze by E. Barlach and, on a column next to it, stands a lively bronze figure of Nijinsky by G. Kolbe. To the right of this can be seen the edge of a wood bas-relief by Hugh Townley covering the height of the wall.

The furniture here, mostly period pieces, obviously plays a secondary role, its placing subject primarily to

95.

115

Within this area is a large square storage cabinet, the back line of which is continued by a stretch of open shelves, all in mahogany. The deep cupboard and the narrow shelving form an angle into which is fitted a nine-foot-long sofa in black leather. At the far end is a steel-legged table serving both the sofa and an oversized ottoman extending out from one end of it. All of this faces an ebonized hanging hearth and mantel mounted on a teak-faced fireplace wall. Other seats are provided by placing cushions on this elevated hearth. At the window end, a backdrop of contrasting texture is pro-

96.

vided by sheer white draperies in an openwork weave assuring plenty of light with privacy. A touch of magnificence is added by an exquisite oriental lamp base in pierced brass, and a hammered brass chest in the fireplace. Other carved pieces, and a large hieroglyphic tablet used as fireplace wall decoration constitute additional interesting accents, together with a couple of

symmetry shattering potted palms, which add to the agreeableness of the overall air. From a practical standpoint, this arrangement gives ample working and seating surfaces, with intriguing views of the treasures stored on and beneath the rear "counter" top.

In 96 the owner's interest is confined to the smaller artifacts of the East which lend themselves particularly well to storage in dust-proof drawers and cupboards.

As far as furnishing is concerned, interest is confined to modern pieces hence the black leather and steel. The ebony-finished cabinet in the foreground conceals drawers and shelves behind its sliding panels which are lacquered in a variety of compatible colors. Behind it is a bed with a sloping, leather-upholstered headboard, and a regular mattress. By reducing the width with suitable bolsters and pillows this can be quickly converted into a sofa for daytime use in this bachelor apartment.

Beyond the bed is a tier table of seating height. This is of mahogany and cane, and large enough for a variety of purposes, including the sorting and inspection of artifacts. The wall is covered with a ceiling-high sheath of mahogany veneer between the silk curtains which hide the French windows. The cubical chairs in seam-tufted black leather, with arms and bases of oiled walnut, are mounted on flush, stainless steel legs, and are a good deal more comfortable than they may appear.

Except for the large round ottoman, the only other piece of furniture is a modular storage cabinet of resin-finished mahogany with black aluminum pulls, and black leather facings to the doors. Color accents are supplied by a half-dozen throw pillows, and a mattress cover which pick up the muted greens and mustard of the sliding cabinet doors. The major color mass, however, is supplied by the huge red oriental rug which adds warmth to the entire décor. The only other gesture toward things exotic lies in the burnished metal lamp, the Burmese elephant, the casually placed snakeskin-sheathed dagger, and the Asiatic pottery ewer.

The furniture arrangement in illustrations 97 and 98 was governed by the owner's need for a living room which could also serve for the recording and playing of music, as an office for personal paper work, and occasionally as a dining room. This multiple objective seems to have been accomplished without the slightest con-

116

97.

fusion or overlapping of functions, allowing ample traffic space, and at no detriment to the acoustic qualities of the interior. The same quiet combination also has been effected between the old and the new in the furnishing, preserving the crisp, clean lines of the modern while finding room for the gracious antique forms and romantic accessories.

Since this was destined to be a busy room, the plaid rug was a practical choice, as was the covering of the long sofa in vinyl suede. Even the necessary shelf space flanking the white-painted piano was made attractive by the adoption of metal-posted étagères whose enameled rods are topped by turned brass finials. The instrument itself is ornamented with old brass candlesticks having bouillotte-style shades.

Another bow to practicality is obvious in the painted

The next example (illustration 99) is an interesting compromise with no frills and in some ways almost stark, though catering to feminine taste in such things as a fanciful ornate bronze chandelier with its four-foot ring of crystals, a display of good china, and the immediate availability of a solid silver coffee pot, sugar and creamer set. Here, too, are mahogany footstools, a mahogany music stand, and a grand piano.

The room itself has some architectural grace with a tongue-and-dart molded and coved cornice, plus a dado with a nicely wrought cap over fielded panels and decorative baseboards. Between the two, the smooth plaster walls are tinted a medium blue, interrupted in one place by a darker, painted panel on which are depicted Chinese willows in golden yellow, and in another by an open-shelved china cabinet whose contents are protected by gold-wire curving mesh. Other porcelain pieces are displayed on stands. The seating consists of two fringed armchairs and a modern version of a wing chair, plus a couple of modern side chairs with rounded backs. There is also a trestle table, and a large Sheraton mahogany drum table on which stands a porcelain-based lamp, whose illumination can be augmented as required by a pair of twin-candle wall sconces, one on each side of the window. Its floor covering is a luxurious fringed rug of almost room size. On a mahogany side table, in the foreground, is a silver-plated lighter, a cigaret "cruet," and a collection of magazines, all of which suggest that this might well be the study-living room of a musically inclined bachelor of either sex.

The next interior (illustration 100) represents an entirely different set of circumstances, where most of the pieces are antiques of various vintages and styles — nineteenth-century English, Louis XV, Regency, French provincial, Louis XVI, and so on. In the beginning, however, there was nothing but an arid interior, all white with no architectural character whatsoever — no moldings, no fireplace, modern or period, to set the style or provide the contrast.

Obviously, the first triumph was accomplished by the huge mural which pushed out the wall and created a vista, supplying a mass of form and color in space that would transform the characterless cell and give it a focal point. The long sofa in a turquoise textured material

98.

metal tables on which stand lamps with bases made from medieval figures. In one corner a Directoire-style desk accompanies eighteenth-century Italian painted chairs and a curule stool, while a large canvas representing a window looking out upon a landscape hangs an inch above a long, dark "sill" — in actuality a bracketed console attached to the light-colored wall — which completes the illusion.

118

99.

119

100.

was made to go under it, and is given added authority by the flanking pair of handsome Directoire bouillotte tables with marble tops and brass galleries. This major group was completed by a modern mahogany coffee table, flat and angular, that contrasts so beautifully with its curvaceous end pair of Louis XV fauteuils in cane and coral satin.

To balance all this, against the left wall an eighteenth-century French provincial chest in fruitwood was centered in the space, and topped by a nineteenth-century mirror painted to match. On one side of this stands an interesting example of an early nineteenth-century English shell-back chair in pine with dolphin arms; on the other a delicately delightful Regency chair in simulated

101. By covering the French windows of a typical sunporch with trellised panels, the designer transformed it into a year-round card-room and sitting room complete with bar. The bar actually consists of an antique armoire containing all the necessities including an ice-box. The tiled floor of the room is covered with closely woven rush matting, and the furniture is oriental rattan in a light finish to go with the white formica-topped game, cocktail, and lamp tables. The rattan sofa is covered in white waterproof sailcloth. The only structural changes necessary, beside the addition of trellis, was to close one arched opening to the living room with mirror to provide the necessary additional wall space.

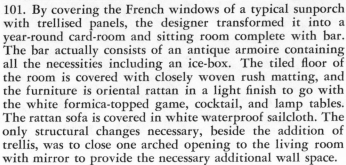

bamboo with a pierced back, and a seat pad. At the opposite side of the room is a twentieth-century flat-topped writing desk in mahogany, accompanied by a tub chair in leather.

Whenever necessary the room can be closed off from the foyer by a tall folding door formed of a four-leaf, louvered screen reaching almost to the ceiling from a floor totally enveloped in a carpet of gray, fitted felt. Around the room in strategic positions are crystal-draped candelabra and lamps with antique pottery bases, porcelain figurines, tiny lifelike ducks on a hunk of driftwood,

102. Sunporch dining, summer or winter, does not necessarily call for either iron or wicker furniture, nor even for loose cushions in these days of waterproof, washable fabrics. The perfection of such materials in a wide variety of colors and patterns has made possible the conversion of many an arbor, gazebo, *pavillon*, belvedere, or plain summerhouse to an all-weather retreat for meals. Here a small sunporch appears after such a transformation with a floor of vinyl slabs in black and white, and one wall covered in waterproofed fabric in a trellis pattern against a brick wall, the high-backed chairs around a black-marble table, upholstered in a similar material whose pattern is repeated in the flooring border. A delicate bronze-and-crystal chandelier over the table, a carved stone fountain-cum-planter, and a deep border of luxurious greenery complete a cool picture of a room once devoted to tropical plants and winter blooms.

121

103.

some exquisite pieces of silverware such as a posset pot, and a leather desk blotter stamped in gold, carefully selected details that not only give the room a lived-in look but indicate that the owner is a person of taste.

A mock-up of a room designed for export to a Greek island where the actual house overlooks the Aegean Sea is seen in illustration 103. It would take very little work, and less imagination, to adapt it to a house or apartment nearer home.

As in previous examples, a great deal of white is used, and the walls are kept plain, except for the arcaded windows which have curtains of a cool white batiste printed with a design of giant pink tulips. Along one wall is a

row of three campaign chests, painted white to match the shelves behind them. These serve as storage units. On the opposite side of the room is a sofa covered in white chintz piped in fern-green, and white-checked gingham. The room's largest mass of color is provided by the area rug which is a Grecian shaggy wool Flokati in avocado green. Next comes the hooded chair which is covered in wild pink and green striped Thai silk.

The furniture is obviously of mixed origins, the desk chair, the rose-smelling cupid, and the coffee table all hailing from Italy. The writing table and the marble-topped bouillotte table are French, and the modified chaises longues American Victorian. Around the room there are plenty of *objets de vertu* including a delightful oil painting of a garden scene, a wall cabinet hiding dancing figurines, rare plates, and old books, an elaborate wrought-iron reading stand on the desk, another stand with a tea kettle and spirit lamp, and so on — something to catch the eye wherever one turns — a happy decorating device in addition to the collector's items on the shelves.

In a great many instances collectors of smaller items such as porcelains prefer to distribute them throughout the living quarters instead of confining them to one room. This practice ordinarily has quite a few advantages since a few pieces here and there can be made to contribute something special to the general décor instead of overpowering it — inviting attention instead of demanding it. Illustration 104 presents an excellent example of this procedure in which a few display pieces enliven one corner of a living room.

This display was carefully planned to suit the architectural features of the room which included a high cathedral ceiling and a tall bow window in the gable end. On one side of the window is a beautiful Louis XV carved oak commode; on the other side is an equally entrancing four-drawer slant-top desk with the same tiny scroll feet, the quarter-columns replaced by lovely tapered moldings that give it a slight bombé effect. Over each of these hangs a narrow, four-shelf plate rack with scalloped sides and an upswept top whose gadrooned edges terminate in a carved floral crest. Each displays a dozen pieces of porcelain.

The semi-circular bay is framed by toile draperies in pink, with a connecting valance of the same material, and fitted with a curved seat. In front of this stands a plain but delicate Louis XV tric-trac table with a shaped apron and drawer front. This serves to display a large blanc-de-chine tureen and a pair of vermeil twin-wick lamps. Other odd pieces may be exposed on the flat tops of furniture around the room, such as the Venetian glass bowl on the desk, and the Spanish figurines on the commode — tiny accents in a room crowded with interest — all in excellent taste.

104.

123

The Entrance Hall and Foyer

Though the terms hall and foyer are often used interchangeably, confusion may be reduced if the term hall is reserved for the usual wide passageway, and foyer used only for the room-type halls — square, octagonal, etc., — off which one or more passageways may open, and which, in effect, is more of a meeting place for guests and hosts, a sort of miniature reception room in the original meaning of the word, or a large one (often at the foot of the grand staircase) in a mansion.

The entrance hall and foyer are considered important to interior design because from them the visitor is supposed to get his first and therefore most lasting impression of the home. For those who get no further than the entrance this may contain a modicum of truth, but others would do well to reserve judgment in these days when every room may be different, and even the traditional may encompass many degrees of informality, while eclecticism can embrace an even wider range of furniture style combinations and decorating moods. Furthermore, one can step from a cold foyer of marble and mirrors into an atmosphere of oriental splendor as the following examples well demonstrate.

One thing to note about these various hall interiors is that, regardless of the style, all may be divided into two classes — the open and the closed. In the former, the hall or foyer opens into other areas so that there are vistas (or maybe only one) due to the use of archways

or ever-open doors, or a passageway to other rooms — all adding to the feeling of space, and to the interest. This is especially so where advantage has been taken of the opportunity to introduce variations into the décor. The closed foyers, on the other hand, are usually self-contained entities that often can be treated as a single small room leading to others.

Any problems arising in such cases are likely to be due to an inability to resist crowding too much into too small a space, or hanging too many things on the walls so that they seem to pull the walls inwards with claustrophobic effects. One of the first things to be considered, then, should be the proportions of the hall which will effect its treatment unless too-high ceilings or too-long passageways are corrected optically. This may call for dividing the walls horizontally by means of a dado or chair rail, making the wall a darker color below than above to give it more weight. It may also call for a deep cornice, a darker ceiling, or a ceiling papered with the same pattern as the walls. Oftentimes a border is more effective. than a cornice because it does not creep out over the ceiling to reduce its apparent width. Tall furniture also helps, as does a suitably designed hanging lantern.

In the case of a high ceiling a panel over a room door may be the solution, whether plain or carved or enclosing a painted design. This can also have a pediment over it

124

if necessary. Ordinarily, these things are quite simple to do to an existing surface and therefore readily removable when the décor is changed.

Another point to note is that the hall will normally need far less furniture than any other space, though it can actually accommodate more without *seeming* crowded. In many instances a table and a mirror may be all that is required; the challenge to the decorator is therefore all the greater. Floors are particularly important, receiving more wear than most in a limited traffic area, but even here the style and materials will have to be governed by the degree of formality, the preponderating period, if any, and the quality of the furnishings.

The basic principle in most instances is to provide an atmosphere of welcome without being too casual, the decoration not too aggressive, but perhaps slightly formal and dignified even though sparsely furnished and using only functional pieces — table, mirror, a seat for changing footwear, and storage space for outdoor clothing. If a chest is used for storage it can also serve as a temporary seat, if not too high. Otherwise it can be used as a table, unless it is of the lidded type which calls for removal of anything on it before opening. In any event, quite a few of the standard groupings consist of a storage piece of some sort, lamp, and a mirror, or a console and mirror with flanking wall lights where the hall ceiling light does not provide proper illumination, together with a small and unpretentious chair. Even with these three pieces it is astonishing how decorative the group can be, depending upon the size and complexity of the cabinet and mirror — and the width of the hall whose primary function as a passageway should be the first consideration.

Injecting interest in a hall often requires the exercise of a great deal of imagination. A trompe l'oeil design, whether executed in paint, wallpaper, or fabric, is always useful and apt to be an object of admiring comment, even if it represents nothing more than a cracked-open door. On the other hand, niches, though less adaptable, are more practical because they can be put to use. They are especially valuable where the perspective would normally terminate in a bare wall, and there is no space for a small piece of furniture. A picture or a mirror in such a spot may look incomplete without something solid under it.

A niche can be made in the manner of a fireplace opening, regardless of its distance from the floor, with a slightly projecting wooden frame or plaster molding, painting the inside darker than the wall to accent its depth. Usually it is necessary to cut into the wall at least half the thickness of a stud. In such cases a small half-round shelf big enough to support a vase can project slightly beyond the frame without spoiling the effect.

Another thing to remember is that, in a hall more than anywhere else, plain doors can be deadly, and if architectural character and interest are missing these can supply it, often by the addition of a little molding, at worst by installing a decorative surround, pilasters or pediment, or both.

Much, of course, depends upon the effects desired as well as the shape and size of the area. In a rather narrow hall the illusion of space can usually be created by the use of mural papers depicting the outdoors with lots of pale blue sky and receding landscape. Where there is a reasonable amount of width, say for two people to walk abreast, this sorcery may not be essential, and even a richer effect can be achieved as in illustration 113, which represents a traditional hallway fortunate enough to be illuminated by windows. Inside this hall there is nothing particularly reflective. The floor is of parquet, somewhat lighter than usual, the wood-sheathed dado painted a medium gray and the ceiling white. The colorful mural in brown, beige, yellow and coral — a nineteenth-century French paper by Dufour of a Chinese river scene — has somewhat of a darker foreground and masses of still darker foliage. Naturally there is an overall light-absorptive effect in spite of the much lighter areas. To counteract this there are antique Spanish rugs in gold adorned with arabesques of green, a rococo English chinoiserie oval mirror above the rounded Adam console table, and a white ceiling, but that is all.

All the furniture pieces are of mahogany, including a Queen Anne knee-hole desk, but the Hepplewhite chair backs and seats are covered with a grayish-brown velvet, the desk stool being an insignificant exception in its light chintz. Though the total effect is luxurious, there is every need, after dark, for both the English three-light bell lantern and a pair of sconces. The desk has its own illumination in the form of a three-candle bouillotte lamp.

105, 106. The hall begins with the entrance door, and the possibilities of establishing the mood at that point are widened by the introduction of carved doors in a wide variety of designs, some of which can be built up from individual panels as these two examples suggest.

126

108. Halls with a beautiful staircase such as this need little further adornment to distract the eye. In this case the owner climaxed the downward sweep of the banister by encircling the plain newel post with a garland of roses modeled in stucco and painted to match the post. The floor is of dark oak with a high luster, the furniture a tall clock, a gold-framed oil painting, and a half-round console supporting a large garden urn, painted the same white as the table, and usually overflowing with huge blossoms and shining leaves.

107. In this classical eighteenth-century hall, the walls are carefully proportioned by the use of a deep cornice and tall paneled dado with the area between whitened for contrast. The front section is divided from the rear by an archway and pilasters, and the generous size of the runner, with its broad borders, is calculated to accentuate the width of the floor. A less-wide carpet would not only have reduced the apparent width of the hall but also have detracted from its luxurious feel.

127

109. The smaller a foyer the more important a vista, here
contrived by opening it into the solarium several steps higher. The problem of adding a second stair to this small area
without reducing its apparent size was partially solved by
using open treads suspended by iron rods from the ceiling
so that the view was unobstructed — a modern device that
seems quite compatible with this eighteenth-century interior.

110. A view from a foyer down a hall should not end in a
blank wall. This is an excellent example of what can be
done to maintain interest throughout a long passageway.
Note that the white cabochons in the black floor lead the
eye down the hall beyond the stairway foot. At the far end
is sufficient room for a small commode under the mirror, a
ceiling lantern lighting the intervening space with its flower
displays.

111, 112. Doorways opening into a long hall can supply the most important decorative note as these two pictures show. In the first, a typical Greek Revival pattern is given height by the addition of a fanlight. The trim, consisting of the molded pilasters and decorated architrave, is surmounted by a deep but simple projecting cornice over which a triangular pediment is suggested by a single shaped board. A pair of sconces give the whole structure extra balance and added importance. The second illustration suggests a rather more modern approach, endowing a plain door with authority by adding ceiling-high pilasters, and decorating it with carved, antiqued plaques. The lever-type handle is a further distinctive note, the whole adding character to an otherwise undistinguished portal.

130

113.

114.

131

In the somewhat darker hall of illustration 114, with only a staircase landing window and light from another room to rely upon, the problem was somewhat more acute and needed to be tackled in a forthright and uncompromising manner. Despite the fact that this is a classical interior, a row of concealed lights was installed. In addition, the floor was covered with white vinyl "marble" decorated only with small diamond-shaped black cabochons. This treatment introduced the further problem of avoiding that aseptic institutional look, especially since the flooring was continued without a break into a reception room through a wide arch. To strengthen the illusion of continuity, the archway itself was decorated with molding terminating in a mask at top center, and the spandrels adorned with floral swags and pendants, the whole painted a pale blue to match the rest of the woodwork.

The hall dadoes are faced with a faux marbre paper, predominantly blue, and the walls, from dado molding to ceiling, papered with antique Zuber panels of the Hindustan pattern which features temples, palm and other trees, camels, and a river scene. The only furniture in the hall is a pair of antique French garden stools in bronze. That part of the staircase which is visible from the hall shows that the carpet is vermillion while the hand rail is covered in antique gold velvet, another unusual and sybaritic touch.

Another long hall (illustration 116) provides a quite different set of problems, since a glass door and two windows, each in its own shallow recess, take up much of the entrance wall, and facing them are a series of arches incorporating three doors and one recess about three feet deep. The flooring is white marble bordered in black, the hall terminating at one end in a wide doorway; at the other four steps lead up to a small anteroom beyond which a passageway gives access to still another chamber.

One of the problems must have been to find wall space for furniture in the hall, preferably on the window side where a pair of wall sconces project. The sconce problem was solved by placing beneath them two Regency chairs which are finished in black lacquer with gold trim. These chairs are flanked by a pair of white ceramic elephants whose howdahs serve as plant stands. Two of the deep

115. Even the simplest entrances can be given character by a small area rug, a clock, and an impressive tiled planter fully stocked. Though the grouping shown is modern it could very well be devised to suit any décor, period or eclectic.

recesses in the opposite wall were made use of by installing in them sofas which occupy the whole space. The recessed walls are papered in vertical red and white stripes to match the sofas' upholstery material. In this same section of the hall the floor is covered by an open-patterned rug

116.

117. A tiny entrance can be defined by a simple translucent glass partition given added decorative value by trailing creeper vines ceilingward from a narrow planter in the adjoining room. The one shown gains both in utility and appearance from the cantilevered shelf which incorporates drawers in its carved and paneled front.

133

118. Where the object of a **screen** is principally to divert drafts from the entrance door opening into a small foyer, textured glass, nicely framed in wood, will admit diffused light while excluding vision, its pattern adding a decorative touch.

with a white ground, and above each end of this hangs a square English-style lantern of plate glass and bronze.

The hall steps are carpeted in light tan broadloom which extends as far as the eye can see. In the little anteroom to which the steps lead there is visible a handsome antique bracket clock on the wall, and below it a small cabinet with two glassed-in upper shelves displaying English china. An upholstered window seat is set against the rear wall. The total effect is one of formality without pretension in a home where practicality and comfort are paramount.

The two entrance halls which are the subjects of 120

and 122 should be studied together because they illustrate two approaches to the same decorating problem, one of them (120) achieving a homelike quality of warmth and friendliness without loss of dignity, while the other (122) accents the more formal, richer and more chaste style with very few but very good pieces which one has an opportunity of examining in detail.

In 120 the horizontal is emphasized by the heavy, dark line of the cornice, and equally dark mass of the dado, both of which stand out sharply against the light ceiling and walls respectively. These horizontal lines serve to reduce the visual height of the room, increasing its apparent floor area in spite of the extra-wide doorways. The floor is dark, the result of treating Southern pine with walnut stain, so that it forms an excellent background for the black Victorian rug with its highly colored bouquets of flowers arranged in a grid pattern.

134

119. Where hall space is at a premium it may be necessary to reduce the furnishing to the smallest dimensions, in which case a more than ordinarily striking ensemble such as this, consisting of a rococo-style mirror and miniature console against an interesting wall finish, might provide the answer.

The major pieces of furniture are a large four-drawer dresser in mahogany, topped by a tall Queen Anne pier glass in its shaped walnut frame, and the eight-legged canapé-style sofa in oatmeal colored linen, given a dash of color by the embroidered pillows. At one end of this

sofa is a butler's folding table, at the other end a mahogany canterbury — and that is all, except for a couple of nineteenth-century genre paintings, plus smaller details such as two miniatures, a table lamp with a silver urn as base, a replica of a dwarf orange tree in a tôle container, and a metal figurine of a stable exercise boy. On the chest is a small silver tray, and chrysanthemums of white and blue in a porcelain bowl, the mirror revealing, quite coincidentally, an old-time mercury barometer hanging on the opposite wall.

The little hall is lit by a pair of sconces alongside the Queen Anne mirror and an English brass lantern hanging from the ceiling's center — nothing extravagant but everything in very good taste, and obviously designed to welcome rather than to impress.

In illustration 122 all the wood trim is painted a fairly light color, the cornice and door trim elaborately molded, the dado reduced to a chair rail decorated with old-time punch and gouge work, and the wall painted white above and below it. The floor is dark with a rich glow, accented by a fabulous Chinese version of an Aubusson rug in maroon, yellow, and white down its center. Above it hangs a bell-type lantern suspended by chains from a bronze eagle whose vertical wing tips connect with the ceiling rose.

Against one wall is a French Empire console with a mirrored back between the platform base and paneled top, the two legs carved with masks. Over this hangs a tall pier glass with a carved frame in faded gold, having the crown and triple feathers for a cresting. On this are disposed a pair of glass and crystal candelabra. Centered in the nearby angled wall is a tall clock, its door decorated in gold in the Chinese manner on black lacquer. Beyond the central door this is balanced by a Chinese painting over a closed semi-circular card table in mahogany, its apron inlaid with satinwood, and its top adorned with a tall, slender, baluster-type wooden lamp with a white shade, and a porcelain incense burner. Next comes a walnut, Dutch-footed Queen Anne chair with a patterned slip seat in colors that match those of the rug.

In the larger halls, such as in 124 and 125, there is much more likelihood of finding the architectural features fully developed, and while these control to a large extent the decorating possibilities they also tend to increase the

120.

121. Halls lacking in width may call for fine carpeting and the slenderest of tables, but where the hall is also long the table does not necessarily have to be surmounted by a mirror. With the looking-glass in a location providing better illumination, a picture could very well take its place over the table, in which case an exotic note provided by the accessories could be enlivened by a modern painting of a shape and size to make the most effective use of the space available.

136

122.

123. Two-piece hall furnishings are commonest, but this does not signify that they should lack in originality since so many practical and decorative furniture pieces are designed precisely for this location. In this example nothing could be more delightful than the triptych-style mirror, its door panels open to reveal decorative detail that might well be 400 years old. And few pieces would go better with it than the shallow, but tall and roomy, and very beautiful cabinet complete with gallery, a sort of console-bookcase that furniture makers tend to lump with other nondescript units as "hall pieces."

137

124.

125.

127. Somehow there is nothing that ties an interior to the outdoors so much as a rugged oak chest in the hall, looking as though it has been there for centuries. This is the kind of piece that would go well with a stone or terra-cotta floor in addition to the plank wall. The mirror, however, seems cast in a less heroic mold, yet because of the Robin-Hood style carving, which almost makes it a trumeau, they go very well together and with the medieval candlestick-based lamp. The accessories are likewise well selected, there being a definite tie between the ancient hunting theme of the mirror carving, the flower holder suggestive of an admiral's hat, and the military bookends.

126. This console-mirror group is quite stately and not a little ecclesiastical in feel despite the plant pots, and well suited to a larger hall with a damask-patterned wall. The console has the advantage of a roomy drawer for gloves, scarves, sunglasses, and the like. In this instance the mirror is finished in a light antique green, the console revealing the charm of walnut and pecan grains. A pair of dignified high-backed chairs would be an interesting addition if space allowed.

140

importance of the interior, endowing it with a more formal character than might otherwise be considered desirable.

As these two views make clear, the architectural features include pilasters and classical pediments on important doorways, together with one double door and a single door trimmed with regular casing. The twin doors, however, are so beautifully designed, with elaborate rounded lock rails to receive the large circular knob escutcheons, and fine panel moldings, that any further ornamentation would be redundant. In any case this door is so tall and so wide that no triangular pediment would fit below the ceiling. The other, and smaller, door is presumably of insufficient importance to warrant elaboration of this sort, and being located in an end wall does not have to match the others.

Another important and unusual feature is the half-domed wall recess, and the low base of which is rounded so that it projects slightly at the center. The top of the base is finished off with a cove molding, and below this is a decorative band of Greek-key ornament, while the base molding of the wall is carried around it. Filled with large-leaf growing plants, this alcove is a striking addition to an already handsome interior, and the focal point of the hall.

With so much molding there is no need for contrasting paints to secure a light-and-shadow effect, so it has been possible to paint the whole of the surfaces white — a perfect foil for the dark mahogany furniture. In contrast, the floor is divided into slate-gray squares laid at 45 degrees to the wall, thereby increasing its apparent width. These are separated by two-inch wide strips, interrupted at each corner by a square black cabochon. The result is interesting without being confusing.

Another beguiling feature is the manner in which the wall, innocent of pediments, has been relieved of its anonymous flatness by the use of box-type pelmets from which to hang the draperies. These are fabric-covered, and project from the wall about eight inches, their decorative outline emphasized by a fancy border with tassels. This gives the draperies three dimensions, isolating the section between them which contains the double door, thereby adding to its visual importance.

This area facing the recess is given greater emphasis by a pair of massive black pedestals supporting bronze busts, each with a black-framed eighteenth-century print above it to raise the eye level. In front of each window is a modern seat of bent round iron with curule-style legs and brass trim. Against the opposite wall, shallow, twin-legged mahogany consoles stand guard on the alcove, displaying specimens of Oriental Lowestoft. Above each of these consoles is a gilded and ebonized wall sconce with twin candles, the only source of light.

At one end of the hall is a flat archway, at the other a splendid oriental four-leaf screen serves to mask the doorway to the domestic offices at a point where a passageway leads off to the right.

Opinions differ as to whether 128 should be considered a hall or foyer, but no doubt can exist that it offers a fascinating solution to the problem of adapting the available space to an effective entrance to a small city apartment. In the photograph the effect is somewhat distorted by the folding door to the bar being open so that the space available for the hallway cannot be fairly gauged. There is, however, ample room to pass the shelf of black slate resting on custom-made brass brackets. This provides room for a lamp in oxidized pewter with a laminated fabric shade, and an antique oak bucket for flowers. Above these is hung a mirror in a weathered wooden frame.

A major feature of this apartment is the fact that, in the absence of any architectural character or embellishments, these had to be compensated for by trompe-l'oeil effects, using a gray-white faux bois paper to cover the walls, doors, and trim, and inserting paper panels of white cane pattern bordered in charcoal. Cornices and baseboards likewise were painted in. On the floor a fitted short-pile wool carpet in oatmeal was used, with a border in regimental red. The lighting, it will be noted, consists of specially designed metal hanging fixtures with castellated edges decorated with smoky-crystal drops, and painted black outside.

In place of the usual coat closet, a custom-built bar was installed. This has a white formica top and a painted finish to match the wallpaper in color and texture. The living room of this apartment, showing the junction of the hallway with the other rooms is illustrated in 29.

The striking and quite unusual entrance hall revealed

128.

129.

in 129 has a variety of novel features which put it in a class by itself. These include a bold combination of marble floor and mirrored walls — on the face of it a recipe for austerity. Details like this, fortunately, cannot be isolated; there are always the adjoining spaces to be considered. In this view the hall is connected to an adjoining interior through a wide, flat-arched opening in-

nocent of trim. One therefore serves as a background for the other, each providing a deeply contrasting vista calculated to add an interesting note, while the mirror undoubtedly increases the feeling of spaciousness in both.

Because of the high reflectivity of the mirror, it is not immediately apparent that the walls of the hall are papered in a pleasing and colorful damask pattern. What

142

does come through is that the whole ensemble gives the effect of a combination old and new, the warm wood tones and tasteful design of the antiques posed against a chaste modern background, an essay which, though daring, is extremely effective.

The furniture pieces consist of a late Sheraton console table with fluted legs and apron, displaying crystal candelabra and a silver-mounted glass bowl, a pair of early Georgian side chairs in walnut, and an exquisitely simple French bracket clock on a mahogany pedestal, the latter set in a convenient angle of the wall. Above these hangs a crystal chandelier of unusual design whose pink-tinted candle shades contribute a mellow glow.

The type of entrance hall one likes to think of as a true foyer is exemplified by 130, which serves a large city apartment. The style is Venetian baroque, and the whole interior has been endowed with some architectural character by the application of fluted Ionic pilasters, the treatment of the doors, and the use of a color border on the coved section of the ceiling.

The doors were painted to give the effect of nicely shaped gray panels outlined in cerulean blue with a border of eggplant. The door trim and the baseboard, and the section of wall between the pilasters, including the pilasters themselves, are all painted off-white, though the pilaster plinths are outlined in the eggplant. The rest of the walls are eggplant color, rich and dark and as fascinating as Royal Purple!

The overdoors in the eggplant area are gray with a stylized design in gold as their centers; that in the foreground is marbleized to match the door panels. Against the eggplant wall is a baroque console of wood, carved and gilded, and set on a marble plinth. Over it is a Venetian mirror in a carved and gilded frame, reflecting a white porcelain bowl and its arrangement of white flowers and green foliage. In front of this the parquet floor is covered with a rug of French linen in colors matching the gray, off-white, blue, and gold of the doors. In gay contrast, the white-walled section is adorned with a putty-colored rug having an eggplant border, the whole thing shaped in the manner of the upper door panels.

Between the marbleized door and each pilaster is an elaborate crystal gilt ormolu sconce, under which has been placed a Louis Quinze stool painted off-white with

130.

gold trim, and upholstered in broad eggplant and gray stripes. Two other chairs of Louis Seize inspiration, in off-white with a border of cerulean blue on seat and back, are placed against the eggplant sections of the walls to complete a sparkling and glamorous tour de force in color and form.

In 131 is a cosy entrance hall to a study, furnished for

143

131.

a person of antiquarian tastes. The background represents the ultimate in simplicity thereby increasing the impact of both the utilitarian and decorative items displayed. The whole interior — walls, doors, and ceiling — is white, the walls innocent of moldings. The floor is of parquet so that it defines the area of the little foyer and keeps the visual weight where it belongs.

In this small area there are many objects of various sizes, shapes, textures, and colors — a recipe for chaos if not handled properly — their individual functions and purposes distinct and obvious. The whole is carefully balanced, and ample space provided where it is needed so that there is no crowding or confusion.

The practical furniture consists of an Italian triple-back settee, turned, carved, painted, and scalloped, and utterly beautiful, with needlepoint pillows for color. Facing it is a cottage-style bedroom chest of fairly recent ancestry with two drawers and a cupboard below, now painted white, and decorated on the sides with a bouquet of roses tied together by a flowing ribbon. The door panels have been replaced by gilded chicken wire, the drawers outlined in color, little knobs of cast brass applied, and the top painted black. These two pieces are tied together across the floor by a white, tasseled rug with flower patterns set in squares and looking like children's cross-stitch samplers of another day.

The lamp tables represent two extremes — a galleried three-tier table, with a top almost coffin-shaped, and a tall stand with a shelf near the floor, a slightly serpentine top inlaid with leather, and delicate cabriole-style legs. On each of them is a shining brass bouillotte lamp with its three trumpet coils and a tôle shade. On the wall behind these lamps are old flower prints in plain, light-colored frames, arranged vertically in threes. These and the settle outline a large wall area in the center of which hangs that massive urn, a rotund creation of tôle in green with gilded laurel leaves and pierced decorative band. Originally made to be stood upon a noble pedestal, it now displays its artful shape against the white of the wall, a third of its roundness having been cut away, and its apparent utility destroyed. Of its effectiveness as the artistic center of this little piece of organized space there could be no dispute, even though it is balanced on the facing wall by a fine old clock on its veneered and banded bracket. Looking at these things one scarcely notices the prim ceiling fixture with its opaline globe ringed by lozenge-shaped crystals, or even the shy pair of pottery urns below the clock, or the Regency chairs with front legs that simulate bamboo, each of which contributes its small quota of interest.

The antithesis in style to the foregoing is 132, where Spartan simplicity achieves a miracle of impeccable taste with two principal pieces of furniture and a huge canvas depicting a scene perfectly in tune with the mood and fascinating as a work of art. There are no trivial accessories here, no bibelots to catch the eye and set fingers to twitching. There is, however, an exquisite chandelier of almost lifelike bronze flowers, set in the frame of the ceiling's

132.

delicately molded cornice. The limited porcelain display discernible in the china cabinet is almost obscured by the heavy gold mesh of the doors whose pattern is repeated in the tiny skirt molding below the plain-paneled cupboards.

The great painting in vivid greens and white is six feet square, its massive architectural frame designed to match

145

the subject, and stand out boldly against walls painted a rich orange above a white dado. Beneath it is a Biedermeier sofa in oatmeal linen with pillows of black and white silk. At either end is a Biedermeier version of a French guéridon in rosewood with brass rings and bands and a *verde antico* marble top, used as a lamp stand. The lamp bases are of black basalt on marble blocks, the shades of opaque white, a modern touch in keeping with the painting. The rich, velvety and receding rug in white on a pale green ground with accents in tan, adds a note of soft luxury that, together with the chandelier, invests the whole display with an aura of charm and friendly warmth so becoming to the entrance area of any home.

133. Small entries do not necessarily demand small wallpaper patterns as this view of such a hall demonstrates. The large Charles X design provides a dynamic answer to the problem of decorating both the tiny hall and the adjacent areas which, broken up with conflicting patterns, or even an indecisive one, would have added to the confusion introduced by the jog in the passage. Such a pattern as this naturally calls not only for a hall piece in scale but one which enters into the spirit of the looping design, and is forthright enough to surmount the challenge. This nineteenth-century hat-stand was contrived from a console and fitted with a marble top, demonstrating the gift of ingenuity which sets such solutions to design problems in a class by themselves.

146

Libraries and Studies

Libraries and studies have a number of things in common. For one, they are mostly masculine retreats for relaxation, contemplation, and even study; or perhaps for the entertainment of a crony, or the quiet enjoyment of an after-dinner cigar. On the other hand these functions may overlap. Books may be called for in any one of them, but probably not to the extent that is demanded of a library where the shelves of bound volumes are the first consideration.

The function of the study, too, may vary, depending upon the occupation and outlook of the owner. Many an interior designer, for example, must have a study in which to do his leisure time planning. To such a one the principal need will be for a good working table or desk, with drawing equipment and perhaps paints and brushes. The writer likewise must have his study to do his research, his typing, and handle his mail, but he may also consider it essential to have a good reference library covering his particular interests. It would, in other words, be his office were it located anywhere but in his home. The study in its widest interpretation, on the other hand, may have to take into account any number of personal interests or the indulgence of any hobby that normally would not involve the use of tools (except perhaps a pair of scissors for clipping coupons or working on a stamp collection), and be furnished accordingly.

In spite of this limited attempt at classification it happens quite often that the terms are used interchangeably so that in designing the interior it is essential to know the actual purpose it is to serve, and what extra features, if any, will need to be incorporated. In the library, for example, the basic requirements might be listed as comfort for study and relaxation, including noise suppression, books arranged within easy reach, and ample lighting both day and after dark for desk or table work as well as reading. This last requirement would involve a number of factors such as sufficient glass area and proper placing of windows, light colored walls, good general artificial lighting (ceiling fixture), table or floor lamps easily maneuverable, and perhaps special illumination of the book shelves.

In some instances the quality of the artificial light is important especially where color illustrations need to be studied and fluorescent fixtures are contemplated. With daylight it may be necessary to arrange for draperies that can be drawn fully aside to expose the whole glass area. Sound and echo may need to be controlled by the use of acoustical ceiling tile, wall insulation, and heavy draperies, and perhaps even cork flooring or extra-thick floor coverings and overall carpeting.

Since most libraries are designed for men, the interior usually needs to be definitely masculine — leather upholstery, paneling, good architectural detail, a fireplace without fussy ornament, good solid furniture, and so on. Colors usually need to be conservative, though colorful plastics may substitute for leather, and draperies can be plain since book bindings and jackets can supply texture and pattern. Although floor coverings often need also to be plain, the truth is that a good oriental rug can generally supply both color and design while adding a note of distinction and dignity.

In the matter of bookcases, these are usually designed to occupy a certain amount of wall space with a minimum loss of floor area, often reaching to the ceiling and therefore necessitating the use of a ladder which presents problems of its own. Occasionally, by careful design, lower stacks can be used, occupying more linear space, but where that continuous space is not available another solution must be sought. One that often works, and at the same time adds to the decorating possibilities, is to substitute several small bookcase units which can be of attractive design and proportion, properly spaced, disposed around the room. These can of course be permanently installed, or be actual case pieces (see illustration 135) which can be moved around as required without damage to the walls. Lighting, however, should not be overlooked.

While some of the foregoing specifications for libraries can also be applied to studies, each will need to be considered in the light of the person's particular and individual needs and desires. Some of the various problems that may arise together with possible solutions will be made apparent in the examples to follow.

The first of these (134) concerns a library that seems to have a little extra of everything — including a bar! The walls and bookshelves are particularly striking because they are sheathed in wood with an exaggerated faux-bois finish in beige. The opening cut in one wall for the bar which occupies an alcove is concealed by a series of shutters with panels formed of patterned fabric. The interior of the bar has the same faux-bois finish as the outside.

It will be noted that the lower edges of the ceiling beams are molded and the timbers painted to match the walls. The floor is covered with vinyl hand-set in a pattern of beige and white giving the impression of a brick surface.

The principal pieces of furniture are a large sofa and a pair of deep easy chairs. All three are upholstered in beige, the chairs having a decorative border in yellow on

134.

arms and seat cushions. The sofa has throw pillows of the same color. Between the big chairs is a lamp table, fashioned in the Chinese manner and lacquered in bright red. Two other square-topped tables are Louis XVI provincial reproductions, but the eye-catcher is an antique Venetian armchair in pale green, carved and gilded. Brass tones are introduced by a tall lamp base, the foot and necking of a shorter one with a Chinese porcelain

148

135. A series of small bookcases used in place of fixed shelves may offer advantages in decorating the library.

motive headlights, it must be admitted that the opening of the screens, like the uncovering of a large picture window, adds considerable depth to the view.

Distinctly more formal, and extremely dramatic, is the library illustrated by two views (136 and 137), in which the architectural aspects are emphasized by the use of simplified Ionic columns having the appearance of black marble, supporting an architrave, dentiled frieze and cornice all in white. The floor is black, the base trim and dado molding being white to emphasize the horizontal. Rich coloring is introduced by the dark eggplant of the walls against which all of the decorative elements stand out boldly. The two principal features of the interior are the bookcase and the fireplace. The former, which extends upward from dado to architrave is set in flush with the wall. Below it is a heavy table supported on twin scroll-shaped consoles, all in heavy white plaster.

On the wall each side the bookcase is a fifteenth-century Roman engraving mounted in a white gesso frame which glows against the dark color. Below these is a pair of terrestrial globes in heavy white stands, gold trimmed, on pedestals of crystal with crystal feet. The same purely classical effect is secured at the opposite end of the room where the fireplace of heavy marble slabs supports the tall, plain pier glass fastened to the wall. On either side are semi-circular console tables, each supported by a shell-like, anthemion-pattern plaster casting copied from one found in the ruins of the Athenian agora. On each of these tables is a silver Chinese mud bird dating from the T'ang dynasty (seventh century).

As might be expected, the draperies are quite formal in a gray woolly fabric, and plain except for silky decorative bands near the hem. They are also set to hang in rigid folds from top to bottom. Equally chaste is the handsome lighting fixture hanging from the center of the ceiling with its gleaming bowl of plain and polished silver, and wide rim of plate glass. From its center projects a solitary crystal ball.

The somewhat scant furnishings are in keeping with the surroundings. The two enormous easy chairs are uncompromisingly square and covered in gray snakeskin with velvet cushions. Between them is a low utility table consisting of three sheets of heavy plate glass, one forming the top, the others disposed vertically at the ends, and

base, and a round brass table and a cradle-like tubular brass magazine basket. The whole grouping is held together by a stunning hand-woven Spanish rug with a pattern of large red and white flowers on a black ground surrounded by a wide multi-colored fringe. It is the books, however, which establish the genteel character of the room with their rich bindings in reds and blues and gold stamping — two sets of shelves at right-angles in a corner. Though one may not be at the moment particularly concerned with the bar or its antique French loco-

149

136.

all held between two simple frames of white-painted wood. On the floor is an almost room-sized rug, sculptured in small and large hexagons which add a degree of light and shade and texture to the monochrome gray. The only other piece of significance, apart from the crystal items on the bookcase console, is a painted and decorated stool with five legs and a ring base — a gentle touch of artless craftsmanship in a setting of cool Greco-Roman classical beauty.

Far less formal is 138, a library of distinction in which the principal decorative feature is the books themselves, and one that betrays continuous and active use. The walls are encased in mahogany veneer in which wide rectangular openings reveal rows of packed shelves flanking a fireplace outlined by flush slabs of gray marble.

This is a room within a room, confined to a narrow platform area by long, wide, and shallow steps of polished wood that can also serve as casual seating thanks to a loose cushion or two invitingly placed. Below the shelves are storage cupboards, above them a row of spaced

137.

ceiling lights that can be used to illuminate the books — in particular those on the upper shelves. At one side of the fireplace is a "café" table of twisted iron rods and marble, with a reading lamp. On the opposite side is a floor lamp for the same purpose, two tub chairs providing the seating, with a low, glass-topped round table in the middle to hold volumes of current interest.

150

Over the fireplace is a large Ben Shahn print — a black-and-white creation in a narrow gold frame that leaps out from the dark mahogany wall. Another striking piece is a carved library chair in black patent leather, brass-nailed. The current art favorite is a framed oil painting on a bamboo easel standing at one end of a long narrow hearth rug in red with a white and black border. This whole grouping has an unusual sense of unity; nothing is extraneous, nothing inessential including the Mayan idol and other small sculptured pieces used as decorative accents on tables or acting as space fillers on an uncrowded shelf.

Somewhat the same general design concept applied to a library in a modern home a thousand miles away is pictured in 139. Here is the same sheathed wall — this time in cherry — extending right up to the high ceiling, the same marble fireplace surround, except for an added slab forming a shelf, and the inevitable work of art gracing the overmantel. But the furniture skillfully combines the antique and the modern — a pair of up-to-date sofas upholstered in yellow fabric, with a huge but low table on the hearthrug between them, a piece made from a section of original parquet from a French chateau, Hepplewhite chairs of a French pattern covered in cherry silk, and English walnut spider-legged occasional tables. The rug is a white Moroccan specimen which these pieces share with a flat-topped writing table, also in walnut, inlaid with tooled leather.

One wall of this room is all window and sliding glass door — except for a small corner area — and equipped with gold-colored draperies. Furthermore, the floor plan is open, the room spaces being arranged around a central glass atrium. The only other wall in this room, therefore, is a partition facing the fireplace. This is painted off-white, providing a usefully reflective area which adds to the overall brightness of the room. Since the room looks out into a fountain court with a yellow-painted brick wall and towering trees beyond, there is little need for pictures on the two walls, and the interior colors are variegated enough to afford plenty of contrast and interest.

An altogether different type of interior is represented in 140 in spite of the fact that the library is located in a southern garden room with one wall almost all glass. The

138.

differences lie in the fact that growing plants form a large part of the décor in addition to a wall-size mural painting of a landscape complete with a pair of tubbed trees that expands the theme; that it is located in a special wing which permits of striking architectural features such as a double-sloped and very high ceiling; and that it is incorporated into an end wall of a tall entrance

151

139.

door with a broken pediment on "ancones" or brackets, the whole accommodated in a shallow, arched recess.

With the large window area, an elegant parquet floor, the mural, the door, and extra architectural features such as the wall-long painted bookcase complete with fluted pilasters, the interior should need little further beautification. The furniture, however, actually adds a great deal.

First of all there is a great mahogany "partners" desk with its tooled leather top and polished brass hardware on both sides. Facing it, with its back to the window, is a large, comfortable sofa, complete with coffee table, and a modern rug patterned with a scattering of stencilled plants and flowers on a field of medium green. By the door is a small but handsome marquetry commode. Else-

152

140.

where a deep tub chair heavily upholstered and tufted in brown leather, and a swivel desk chair also in leather decorated with brass nails, plus one American Chippendale-style side chair and a cherry drop-leaf table used as a working surface auxiliary to the desk complete the ensemble.

A library in which the books do not form a part of the décor is the subject of 141. There are a great many books, and some fine bindings, but all are sequestered behind wood-panelled doors. The rest of the room also is panelled, except where the walls give way to the big windows and glass door overlooking the garden. In the daytime these flood the room with light, enough of which is reflected from the cardinal-red carpet to give the pan-

153

141.

eling a warm and friendly glow. After dark, a somewhat similar effect is produced by the big globular lighting fixture hanging over the games table, and the smaller table lamps.

Besides the paneling, other partially reflective surfaces within the room include the Roman window and door blinds with their white and black stripes, the red and white houndstooth upholstery of the game chairs and the wing chair cushion and back, plus the glass top of a round coffee table whose base is of polished brass. The rest of the furniture is more or less dark, including a Louis XVI bureau-plat, whose top is inset with black leather, and the reproduction Louis XV high-backed fauteuil which is upholstered with the same hide. Other dark surfaces

154

are presented by the games table with its antique cast-iron base and black slate top, and the sofa which is covered in black felt.

The armchairs used at the games table are reproductions of unusually handsome French provincial carved ladder-backs, with two bearing arms and beautifully shaped splats and top rail, all in walnut. The games-table lantern has a conical shade with a cut-out apron decorated with fiber tassels, the whole thing painted white inside while the exterior is antiqued red tôle. The desk light, on the other hand, is an antique of columnar style in polished brass with a railed and stepped base, a painted oblong metal shade, and a large eagle finial.

The overall effect of this room is both impressive and cozy — and a little surprising — the bare paneling being far less bleak than the picture might suggest, thanks to the color treatment and the variegated and unusual shapes of the furniture pieces which, though diverse and exotic, are utterly compatible.

The study — half-brother to the library (since there must be plenty of reference books and trade magazines on hand) — can be actually more interesting from a decorating standpoint since the problems are likely to vary even more widely. In a room such as 142 and 143, for example, the results of careful design can be positively delightful.

This particular room is located in a city apartment, the study originally consisting of a somewhat stark, all-white interior of little architectural merit except for a dark, polished parquet floor. A start could conceivably have been made with the oversized window, painting the trim black, and applying a narrower band of zebra-wood veneer so as to leave a border on either side. The glassed area could then have been obscured by hanging translucent shades inside the trim, the whole forming, in the daylight, a luminous background for the principal furniture group.

This group logically consists of a modern swivelling desk chair, a highly decorative table-type desk (actually a Louis XVI Italian piece), and a small telephone table to one side, all framed by a couple of tall, growing plants for atmosphere.

On the desk top artificial lighting could be supplied by a colorful Chinese vase-based lamp, balanced by a crystal obelisk at the other end to help dissipate the air of practicality.

This would be the focal point of the room, the rest arranged for study, conversation, and relaxation. The essentials of a second grouping then would be a sofa, tweed-covered and masculine, set against the plain white wall and flanked by solid and ample end tables with room for more than a lamp, a handsome though practical rug, plain with a varicolored striped border, a tasteful, sturdy, and unusual coffee table of the marble-topped variety with a tubular brass base, and a comfortable commodious bergère in walnut covered with a dark nubby fabric.

One of the walls (in this case that opposite the sofa), incorporating the entrance door and a storage closet with a shallow recess between them, might well be sheathed in wood with panels of dramatic vertical zebra-wood grain bordered in black. In the recess there would be room for a narrow black-topped shelf, projecting at the center and there supported by a pair of tapering brass legs. The thick edge of the shelf would be finished in the same zebra-wood, and beneath it a pair of brass-legged stools stored as emergency seating. This unit would be completed by a vertical oil painting at one end of the shelf — something with a masculine feel such as a lion among the veldt grass, a receding picture in soft yellows and greens, at the other end a columnar lamp in black and gold for visual balance plus minor curios.

A third group could be arranged by the entrance door — a tall metal-framed modern table in brassbound black with a central zebra-wood panel continued over the doors, a leopard skin on the floor, and a small painted hall chair with a brass-framed medallion in the back panel placed to one side. Over the table a plain black-bordered mirror would incorporate narrow strips of zebra-wood, top and bottom. A table lamp would serve all normal occasions, but a tôle lantern, almost Moorish in design, hanging from the ceiling by the door, would serve to welcome visitors, while a row of decanters on the table suggested further hospitality to come. Judging by the photographs, most designers would vote such a study interior an unqualified success if not inspired!

A large, heavy and impressive country-made bureau-plat in French cherry is the most important single piece in the richly decorated study depicted in (144). Leopard

142.

143.

skins on chairs and floor vie with the lavishly beautiful window hangings and their swagged pelmets of hand-printed English linen which has a floral pattern in red, ochre, and blue wool.

The setting is particularly exciting because of the inspired combination of a Zuber French wallpaper of gray and ochre stripes, with a dado paper in balustrade design

combining white marble with various leaf-greens. The wallpaper, it will be noted, covers the door trim, and both papers entirely hide a closet door. The hall doors, on the other hand, are painted gray and the panel moldings accented with white. The floor is of vinyl representing Carrara marble with a narrow border line of black, in pleasant counterpoint to both draperies and the leopard-

144.

skin rug with its lining and border of black wool.

As usual, the desk is arranged so that the user can sit with his back to the window, and, luckily, there are two windows so that he does not have to work in his own shadow. After dark, of course, it is necessary to rely on the tall lamp with its urn base and bouillotte shade which casts a wide beam, uninterrupted, it is to be hoped, by the foliage and flowers springing up from its bronze stem. The winged desk chair is an antique Biedermeier upholstered in Somalian leopard-skin and, because of its solidity, seemingly perfectly matched with the sturdy desk.

Between the two doors is a tall and narrow book cabinet which once was an antique French clock case built by some eighteenth-century cabinetmaker. The

145.

146.

it is not explained, nevertheless this is one study that will not suffer by comparison with any other room in the house.

Libraries vary as much in size as they do in the quality of their furnishings, two factors that are entirely unrelated. In 145 and 146 the room is not large and the furniture consequently is limited to a few essential pieces, nevertheless everything is of the finest quality and well chosen so that the styles could be mixed without any loss of compatibility.

The principal pieces consist of a pair of Louis XV cane-backed and seated fauteuils without arm pads (possibly Swedish adaptations), a New England flat-topped table with plain cabriole legs used for writing, plus a lower table with tapered square legs and Egyptian hieroglyphs painted on the apron. There is also an excellent Chinese-style lacquered coffee table ornamented in gold, in addition to two end tables, one with a tray-top and drawer, the other round and swathed in velvet. On the writing table stands a bouillotte lamp in bronze, and on each end table a lamp with a columnar tôle base painted

small cane-backed side chair next to it is also an antique — a signed Louis XVI piece in leopard-skin upholstery. Along this same wall is an excellent reproduction of a French daybed or *lit de repos à crosse*, upholstered in pale gold Belgian linen velvet, the cane-paneled ends and the aprons decorated with faux marbre in ochre, blue, and charcoal. The gilded horse-laugh on the wall above

158

with eighteenth-century scenes and topped by a reservoir.

The seating is modern, consisting of a sofa upholstered in linen, and an upholstered armchair and ottoman in a cotton check. The white rug has an open pattern in brown and blue, and the floor-length draperies are of yellow silk which contrasts interestingly with the pale blue of the walls and woodwork.

This interior has a great deal of architectural character thanks to a deeply molded cornice, and the paneling of one wall which is devoted to cupboards and bookshelves. Some relief from the strict formality is afforded by a modern painting over the sofa with its gilded baroque frame, and a framed cast of an Indian sculptured fragment over the writing table. Above the narrow double doors to the room is an equally exotic carving of a holly wreath and sugar cane tops, this and the sculpture both hinting at the wide range of interests of their owner.

It will be observed from the illustrations that this room does not, like so many libraries, have pieces of furniture placed so as to block access to the shelves merely because the things look better that way. In other words, its function as a library is pre-eminent as it should be.

What many will consider the ultimate in private library design is represented by 147, though only a corner of it is shown. The interior itself is lovely enough to serve as a drawing room even with its ceiling of massive beams from which an antique copper chandelier is suspended. The paintings are rich and rare and old; the fireplace wall is sheathed in dark wood to match the posts and beams of the others. The open walls between them are hidden beneath an exquisite pattern in dark mauve and white of birds and flowers and foliage enframed in undulating vertical columns on a ground of deep yellow. The floor is of brown vinyl glowing darkly in the artificial light, its elongated blocks reminiscent of old English parquet.

The bookshelves occupy one corner which extends into a deep recess, and in this angle is erected a metal winding, open stair that gives access to shelves up to ceiling level. This whole structure, its risers perforated in diamond pattern, is painted a bright yellow, matching the color of the bamboo furniture and its leather cushions. By one chair stands an antique copper fireside footrest and ale warmer; beyond it a tall, leafy palm adds its feathery quota of contrasting green, but nothing can

excell the glowing blacks and reds of the leather bindings, richly embossed in gold, that fill the shelves, completing a picture of undiluted excellence.

In illustration 134 a library was examined which contained a bar. In 148 and 148a is its anthithesis — a bar containing a library! — a combination of functions that many might wish to adopt without finding so felicitous a solution. Actually this is designated as a cocktail room and its decoration is based on a theme established by the living room which is shown in illustration 51.

Though the books are very much in evidence, the bar, centered between bookcases and projecting in a semi-circular sweep, dominates the picture. The book-section doors and the bar front are paneled, the three units being separated by fluted pilasters. All of the woodwork, including the interior of the bar, the room's folding entrance door and its trim, are painted white; the floor is of quarter-sawn oak, dark-stained.

This room is fully and comfortably furnished for relaxation — and reading — with two deep upholstered occasional chairs, two cane-backed library chairs in mahogany, and a long, deep-cushioned sofa with a center arm. The drapery fabric, patterned in gold on white, is also used to cover the occasional chair. The remaining pieces consist of a pair of rosewood lamp tables in the Chinese mood, a cocktail table of plate glass on a bobbin-turned wooden base, a Chinese garden seat in black lacquer, used as a table alongside one of the upholstered chairs, the other small table being of that rare type designed to look like a pile of books in rich bindings atop a low stool. Another one appears in illustration 100.

The most decorative accessories are undoubtedly the two lamps made from large Chinese metal tea canisters of a lacquered black decorated in gold, with plain black shades. The wildcat skin on the floor adds a casual outdoorsy note, but the mounted head would seem, in these close quarters, an unnecessary hazard. The total impression here is of a light and airy interior, intimate and cosy, adaptable either as a study or for the entertainment of a small group of intimate friends to whom comfort is the first consideration.

The most comfortable studies are often the smallest, with everything within easy reach (so that, for one thing, it is easy to be tidy), the furniture comfortable and pos-

147.

148.

148a.

149.

sibly well-worn, the air masculine, with familiar things all about. The room should be devoid of exciting colors and patterns, the surfaces simple and sincere.

Such a study is presented in 149, a room with a wealth of plain wood, old leather, deep cushions, and with a grate for fall, winter, and spring fires; soft under foot, and quiet, thanks to a large, fleecy carpet, brightened by the rich, warm pattern of a Feraghan rug.

The wood is a rich-grained birch, only slightly darkened with a sealer and wax finish, architecturally pleasing with its mantel moldings and flanking pilasters, its panels, and a round-topped door. Over the mantel is a colorful map of the world, and between the shelf and the bolection molding hangs a dress sword as ornament. The hearth, with its black slate surround, has its fitted spark arrester, its tall brass andirons, and high fender of pierced brass. In one corner is a brass bucket for logs, besides the brown leather-covered, nail-studded Queen Anne style wing chair with its accompanying floor lamp for reading.

Over the single window is a wooden pelmet, straight-

edged, with its simple molding, holding up the floor length curtains of a Fortuny type fabric of brown, beige, and blue. Under the sill is a Queen Anne walnut table with a marble top, and on it a bronze of horse and armored rider serving as a base for a lamp with a large rectangular shade of beige silk.

Against one wall is an upholstered easy chair and ottoman (for moments of deeper concentration) and a bookcase, neither of which shows in the photograph. Behind the sofa is a stand to hold a bowl of cut flowers, reducing the distance between sofa and fireplace but leaving ample room for a butler's tray table with its cargo of smoking utensils and reading matter.

On warm days a folding door is opened on a flagged terrace with its wide awning to let in breezes from the garden. Who could ask for more? (Note: The living room of this house is shown in 52 and 53, the dining room in 62).

Obviously not every study is a place of relaxation. Many who work at home need both the privacy and convenience of such a room, particularly those engaged in the art of writing. In such a room no tools should be needed beyond a typewriter, thesaurus, and eraser, though almost always it seems that space has to be found for reference books and files to hold the records — or rejects! These requirements, however, do not — or should not — militate against the room being attractively designed as well as conveniently arranged, as 150 should serve to demonstrate.

This is a study created for a feminine writer. It occupies very little space but represents the ultimate in convenience in an atmosphere of artful grace that should be inspiring.

As far as the practical aspects are concerned, the designer was fortunate enough to find available a sealed-off doorway that could be used to accommodate file shelves, and these, in turn, dictated the location of the working desk. This, luckily, could be placed alongside one of the room's two windows, allowing space for a work chair between the desk and the files. For night work, a tall table lamp in yellow and bronze was installed by the window atop a fascinatingly garish bronze stand.

Between the two windows is a fireplace with a Louis

162

150.

which is tied back within two feet of the top, reminiscent of the (very) high-waisted gowns of the Regency days. The pelmet is of wood, pierced, carved, and painted to represent blue tassels on yellow fabric. Against the glass are venetian blinds whose slats and tapes are covered with the yellow and blue fabric used to upholster both the desk chair and a chaise-longue in the opposite corner. Other interesting details are the French *serviteur fidèle* with its three brass-galleried trays, two of which revolve, and the white fur rug — Polar bear? — in front of the little brass-rimmed fender. A fabric-covered box on end not only makes an admirable tea table alongside the desk, but typifies the ingenuity that went into this whole decorative scheme.

A much more businesslike and rugged approach to the design of a working study is illustrated by 151, though adequate provision is made for comfort and the strict functionalism is tempered with a bow toward the traditional as represented by a beautiful French commode, displayed like a picture. This is not in the least compatible with its setting, in spite of the other objets d'art spread around the room — the copper, wind-vane horse, the carved geese, the brass French fire helmet below it, the miniature mahogany chest, the marquetry box or the brass candlestick. The "great leveler," however, is color, even the daylight being screened through venetian blinds, yellow even to their tapes. The walls are terracotta, the floor saffron vinyl with yellow striping, the working surfaces and the chair and stool cushions white, the cane-back sofa upholstered in stripes of copper, saffron, and pale yellow. Wood tones also abound in the cypress and the cedar boxing in the windows, and shrouding the ceiling lights over each recess thus formed.

From the practical standpoint, the room has plenty of shelf space with provision for adding a great deal more; the principal working surface is long and uncluttered, and cantilevered out so that there are no legs to obstruct the seating position. The television set is unobtrusive, and the sofa well placed for viewing. The Victorian hanging lamp is a thing of beauty whose polished brass, along with that of the tabourets, adds an attractive gleam that defies the aseptic whites and dirt resistant glow of the vinyl floor.

More often than may be generally realized, a study

XV mantel, and these three units together form an extremely attractive focal point in the decorative scheme. The mantel itself is in Italian verde antico marble, small but boldly carved. On it are displayed a row of English majolica lidded vases, and above them is hung a massive antique Italian mirror.

The tall windows are unusual in several respects. Each has but one heavily tasseled, white silk curtain

151.

the designer has gone a step further and allowed for occasional possible use of the room as an overflow bedroom. Two beds are therefore installed permanently, foot to foot, so that together they form one large seat yet can quickly be rearranged if necessity requires. On the wall over each head, in their normal position, there will be an antique twin-light fixture, one of which can be seen.

Incidentally, this room is made bright and interesting by ringing the changes on three major colors — red, gold, beige — and also black. The beds are covered in red with gold welting. The draperies which can be used to separate the sleeping area from the study are in gold, and the hand-loomed Spanish rug is gold and red. The desk, chairs, and table in walnut or black lacquer add further contrast in a room that has all the color variety it needs to eliminate the workaday atmosphere common to rooms designed to serve so mundane a purpose.

The music room (illustration 153) successfully combines eighteenth-century French and Victorian American furniture in a setting whose color scheme of red, white, blue, and black derives from the French Empire period, and that may be said to be something of a triumph in itself.

The background is composed of a deep-red wallpaper patterned all over with tiny flowerets and dots in pale pink, a fabric in the same design being laminated to the venetian blind tapes and used as a border on the pale-beige draperies and window valance. The floor is covered with black and white tiles, and in the center is laid an oval, shaggy rug in a medium blue.

In this setting, the Victorian, double-crested sofa in scarlet fabric fairly sparkles. Alongside it is a Louis XV-style provincial table and a beautiful eighteenth-century ladderback chair with a rush seat. The modern, miniature grand piano is in ebony, and in the foreground is a black lacquered chair whose seat picks up the wallpaper color and design. The little stool, half under the piano, has a plain steel frame and a scarlet cushion, a striking combination that endows it with a certain individuality.

The round Victorian table is covered in white with an embroidered border in black. The antique pendulum clock, the mid-nineteenth-century portrait, and the re-

will have to include emergency sleeping quarters for an owner who must work at night, and will not wish to disturb the household when he (or she) retires. Such a study is depicted in 152, this one actually located in a penthouse apartment with a window wall opening on to a terrace. During the daytime ample light is ordinarily reflected from the whitewashed wall of the adjoining building. The intensity and location of this light can be controlled by a series of wood-framed blinds on casters which can be slid along a brass pole, singly or together, to create areas of shade, and the slats adjusted accordingly.

The single desk can either be backed up to the window or turned from it. In either case, night work is possible because of the large, four-light chandelier suspended above. Floor space is economized by hanging the bookshelves on the wall, and putting the filing cabinets below them. The placing of a single bed ordinarily offers no problem since it can be assumed it will take the place of the usual sofa. In this instance, however,

164

152.

153.

production lamps are indications of the quarter-millennium time span covered by this small interior which seems as fresh as tomorrow.

To turn a sunporch into a study-sitting room, as in 154, an extraordinary conversion was carried out. This involved the adaptation of the beams and posts, which divide the ceiling and wall into three sections, to the support of wall and ceiling panels of glass. Inside the glass these large areas were then covered by venetian blinds which give complete control of both light and air during the daytime. At night, with the blinds closed, lights concealed in the beams fill the room with a warm glow. For reading, et cetera, the usual table lamps provide local illumination.

In order to provide the desired quality of light during the daytime, the matte-white slats of the blinds have their edges tinted in colors keyed to those of the room. By arranging these colors so that three slats in hyacinth alternate with two slats edged in cerulean blue, the effect of a Roman shade is obtained, together with a decorative pattern that seems to give height to the room.

The pine walls and timbers are given a natural finish so that the color and grain pattern go very well with the black and white floor tiles, and the pinkish blue of the sofa. A touch of gold is provided by the brass-legged tray-table, the sunburst on the wall, and the trim of a Franklin stove for which a small cabinet might very well be substituted. The tall table lamp is an antique reproduction in white trimmed with gold.

Somewhat suggestive of the foregoing at first glance, but quite different in actuality, is the studio in 155, which provides a sixteenth-century background in exquisite coloring for modern pieces of furniture. One of the major problems here was what to do with the pitched window-wall of a mansard roof topped by an Italianate cupola. The solution was to stretch three venetian blinds, with stark white slats and black tapes, the full height of the windows, using the slat setting to control the amount of light admitted. Access to the cupola was provided by a circular iron stair painted white. This stands out strongly against the dark-stained wood of the fireplace and becomes a truly decorative feature of the room.

The fireplace itself is lined with tiles to accommodate

an electric fire, and fitted with an insulated, oxidized iron hood adorned with a ceramic deer-head in a natural looking fawn color. The floor is covered with heavy linoleum to match the tiles which are of a stunning antique blue on white, a color picked up by the two highbacked armchairs. The modern round table has a top of white formica, but the smaller one is a copy of an antique piece in pine. The console beneath the contemporary painting is swathed in dark-blue felt enlivened by black braid trim. In addition to the picture, modern art is represented by a charging bull on a pedestal in the window, and modern design by the twin chairs in steel and black leather, symbolic of the clean-cut design of the whole interior.

Two very different styles of occasional rooms are represented by 156 and 157, the first of these being modern in casual country dress, the other constituting an exotic retreat within a house whose interiors may be of any vintage or style.

In 156 Nature's colors and natural textures emphasize the informal air of this conversation corner (which actually might be part of a living room) with its modern fireplace in gleaming copper. This fireplace wall is papered in very broad stripes of sky blue and white, the color being reflected in the hooked carpeting of delft blue and white that covers the low, castered fireplace bench. The sofa, with its slender cross-stretcher base of ebony-finish mahogany and brass, is upholstered in houndstooth checked cotton in contrasting shades of blue. The linen covering of the armchair is also blue, and even the hearthrug of bulky tweed displays the same hue in three different tones. Jute and linen cover the walls, and the window curtains are of sheer wool, completing a tweedy looking room for tweedy people.

In 157, chairs, as well as cocktail table and sofa of rawhide bound rattan, made in Hong Kong, together with the corner heating stove — not so portable as it seems — give the interior a somewhat exotic flavor, which is quite in keeping with the international air contributed by French prints, a modern painting, an American armchair and antique tripod table, the French country-style ladder-back chair, and the oriental rug.

The background for the most part is white, the floor a warm brown, the armchair a medium red, the sofa a

154.

155.

156.

157.

158.

hideaway, and 158 is a very good example of such a "no-fuss" workroom. Even the floor is easily cleaned, hard-wearing travertine vinyl in a large hexagon pattern, with no rugs to trip the unwary preoccupied scholar.

Most of the furnishing consists of bookshelves, with deep leather boxes in which to file collectors' items, and a sizable niche for a monkish medieval wood carving that gives character to the whole room. A spacious desk set into a well-lighted recess can be pulled out and its leaves extended whenever necessary, and in one corner stands a tall ladder-chair on which to perch while consulting volumes from the upper shelves. A thickly cushioned, oversized stool that never has to be moved serves as a desk seat. There is also a high-backed armchair for more relaxing moments, a bureau, and a games table for solitary diversion.

Wide, dark-stained pine boards screen off the doorway, otherwise the predominant colors are rich and warm — the walls purple, the armchair in checks of red and mustard, the latter coloring imitating that of the leather files — the whole constituting a satisfying and comfortable retreat for one with an intellectual bent.

In a study such as 159, where sporting art is the principal interest, ample daylight is essential, whether or not the windows overlook a panoramic view as they do in this case. A major problem here arose out of the location of the windows in a corner of the room instead of being centrally placed. Fortunately they were large, and it was possible to take full advantage of the whole glass area by using venetian blinds and eliminating draperies entirely. These had to be controlled by merely tilting the slats.

To help in securing an even distribution of light, the ceiling and walls were painted white, a predominately white throw rug was used on the floor, and the use of bulky furniture which might throw shadows was avoided. To soften the transmitted light, the slats were made a deep red so that when the blinds are wholly or partially down the room is infused with a rosy glow. At the same time the large expanse of color rendered any further decoration in that corner unnecessary.

In the window area, furniture was reduced to a minimum and the window bottom used as seating by the addition of flat cushions with removable pillows in

checkerboard of browns and reds, and the rug red with light beige and a sprinkling of white, yellow, green, and blue, plus a geometric border figure in black — a totally masculine cosy corner whose highlights are provided by a variety of pillows on the sofa and platform wall.

A study that is really for studying requires a much more sober and practical approach than the dilettante's

170

159.

a variety of colors. The movable pieces were confined to the wall areas as far as possible. A bamboo-legged table and its roundabout chair stand against the dining platform; a tubular brass what-not with glass shelves housing a cactus collection sharing the left hand wall with the only bulky piece — a seat upholstered in a modernized paisley pattern in tan, red, and white.

The fourth wall is confined to the display of canvases, with a small, marble-topped, horse-legged table featuring contemporary sculpture. The shadows cast by a tiny pair of bamboo-legged folding tables are minimal so that they need rarely be moved. With high-level general lighting, and a single table lamp for study, the whole arrangement is more than satisfactory both day and night.

171

The Bedroom

In that most personal of all rooms, the bedroom, the décor can often run riot in the owner's search for self-expression — and often does — on the theory that here at last one can be oneself and give outlet to one's true nature and express one's secret ambitions without let or hindrance. This is far from the truth if the room is to perform its true function of providing the atmosphere and facilities for comfort and relaxation both physical and mental. In such a room there should be no place for busy wallpapers or fabrics, and strong colors should be avoided.

Here, too, the placement of furniture is usually more restricted than elsewhere because of the necessary consideration of light (both day and artificial), drafts, and convenience. This may be further affected by the modern tendency to replace certain movable pieces of furniture with fitted closets, so that wall space must needs be sacrificed to doors, and the decorative possibilities of the room consequently modified.

Normally, in designing such a room, it is best to choose the furniture for its basic quality and pleasing individual style, using color and pattern to establish the mood, and relying upon accessories and bibelots to take care of the revelatory expression. In some of the rooms shown here the latter items have been omitted, pending the owner's personal ministrations, and the interiors may consequently seem a little bare, formal, and austere. In others there are sufficient items to indicate both the sex and the predilections of the prospective occupant, though there are often tell-tale details that suggest modifications made as a concession to a husband or wife occupying the same room. Such a room, fortunately, can have just as interesting a personality as that which represents the taste of only one of the parties, providing the compromise is skillfully handled and no attempt is made to marry two opposing and incompatible schemes. As a rule all that is needed is the suppression of an urge to prettify at the expense of practicality or, conversely, confusing beauty with feminity and a touch of luxury with waste.

The first of these exhibits is 160 and 161, a twin-bed room with French Empire-style beds carved and painted a warm gray with gilt ornamentation. The other furniture pieces comprise a Louis Seize commode with a gilt and painted trumeau above it, an Empire *secrétaire-á-abattant* with ormolu mounts, one fruitwood armchair, and a Louis XV side chair, both in yellow bird-and-flower print of enchanting delicacy, with a small, brass-galleried Louis XV oval table in the window. Small decorative items include a pair of porcelain urns on the commode and Meissen candlesticks on the secretary. Over each bed is a large English aquatint, and flanking the mirror is a pair of French tôle sconces.

After dark, the room acquires a cheerful glow from the lamps thanks to the almost white rug and the yellow striped fabric which covers both the walls and the beds.

172

160.

On the other hand, nothing dresses up the room so much, night or day, as the stunning lace-and-tassel bordered toile drapery which forms a swag over the window, descending on either side in a graceful cascade. The translucent white, floor-length curtains, which have toile tie-backs, are finished with the same deep ball-fringe. This glistening ensemble stands out against both the yellow of the walls and the darker wood of the louvered shutters with which it is in perfect harmony, forming one exquisite whole with the black-framed pictures and the beds. This interior is indeed an excellent example of eclectic furnishing at its best.

It is interesting to compare the foregoing with 162, which shows the owner's bedroom in the same house. The principal piece of course is the prim and precise bed with its stiff fringed canopy, all in white to match the square-topped head posts, the headboard and the coverlet. The bedposts are round, fluted mahogany, mounted on square, pedestal-type feet which are painted white and outlined in gold. This bed stands on a late

161.

eighteenth-century Aubusson rug which adds a great deal of warmth, color, and pattern to the room. The dresser is an Empire serpentine chest, dating from about 1780, with carved chamfers and bracket feet. Over it hangs a carved and gilt French mirror and candle branches. In the window corner is a low screen paneled with old paintings on canvas, the frames being supported

162.

163.

on typical "spider" legs. In the window is a small mahogany commode with a table lamp in white porcelain under a white silk shade. The armchair is a Hepplewhite adaptation of a Louis Quinze type, its oval back inset with a white leather panel bearing a floral decoration.

With so much white, including that of the dado, plus the pale beige of the walls and the bed drapery, the room

fairly sparkles, a romantic note being added by the beige, greens, purple, and yellows of the rug, the colorful nosegay of the chairs and lamps, and the gold-framed cherubs placed either side of the mirror. This betrays the feminine touch in a room that is otherwise eminently uncluttered and practical, even to the light walls which make it seem larger than it is.

In 163 an attempt is made to recapture the atmosphere of an early New England bedroom using both antiques and contemporary interpretations of original pieces. These include a Queen Anne lowboy, a four-poster bed, and a pair of Victorian basin stands, one of which is given a touch of authenticity by an added pot de chambre.

The problem in all such rooms is to achieve the air without losing any of the advantages of modern living with its attendant comfort and convenience such as restful seating, up-to-date lighting, and the use of present-day fabrics, and even patterns and colors. In a room such as this, one also has to distinguish between country

174

furniture and the designs and workmanship of the trained cabinet maker of the period.

In this instance, a very good job has been done in making use of the antique styles redolent of another era but enjoyable today as things to live with. The huge braided rug, for instance, is all of wool, but in a wider variety of colors (plus black and white) than one would expect in an eighteenth-century product, and probably far better made than the handiwork of any country housewife. The draperies, too, are of an old-time pattern, but machine woven and printed in splendid gradations of color not available in bygone centuries. Their gently scalloped pelmets also are not exactly cottage equipment, and beneath them are ruffled glass curtains which are necessary intruders.

The bedspread is of white quilted cotton with a pretty cherry pattern in appliquè. The front bedposts are of a vase pattern and spirally reeded, the others remaining plain, the whole being topped with a valance of white muslin which is duplicated in the dust ruffles of the bed frame. The pillows are dressed up with organdy ruffles, adding a final delicate touch to a delightfully feminine confection.

The small easy chair is upholstered in beige broadcloth, a modern touch in keeping with the two table lamps which have green-bordered white silk shades, and employ white ceramic roosters as bases. Over the antique lowboy a primitive painting of a little girl adds a nostalgic touch that the pair of brass candlesticks and china fruit plate can hardly equal.

The furnishing and decorating of such a room to recapture an early eighteenth-century air is capable of almost infinite variation depending upon the degree of authenticity required, but today many liberties are taken in mixing the old and the new, adapting the old to new uses, and substituting modern variations, as this example can only faintly suggest.

There are many and varied ways of furnishing a bedroom, all depending as much upon the space available as the mood to be created. That otherwise anonymous bedroom designated by 164 is particularly interesting as an example of what might have been done as well as what actually was done. It is a large room and in the hands of a less competent designer might well have been broken up into an agglomeration of small areas defined by a scattering of rugs, reducing its apparent size and endowing it with an air of busy-ness if not downright confusion. As it is, the room is airy and light and obviously spacious, the overall carpet serving to unify the several isolated and somewhat disparate elements — the beds, the dresser ensemble, and the chaise-longue-lamp group, and others not appearing in the picture.

In addition to the floor covering, color is an important element in holding the units together and creating a feeling of pleasant uncrowded homogeneity. The basic colors are yellow and white, the multiple swags and cascading ends of the wide window pelmets setting the pace with contrasting depths of color. Blinds are fitted so that lacy curtains can be used over the big window. The walls are pale yellow, with large panels delineated upon them giving importance to the pictures and furniture groupings that they enclose and extending their area of influence.

One result of this is that fewer decorative items and pieces of furniture are needed to eliminate a feeling of bareness throughout the room. The Louis XV-style mahogany dresser, for example, is grouped with two eighteenth-century chairs in black lacquer with rush seats, and a gilt-framed Napoleonic-looking mirror between black-iron and crystal three-candle wall sconces.

Adornments here consist of the dresser lamp with its intriguing base composed of a metal musical box with revolving figures, together with a porcelain basket of flowers and a piece of modern sculpture consisting of three headless but otherwise engaging female torsos. In the little corner group the chaise is covered in a striking cotton print with white background. Paired with it is a tripod tablelamp, and three pictures, making use of two of the painted panels. The dressing table proper is the other side of the window. Enough, however, can be seen to indicate the principle involved in securing balance and adequately furnishing the whole with a minimum number of furniture pieces.

An entirely different sort of problem is imposed by the small bachelor's bedroom depicted in 165 — a unit of the apartment seen in 142 and 143. This actually is a dual-purpose interior, a library by day, sleeping quarters at night, the steel-framed French bed masquerading

164.

as a sofa when required, and the conversion being effected without disturbing the rest of the furniture.

The apartment is located in a penthouse with a large outside terrace and ample window areas so that with plenty of available light and a white ceiling, a certain amount of dark wood on walls and floor is no detriment.

The unpainted wall areas are sheathed in zebra-wood, as are the window trim and ceiling-high doors. These double doors, with their attractive hardware, are flanked by black-painted bookcases in which the books themselves suffice to decorate the entire wall.

There is really little furniture in the room, and not

176

165.

166.

which is perched a white-shaded lamp having a porcelain vase as base. The general illumination is taken care of by a tôle ceiling fixture — a wheel-type chandelier in black and gold, with four shaded electric candles.

In the corner behind the drum table, a paneled stand, painted in faux-bois, acts as a shelf for a small decorative palm. On the dark floor the eye-catcher is a rug of leopard-skins as splended in its way as the painted Louis XIV bergère which stands upon it. Other furnishings are restricted to sculpture including the famous "Thorn" (visible in the photograph) and a variety of growing palms and ferns which serve to bring the garden-like terrace indoors.

It is interesting to compare this bachelor's bedroom with its feminine counterpart in illustration 166, where a sort of sophisticated simplicity. has taken over. The elaborate crystal chandelier and the rich Austrian shades in silk contrast strangely with the simple French bed in walnut, and the unpretentious portrait above it. The lamp is a small one, porcelain-based, keeping company

much is needed in this limited space. What is lost in variety is therefore counterbalanced by an increase in intensity, evident in this compelling décor where so much is done with so little. The sofa seat-pad mattress, cushions, and bolsters, are covered in a dark brown material enlivened by throw pillows in light beige. At one end is an antique drum table with a marble top on

177

167.

bronze appliques hold candles (obviously used) athwart the gilded oval mirror. By the side of a satin-covered daybed is a kidney-shaped table with a leather-inlaid top and a shaped apron scalloped along the face, its sole burden a silver Louis XVI bouillotte lamp. The little tub chair which counterbalances the daybed is covered in sprig-dotted white muslin.

In spite of the predominance of white, the room has more life than shows in the picture, the overall carpet being of a warm mauve color, the walls a delicate purplish pink, the bedspread ecru with sculptured quilting adding a three-dimensional effect — altogether a pleasantly unexciting retreat with the fringe benefits of a place to relax in solitude, to read, to telephone, or to dash off a note to a friend, always with that fabulous chandelier to give the girlish spirits a lift.

While simplicity may have its appeal, it would seem that a touch of the exotic is more often found preferable, particularly in the warmer areas of the country. This urge may present itself in varying degrees from an all-out attempt to duplicate the bedrooms of the Orient to the mere inclusion of a single alien note. A good example of the former is represented by 167, which speaks of the Far East in general and Hong Kong in particular.

The bed, which of course is the most important feature, is made of rattan, painted a light yellow, and held together by rawhide thongs. The walls are covered with striped linen in orange on white, the locale being California and not the tropics. The window is covered by a sliding curtain of the same material, spaced slightly from the open window for air circulation in which the high, coved ceiling helps.

The bed canopy is a fragmentary affair, the bolster and bed-covering daytime dress-up features. The bedside table, painted the same color as the bed, is of rattan with a wooden frame, the lamp a termite-proof cone of iron mesh and an opaque shade in blue. The rug is a Chinese oriental, the decorative porcelains and the tall vase collector's items from Hong Kong. These pieces rest on a black-lacquered wooden shelf, in a room where everything is perfectly compatible and convincing.

If a Mediterranean atmosphere is preferred, 168 may appeal as combining simplicity and elegance with an aura of uncluttered coolness. The background is one

with a white telephone, leather-bound address book and a crystal perfume bottle.

The rest of the pieces are not gaudy but good. The round stand by the bed is actually a Directoire bouillotte table with a faux marbre top and brass gallery. Between the windows is the dressing table with delicate legs, in reality a Parisian *table-de-dame,* while a tiny pair of

178

168.

of whitewashed walls and pecky cypress beams, a floor of white tile with black insets. In the wall is a gothic niche, painted black inside, the better to show off a white vase of yellow, blue, pink, and white flowers. The three floor-to-ceiling openings to the room are fitted with venetian blinds in three different colors — tangerine, citron, and olive-green. The design of the beauti-

fully carved bedstead is Moorish in origin, shown in its daytime wear of bittersweet mattress and bolster covers. In pleasant contrast are the glass-topped iron table, the Venetian version of a Louis XV fauteuil, and the fixed-top game table with its inlaid checkerboard.

From Morocco to Central Africa is but a short step in the decorating world, and here again Asian rattan

179

169.

can be used to good effect, as illustration 169 shows. The rawhide-bound rattan is given a darker finish without the aid of paint. In the bed this color is combined with a medium blue sailcloth decorated in white; on the chairs the covering is heavy, undyed antique satin, and on the stool, dacron.

On the occasional table is a brass lamp of oriental flavor; on the night-stand a brass-based hurricane globe protects an everyday candle which is more atmospheric than practical. This stand has a white plastic top. On the far side of the bed is a mahogany chest ornamented with mitered rattan, a distinguished looking piece harboring a footed tray with a pierced gallery, and several other items of pewter, plus a Chinese white vase full of California tulips. Above this hangs a mirror with a frame of mitered rattan.

The room's only window is covered by a blind of rice-straw, while on the floor a thin rush carpeting insulates a full size zebra-skin from the stone floor, completing an unusual and intensely practical interior that would be interesting in any climate.

On the East Coast, many a bedroom borrows its Oriental flavor by more subtle means, certain designers being satisfied with wallpapers of Chinese inspiration, perhaps a single coromandel screen, or mahogany furniture of the so-called Chinese Chippendale pattern. In photograph 170 this method is taken a step further with admirable results. Above the white dado of this bedroom, a pale blue paper of Chinese inspiration displays willow trees in browns, yellows, sage green, and white in the usual Chinese undulating rhythm, interspersed with birds in blues and grays with touches of orange — a growing practice in America since the days of the clipper ships. What has been added in this case, however, is the suggestion of pagoda roofs incorporated into the cornices of the bed and the window frame. The illusion is heightened by the annular bands on the bedposts faintly simulating bamboo joints, and painting the whole a yellowish white.

A further exotic note is struck by the use of red lacquer on the frame of a Queen Anne mirror, and stencilling in gold thereon suggestions of birds and foliage in the Chinese manner without adopting the old Chinese techniques. To this is added a Chippendale-style console table, lacquered black, and a twin-leaved firescreen in the same finish with fretted panels and spider legs, plus a Chinese ginger jar or two.

The bed and window draperies, together with the bedspread, are of smooth white Thai silk, and the pelmet, tester, and spread are edged with raspberry-shaped tassels in the same red as the mirror frame, this color again being picked up by the upholstered easy chair in a somewhat lighter tone. In contrast, the long-looped rug is a pale beige.

In the next two pictures, 171 and 172, the Oriental accent is purely incidental, being confined in 171 to the window pelmets, and in 172 to the wallpaper, and the same bell-type tassels which adorn the beds. In the first of these the pagoda theme ties in with the prints over the twin beds and has a suggestive relationship with the landscape in the trumeau picture with its wild trees and twin volcanoes. Otherwise the room is wholly American in feel, even though the beds are French, painted to suit the décor. In spite of these minor exotic touches the room is quiet and restful, thanks largely to the plainness of the surfaces and fabrics, and monochrome rug, and the familiar antiques such as the French-footed Sheraton mahogany chest.

In the master bedroom of this house, a sense of continuity is established by using the same bell tassels, but this time on the beds. These beds are fully upholstered, otherwise quite plain, having the general appearance of a modern version of the old-time sleigh bed, the curves of head and foot being carried down to the feet. The "bells" therefore are particularly appropriate. The Oriental flavor is further captured by the use of a Chinese-style wallpaper, mostly pale yellow and white on pale blue. This wide sweep of color and pattern, restricted to the wall area above the dado, is interrupted only by the wide chimney breast of vertical wood sheathing painted a jonquil yellow.

Above the mantel is a large trumeau in which the painting occupies two thirds of the total glass area, giving the whole piece greater impact and weight. On either side of it is an unusual twin-candle sconce with a brilliant cut-glass mirrored plate, glass branches and mirrored drops — sparkling accents that the plain wood surface needs.

170.

171.

172.

Among the most interesting features of the room is the design of the upholstered armchairs alongside the fireplace. Each of these has the arm nearest the fireplace cut off short so that the chair's occupant can benefit from the fire's radiated heat on that side. A somewhat bolder accent is provided by a tall five-panel screen of striated mirrored glass, and a touch of elegance by a bouillotte table with its faux-marbre top.

The twin-decked bedside tables are painted a deep rich yellow, the drawers outlined in brown. This yellow complements that of the overall carpet which is somewhat lighter in tone, setting off the mauve masses of the chairs and ottoman, and pleasantly counterbalancing the blue of the walls.

In 173 is seen the bachelor bedroom of the apartment whose living room was illustrated in 29 and whose hall was shown in 128. Here the exotic touches are supplied by the bed — in particular the bed-head carvings — and the modeling and styling of the bedside lamp, both of which suggest Mexican handiwork. The table to one side of the structurally heavy bed, and the dresser at the other side, as well as the round occasional table, are all substantially made with heavy legs or feet typical of the workmanship of that Spanish-Indian civilization. Actually the headboard is a reproduction of a country Spanish piece, the carved posts finished in antique ochre with a central panel of dark rush. The ochre of the posts is repeated in the dust skirt, which is striped in white and makes a strong contrast with the regimental red of the coverlet. The chanticleer lamp is made of pewter with a striped, laminated shade which is extremely shallow and adjustable as to height. The other lamp, which has a massive urn base, is of brass with a felt shade, both of them designed and made by the decorators. The table on which the lamp stands is a reproduction in walnut of a Jacobean original. In keeping with this solid furniture, the custom-made swivel chair is heavily upholstered, showing neither frame nor legs, and is covered in ochre wool hopsacking with red welting.

In contrast with the buttermilk-white of the walls, the interior colors stand out boldly. The carpet is the same regimental red as the coverlet, while the draperies and valance copy the bed's dust skirt, the valance being trimmed in red in addition. The total result is an attractive and comfortable interior, much more restful than it sounds (largely because of the compatibility of the colors), and masculine in every respect.

The skins of tropical animals on floor and walls constitute one of the simplest means of imparting an exotic touch to an interior as will be recognized from 174. And since they formed the first known beds for humans they (or reasonable facsimiles thereof) should be recognized as fitting furnishings for these quarters.

In this picture, leopard-skins provide a handsome and luxurious combination of color and texture as wall hangings behind the bedheads, and look equally well on the floor. Everything else in the room therefore can be plain. If the color and pattern need to be picked up for accent nothing would be more effective than the large canister on the dressing table which has a bronze leopard as handle and is wrapped in the skin.

As for the furniture itself, the walnut veneers, accented with burl panels and brass fitings, are in tune with both the yellow of the skins and the pattern of the spots. Contrast is afforded by the deep green of the draperies and coverlets, the white of the bookshelf recess, and accents provided by the throw-pillows on the beds, plus the palm leaves and other foliage in the brass urns, the shafts and shades of the gilt-brass mounted dressing-table lamps, and that attached to the wall over the beds.

The furniture itself is modern of Italian inspiration, columnar, and rugged, with brass fittings, finials and mounts. The beds are tied together by a hinged octagonal post at the head so that they can be swung apart for making up. At their foot, stands a cocktail table which provides a certain amount of storage and furnishes a handy seat. Not far away is a high-backed slipper chair, with a marble-topped pedestal table for the matutinal coffee and similar occasions, adding a final touch to an interior of restrained elegance that needs no expensive bibelots to bring it to life.

Another kind of exoticism is represented by fabric-paneled walls with heavy draperies to match, as a background for one or more unusual pieces as in 175. This material, which is obtainable either in a solid color or as a patterned print, is applied to the walls in alternating panels of varying sizes. The printed design is also used for the window curtains. The floor is covered in a vinyl representing boards of different widths. This arrangement provides a spectacular background in tones of rose, mustard, aqua, and brown interspersed with areas of mustard. This mustard color is repeated in the felt coverlet of the bed which has a fringe of brown and rose.

The most conspicuous piece of furniture is the glass-

173.

enclosed étagère with its display of porcelains, topped off by an antique teapot full of gay, though artificial, flowers. Both this and the twin-poster bed are accented in Renoir blue, the latter having an elegant scalloped headboard adorned with brass finials. Three other important pieces of furniture are included — a circular commode acting as a storage cupboard and lamp table, the twin tables on casters which have bottom shelves for books, etc.

In the corner by the commode the panel of plain silk emphasizes the three small, old-time pictures displayed on it, and acts as a background for the bouillotte lamp

(that universal favorite of the interior designer!) in bronze and tôle. Over the bed itself is a portrait in oils by Gaggetta which puts the finishing touch to an interior both novel and colorful as well as highly dramatic.

In designing bedrooms, tastes and requirements vary as much as budgets, and it is astonishing how much can be done with so little. There is not much in the bachelor (boy or girl) bedroom of 176, yet how utterly satisfactory it could be to one who had to choose between this monkish yet tasteful cell and a room furnished with everyday castoffs that so many have to endure.

Genetically, this is a French country bedroom, a label that at once lifts it out of the common run. There are only three pieces shown, and these should suffice with the addition of storage space and a mirror. Even the background can be created with little expense by anyone digitally adept. For the window wall, all that is needed is a pair of candystriped sheets, while a matching pillow case can be converted into a café curtain. The window, its sill and trim, should be painted French blue. The multistriped, translucent shade, finished with white-moss fringe will doubtless have to be bought, and those who want the little feminine touch can make and apply their own blue bow to match. The other wall is whitewashed brick and where such does not exist, a ready-made duplicate in tile form can be acquired, or a plaster wall simply painted white. The painted, or tiled floor also is white to receive a lovely bushy area rug in raspberry color. The footless bed, or at least the headboard, must of course be found in the flea market, or elsewhere. The one shown is an old-time cane-paneled piece with nice carved finials, and this, too, is painted blue. The coverlet is easily made from another of the striped sheets — if a quilting accessory is available for the sewing machine. It should then be edged with the same fringe as the shade, and white pompons on a twisted cord added to the bottom corners to make it "form-fitting." The dust ruffle can be made from a French-blue sheet. The rest of the ensemble consists of an old carved chest and a handsome French ladder-back chair, with perhaps a few pictures and an accent piece or two such as a red box on the blue sill, and the necessary lamp in sparkling white to emphasize the tricolor flavor of the thrifty Gallic room.

Formal and luxurious but not overly imposing is the

186

174.

175.

176.

impression one would get from 177 with its rich adaptations of old traditional American bedroom pieces, for while the dresser and chest are comparatively solid and heavy, the small-scale lowboy, with its slender, shapely legs, and the gorgeous pencil-post bed, have an air of delicacy about them that counterbalances the rest. Actually, they are a little too refined for the beamed ceiling,

particularly with that sumptuous carpet on the floor, yet under it, and against the plain white wall, they acknowledge their origins, even though embellished with matched veneers and expensive bandings. Not only the mirror (in spite of its gold-trimmed mahogany), but the brass sconce and the wing chair are in Queen Anne style, benefiting from modern materials and methods so that everything is wholly compatible, including the oriental rug and the pattern-quilted bed coverlet.

This grouping is well suited to the L-shaped room which introduces a note of informality and calls for no extravagant collection of pictures to make it seem fully furnished. The tall, brass-columned lamp, with a glass base serving to diminish its apparent weight, is nicely calculated to visually balance the chest. (It is to be hoped, of course, that its switch has been installed within easy reach of the bed; decorators can sometimes be so impractical!)

The colors here are: Wall, off-white; carpet, dark

188

177.

178.

179.

green; bedspread a lighter green; dust ruffle and valance, white; rug, beige ground with reds, blues, yellows and tans, a setting in which the red roses on the dresser should look their lovely best.

Bedrooms with an exotic air often delight the artistically minded, and illustration 178 is a good example based on artifacts brought from Burma. The walls are sheathed in satinwood, the floor covered with padouk laid in squares like tiles and framed in satinwood strips. In this setting is assembled a collection of elaborately carved furniture — a bed, chest, seat, and low table, mostly in teak, together with rattan chairs having cane backs and rawhide bindings; a circular rattan table and

tall plant stands also in rattan. These tend to make the Queen Anne dresser seem slightly out of place.

On the wall is hung a tall Burmese painting which is narrower at the top than the bottom, as is the carved, double-doored, turtle-footed cabinet which stands beneath a small painting on the adjoining wall. Other wall decorations consist of icons in the form of praying figures,

190

carved in the round, and about 18 inches high, which apparently once graced a pagoda and now are grouped around a large one in the form of a framed relic. On the tables are additional decorative items such as bronzes and small ceramics, Burmese heads modeled in stone, a huge carved fan, and exotic plants. Arrangement of the principal pieces is apparently of secondary importance, the more informal the better, the draperies, seat pads, cushions, and bedspread being relied upon to provide a desirable quota of color.

An interestingly "different" bedroom interior such as 179 can be contrived from the simplest of materials and the liveliest of color schemes. This is the basis of a décor particularly adapted to rooms having built-in closets which normally would be aggressively obvious and add nothing to the total effect.

The doors to these closets are of the flush type, and there are three in a row, each covered with a plastic fabric of the same pattern but in a different color so as to distinguish the contents. The color used on the central door is that employed for the rest of the wall areas since the two could not be confused in any event. Each closet door is ceiling high and has a purple glass knob at its center, an arrangement made possible by the use of spring latches.

The bed-head is formed of a single sheet of half-inch plywood attached to the wall. At its top, supported by triangular plywood brackets is a light trough with a frosted-glass base, which contains a pair of fluorescent lighting fixtures. The bed itself consists of a simple box frame on gliders to support the spring and mattress, with a pair of hooks to hold head and bed together.

In the picture the bed is shown with a spread in deep yellow with purple trim, reflecting the colors used on the walls and two of the doors. The floor is covered with plain gold vinyl representing floor boards arranged in rectangles, giving a sort of exaggerated parquet effect. A plaid mixture of deep blue, yellow, and brown is used for the upholstery of a steel-footed easy chair, with a contemporary rug streaked in shades of brown beneath it. Alongside this stands a round marble-topped table with an iron pedestal — one of the most modern units in the room, serving as a stand for the oldest piece — a carved wood statuette with ecclesiastical connotations

apparently made centuries ago. Over this hangs a small metal chandelier like a somewhat clumsy halo.

The rest of the furniture consists of plain, country-style wooden chairs with seats in dull-gold fabric, and an antique dresser on which a leafy growing plant spreads a touch of Nature's green, and a nicely carved old-time little commode supporting a tall painted candlestick and a cluster of geraniums in a pottery bowl.

Not many will want to copy the chandelier, but there are several more practical ideas worth adopting, or, better still, adapting to one's particular needs.

Small but neat is bedroom 180, which has a great deal more to it than may be obvious. The secret lies in the hidden doors in the dressing-table wall which the heavily striped wallpaper helps to conceal. When open, these reveal a television set, a high-fidelity phonograph, storage room, and a built-in chest of drawers. This arrangement provides desirable extra features while maintaining an uncluttered appearance and preserving the attractive décor of a room designed for one principal purpose. Opening up the wall to throw the extra space into the room would have been far less satisfactory, resulting in the addition of extra furniture including storage pieces and probably others totally incompatible with the rest.

Apart from this, the interior has much to recommend it. Green and yellow are the key colors, combined with white, and the walls are given some architectural character by the paper border and the neatly pleated draperies with their rigid top line. Between them can be seen the Roman shades which repeat the wallpaper pattern. The furniture consists of excellent reproductions of antiques, mostly Louis XVI French, combined with modern pieces selected for their compatibility as well as their contribution to the desired mood of unpretentious comfort.

The combination of a bedroom with a sitting room may offer decorating problems depending on the amount of space available for each, and the necessity or otherwise of separating one from the other visually so as to conceal the room's dual nature. Storage requirements likewise will, ordinarily, have to be considered together with the resultant problem of making doors and drawers a part of the décor.

In 181 and 182 the designer, faced with an odd-shaped room, tackled the last problem first, lining the interior

180.

with somewhat bizarre wallpaper representing vertical sheathing in white boards with a black grain. This not only provided a dramatic backdrop to the furnishings but effectively hid the numerous closet double-doors which are betrayed only by insignificant knobs easily mistaken for knots in the wood.

For "live" storage, however, it was still necessary to provide a wardrobe. This took the form of a particularly handsome eighteenth-century French provincial armoire in fruitwood which thereby became the key feature of the room, and the most decorative. Another important innovation is the use of accordion-type black-leather curtains which slide on brass rods, top and bottom, and fasten with buckle closures. Nearby, on the specially-

181.

182.

shaped rug, is a modern chair and ottoman in white leather, with its own brass standard lamp.

In the facing corner are twin sofa-beds with white-painted metal end tables, sized to suit, one of them shaped to accommodate the wall angle. The use of bolsters instead of fixed backs to the sofas adds both to their comfort and adaptability, while throw-pillows in red and black provide colorful accents second only to the large and shapely porcelain lamps that complete the décor.

It is probably no more than natural to complete this section on bedrooms with a dream room designed for a little girl (illustration 183), especially since it contains a number of novel ideas appealing to the youthful and feminine. Because children love vivid colors, bright hues are employed over large areas. To act as a foil for these the walls are white, except for that behind the bed which is peppermint red.

The three colors selected for the room — red, pink, and gold, plus white — have been dramatically combined in ceiling-high storage units which are arranged one on each side of the bed. In place of doors these spaces, which contain both shelves and hanger rods, are enclosed by venetian blinds in white-painted wooden frames. One of these is reserved for clothing, and is therefore distinguished by painting alternate pairs of slats in red, white, pink, and gold-on-white. The other one, which is used for toys and books, has blinds of the gold-on-white pattern only. Interior lighting is supplied for both and

193

183.

184.

the slats can be set to reveal as much or as little of the contents as desired.

As the picture shows, the room is warmly floored with a thick woven carpet, plus a play area in light tiles with a colorful widely-spaced design. The bed is a two-poster with a definitely antique and grown-up air, that any pre-teener of the fair sex would love.

The Beds

Since color plays such an important part in the bedroom décor, and since the beds themselves are the most important items in that room, it is quite necessary to suit the bed coverings and pillows both to the style of the bed and the principal decorating tones of the room. This is perhaps best illustrated by views which relate certain spreads, throws, sheets, and pillow cases to their settings.

In the first of these (184), the bedspread, which may appear to be white, is actually a two-color contrast weave in white against a background of light beige, and this

185.

194

186.

intensifies the pattern. The draperies of both window and bed are of Thai silk which dyes a mottled brown showing up the rich mahogany of the furniture, particularly the bed head which is silhouetted against a striped paper in lilac and white.

The same method of analysis should be used in appraising the next three views of the beds and throws. That of 185 is a richly printed and quilted one with an oriental air in dark green and royal blue. The corners are rounded so as to drape at the foot more neatly. This throw could very well be used with carpet and draperies in one of these two colors or with a deep yellow. The blue of the pattern might also be picked up by the accessories. The bed head shown is a rather severe modern Gothic style in birch to contrast with the rich coloring of the material.

Lighthearted in comparison is 186, which has the look and feel of antique silk. The graded quilting of the center is finished off with a gathered flounce that adds a gay

187.

189.

188.

190.

192. A lesson in the charm of simplicity — a fabric gay with bouquets in yellows and golds enlivens the table, the bed and the window, against the deeper gold of the bed's flounced petticoat, the draperies, and the wing chair, with tiny pillows as accents. The white ball-fringe of the quilted spread is repeated in the draperies which also have white tiebacks, and enframe a window softened by crisp white café curtains on shining brass rods in keeping with the old-fashioned charm of this delightfully feminine bedroom corner.

191. An equally formal but unquilted throw with fitted corners such as this represents a paneled effect on all three sides. This has a Spanish air, constituting a fine example of sheer decorative pattern that contrasts perfectly with the plain fabric of the head board which, in turn, duplicates one of the colors in the cover design. The throw material, it will be noted, is also used for the draperies which are edged with the same braid.

note and renders it equally compatible with French provincial walnut or Louis XV fruitwood pieces, or a bed-head inspired by either.

Different again is 187, with its flap corners which allow it to be used on beds with or without foot rails. Quite incidentally these add a prim tailored look which would recommend its use with a modern décor — a metal trimmed bed-head, for instance, though its apparent weight suggests that the spread would do equally well when dominated by a bed showing a sturdy wood panel and posts.

In the matter of decorated sheets and pillow cases, suitability is largely a matter of mood, and the color and

197

193. A riot of form and color is this exotic Florentine bedroom where autumn reds, browns, and golds are accented with the leaf-greens of cushions, and table cover, emphasizing the dark glow of antique woods, a seventeenth-century New England chest vying for attention with the Italian chairs and spool-turned twin bed heads. An important feature is the window draperies which repeat the colors and tile-pattern of the quilted spread overflowing so luxuriously on to the tufted rug. Here the accessories and pictures and the low-hung curtains add to the cozy feeling without encroaching on the limited space.

198

194. In this large airy room the feeling of space is augmented by the low headboard and picture arrangement, the horizontal lines of the wide bed and the daybed, the overall
carpeting and the extensive wall areas that emphasize the
vertical sweep of the window draperies under a deep pelmet,
in a dark green to match the table cover, which reduces their
visual height. The bed is unified by upholstering the head
in the same material as the yellow-and-white spread. The
identical material is used for the ceiling-high draperies over
the misty sheerness of white, embroidered French curtains.
In contrast to the bed, the chaise longue and the side chair
are covered in a solid yellow of a darker hue. Here, again,
the throw pillows in pinks and greens provide pleasant
points of contrast that enliven the whole décor.

pattern can quickly introduce a false note if they are tied into an overall scheme to which they are not wholly suited. In 188, for instance, the sprays of roses and scattered rosebuds are decidedly feminine, expressing a dainty mood yet not present in sufficient volume to determine the total character of a room. They need to be emphasized by picking up and repeating the colors and forms in accessories, and perhaps in a rug, or even the background of a sufficiently large painting. The bedside telephone color would help, also the valance (which is not obvious) and perhaps even with the bud pattern repeated in the under-sheet. In the picture, the green of the blanket — the color of spring leaves — adds a perfect counterpoint.

The masculine counterpart to the foregoing might well be the striped percale of 189, the pillow stripes of pink, red, lilac, and two yellows running crosswise, and both sheet and case having a wide pink band at one end. This assembly is shown against a wall of deep red, the iron bed-head being painted the same color, but relieved by the brass knobs, gold picture frame, and gold shade and trim of the red lamp.

Less aggressively partisan is 190, despite its associations with Harlequin, and the uncompromising quality of the blood-red plank wall behind it.

This rhythmic arrangement of squares in golds and oranges on white is mild in comparison and therefore more appealing. One of the darker oranges being used for the body of the sheet and dark gold for the valance, smooth transition is attained in the bedding colors. This time the bed is white and gold, and the gold-mounted red lamp, a red flower vase, and mahogany table are outlined against a white, rough-plastered section of the wall. There is action in this pattern, but not sufficient to be disturbing, and it should be easy to imagine it in a much cooler setting.

In each of these instances it is necessary to remember that these are not colors and patterns in a vacuum — they relate to the rest of the room, or should do so, even if they are intended only as accents in the general décor.

200

The Bathroom

The biggest challenge to the decorator in designing a bathroom with individuality is to find some means of making it look like something it is not. And in this the handicaps are tremendous because of the simple fact that in most houses and apartments the space is not available to permit of interesting juggling of the pieces, and, regardless of color or details of shape, the products are, by their intrinsic nature, everlastingly the same; their function is obvious and cannot be disguised. Two things in the designer's favor, however, are the attractive design of modern units and the variety of colors in which they are obtainable. This, unfortunately, is not enough, and the first requirement in killing the totally utilitarian aspect of such a room is space. For this reason, if the bath and dressing rooms can be combined, the problem is simpler. But since that solution is not always possible, the simplest alternative is usually a resort to trompe-l'oeil features.

Much can be done by using wall coverings that emphasize the open air — outdoor space. Next comes the illusion provided by painted-in windows, perhaps illuminated from behind, or covered with sheer curtains, and the alteration of the shape of the interior space by adding painted-in draperies, furniture, screens, etc., and in this way not only eliminating the causes of claustrophobia but creating active interest. In the modern bathroom, in other words, we need fewer representations of denizens of the deep and more trees, flowers, and distant vistas!

Turning to the practical aspects of the situation, the sad truth is that, in spite of all the advances that have been made in the design of bathroom equipment, the really handsome room is a rarity that few besides professional decorators take the trouble to give the attention it deserves. This does not mean that the palatial bathroom is unknown; indeed where funds are unlimited there is no problem. One can have beautifully tiled floors and walls, tubs of solid marble with gold fittings, and so on. But for the average home such extravagances are highly unnecessary. As a rule, much more important is careful investigation of the types of fixtures and materials available, and equally meticulous planning according to the space required and the needs of the family.

In many instances the efficiency of the bathroom can be increased by separating the water closet from the rest of the room. It may also be advisable to add a second lavatory, or even duplicate the closet and lavatory and enclose the tub by itself, an arrangement that is illustrated in 197. In this example each unit can be separated from the rest by means of a sliding door at each end of the tub.

In planning such changes and additions there are obviously a number of technical considerations to be taken into account, such as the location of doors and windows and the possibility of installing extra water supply and waste pipes in the areas selected. On the other hand, simply duplicating fixtures — a popular procedure with large families — rarely offers problems, and the designer

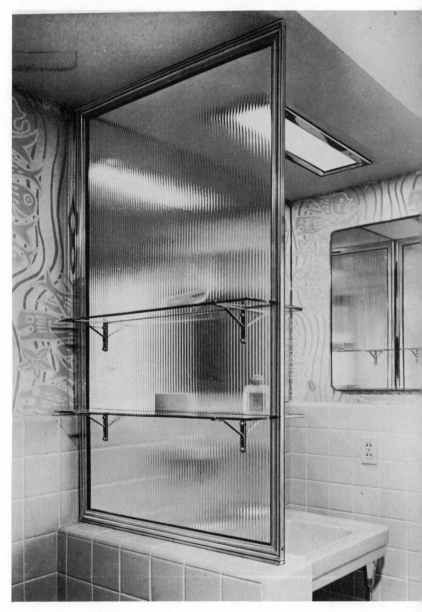

196. A neat and simple method of dividing the bath from the lavatory without loss of light from the ceiling fixture calls for a glass panel which incorporates shelves on either side. The cabinet door swings open to reflect the image from the larger mirror facing the user. Plain ceramic tiles are topped by a decorative vinyl wall covering.

195. One of the major difficulties in designing a contemporary bathroom is that of suppressing the wholly utilitarian aspects, adding glamour and interest and aesthetic satisfactions without extravagant waste of space, problems to which few but the professional decorator give the attention it deserves.

197.

can concentrate on the decorative aspects of the installation. In some instances, of course, this will make it advisable to replace the old units with new ones, not only for better efficiency but also to substitute those of a more desirable color. This can be quite important in contemporary bathrooms where delightful results can be achieved by having one of the three (or four) units in an accent color and the others in contrasting or neutral tones. Actually this is only one of the many ways in which advantage can be taken of the new designs and new materials now available, from lighting fixtures to wall finishes, and supported fixtures which simplify the use of overall carpets, all of which can help to make the bathroom one of the most glamorous interiors of the home.

Two very good bathroom designs of entirely different styles are represented by 198 and 200. The first two of these (198 and 199), illustrate the basic features of a French provincial interior with its splendid ceiling-high doors and bath surround, beautifully paneled and carved

in natural fruitwood. The square-edged tub is rimmed and enclosed with tinted French tiles in military motifs. The ceiling has a heavy cornice of wood which ties together the door frames and wall panels, spanning a recess into which is set a bow-fronted dresser topped by a huge mirror.

The floor is of white marble, and the dresser is topped with the same material. In front of the dresser there is a Louis XVI-style carved stool upholstered in a decorative waterproof fabric which is also used as a wall covering at the end of the room visible in the mirror. The style of the lighting fixture also is of importance, this being a four-light chandelier in gilt-bronze of the Empire period. The dressing table naturally has its own pair of candlestick-lamps in silver with translucent white shades.

In illustration 200 the setting is contemporary and the dressing area quite separate from the tub. This floor is of white vinyl tiles with an occasional floral decoration in the center, in ultra-modest contrast to the walls, the ceil-

198.

199.

ing, and even the sliding closet doors and interiors which are completely covered with zinnias in pink, yellow, orange, and green, thanks to a lavishly patterned Zuber wallpaper from Paris. The dressing table is a Napoleonic piece in polished steel with a glass top and metal-framed mirror, whose posts terminate in swan-neck light brackets with fringed shades. Other lights are concealed in adjustable ceiling fixtures. The table's matching seat is covered

in white damask with colorful tassels. On one wall is a floor-length triple mirror with swinging extensions. In front of it rests a French doll's bed in brass, trimmed in white damask and occupied by a lifesize porcelain cat — the whole thing a family heirloom that constitutes a fascinating conversation piece. In the wall mirror can be

204

200.

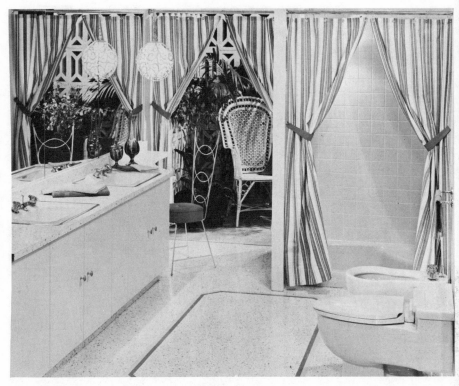

201.

seen a white porcelain French stove which decorates the bathroom area.

A thoroughly up-to-date bathroom grouping, both as to style of fixtures and arrangement, is that of 201, which shows not only a sunken square tub and modern floor-type toilet, but also a bidet — now all the rage in America — without which no Continental bathroom would be complete. The twin lavatory basins are of the flush,

counter type set in a gold-flecked, vinyl plastic top which matches the flooring, and sets off the delicate pink of the fixtures and the ceramic-tiled bathtub walls.

In this area the floor is decorated with a panel border in pink and red-orange. Both the tub and the dressing-room archway are equipped with waterproof curtains in gold and white stripes. These have orange-red tiebacks, a color picked up by the seat of the steel chair and some of the towels, the rest of which are either pink or green. The lighting fixtures consist of spherical opal globes in gold filigree, suspended by chains from the ceiling.

Much less gay than the foregoing, somewhat more formal, yet quite colorful in spite of the white fixtures, is 202 with its rich-looking vinyl-coated wood-grained wallpaper and an overall carpet in royal blue. The ceiling's translucent lighting panels, the rattan blind, and the perforated screen facing the left-hand wall — not to mention the bamboo plant — give the room an oriental flavor. The towels are a light blue, the mirror frame a silvery white, and the shower curtain — removed for

202.

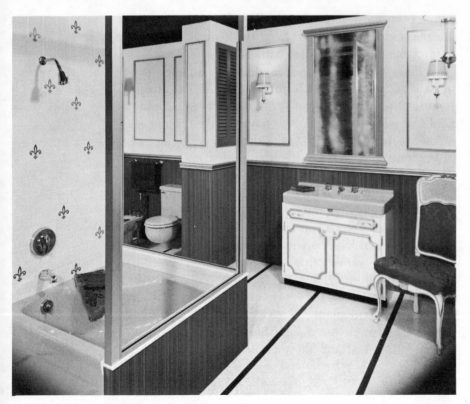

203.

photographic purposes — presumably could be blue with a lighter pattern, or a contrasting orange yellow to add a frivolous touch.

Blue is also the key color in the French provincial bathroom of 203. This contrasts nicely with the white of the floor and upper walls as well as the tub tiling. Gold accents are introduced in the fleur-de-lis pattern of occasional bath tiles, and also in the panel molding of the lavatory cabinet and walls, the dado cap and mirror frame, and the white-painted chair which is upholstered in a golden brown.

This bathroom has two entrances, and a sliding door separates the bath and lavatory area from the other compartment. The tub itself is square and enclosed in glass. This whole floor is of white vinyl, inlaid with black stripes, emphasizing what is actually a cool and clinical décor.

The so-called Early-American bathroom (illustration 204) gets its characterization from the wood tones of the floor, one cherry-sheathed wall, and the lavatory cabinet with its louvered doors. There is also a triple hanging shelf in antiqued pine. Other brown tones are supplied by the nutmeg-colored ceramic tile of the tub recess and lavatory counter, and by the fixtures themselves which are colored a pale tan.

Apart from the cherry sheathing, the walls are covered with a red "bandanna" paper of an early design with a tiny pattern in yellowish white, plus a starry border in black and yellow. Other colonial touches are a small braided rug in black, red, and white, and a splint-seated ladderback chair. In addition, a pair of tombstone-shaped mirrors are placed over the lavatory bowls, flanked by two tôle-shaded lamps in Victorian cast-iron brackets made to hold glass-bowled kerosene lamps. Regardless of the details, authentic colonial or otherwise, the total effect is quite pleasing and the wall-mounted toilet impressive.

Though it may seem a long leap from early America to late eighteenth-century France, the range of interest in bathroom design seems to know no limits. At any rate there is no reason why the Louis XVI period should not have just as great possibilities for a bathroom as for any other interior, as illustration 205 should bear witness. This is a particularly good example of what can be done in interpreting that period, and one that should appeal to those who are looking for something both nostalgic and different.

The bathtub itself is a luxurious creation encased in Mexican onyx, the same material as is used for the top of the half-round cabinet, complete with splash-back, which houses the oval lavatory bowl. The fittings for both, together with the towel bar, are of the same period, exquisitely modeled and finished in gold. The half-round

204.

cabinet is enameled white with gold trim, and the basin interior is decorated with a leaf design which matches that of the large panel let into the black mosaic-patterned vinyl flooring.

Above the lavatory is a gold-plated recessed medicine cabinet whose mirrored door is molded in the reed-and-ribbon motif. This ancient pattern is repeated in the frames of the mirrored wall sconces which flank it. The walls are covered in a gold-tinted vinyl silk of ripple pattern, against which the bath towels stand out as projecting rectangles of antique blue with a striking woven de-

sign in black. The ceiling fixture is a crystal-beaded basket with bands of gold that echo the rich yellow gleam of the metallic surfaces around it.

The hexagonal twin-lavatory cabinet in 206 is a good

205.

example of the originality that can be displayed in bathroom design. This structure, approachable from all sides,

207

206.

has a black-marble top in which two gold-banded basins are countersunk. The cabinet itself is white with gold-lined paneling, and the faucets are in gold plate with cut-crystal knobs. Suspended above this unit is a double mirrored medicine cabinet in gold plate, operable from either side. Centered above it is a lighting fixture which illuminates both sides and the basins below.

The wall to the right of this lavatory cabinet contains a mirror-lined and illuminated recessed shelf. Under this are two smaller units let into the wall, one accommodating a drinking glass, soap dish, and tooth brush-holder, the other a tissue dispenser. All are finished in gold plate.

In this washing area the floor is covered with white marbled vinyl inlaid with a geometric design emphasiz-

208

207.

208.

ing the shape and location of the cabinet. In the areas occupied by storage cabinets and chests, a waterproof carpeting with a tweedy surface in dark green supplies the desirable color contrast repeated in lighter tints in the wallpaper's floral panels.

A rich medieval tapestry was the inspiration for the vinyl wall covering used in the bathroom in illustration 207, which has a floor of white marble and a glass-enclosed shower. The wash basin, which is decorated in a bell design, is countersunk in a large and beautifully shaped marble top with a deep apron and twisted crystal legs. The fittings and the towel bar are of Louis XV design, and gold-plated to match the frames of the recessed medicine cabinet and its flanking mirror-lined shelves,

209

and the mirror-trimmed valance light, as well as the crystal-decorated chandelier.

In spite of the design of the fittings, however, it should be noted that this is not necessarily a classical interior. In 208, for example, the fittings and cabinets are plated in pewter which allows of an entirely different color scheme. They are of the Louis XVI acanthus-leaf design, but the basin, with its top and oval splash plate of white

209.

210

statuary marble, is actually Victorian in style despite the fluted crystal legs.

The waterproof flooring is heavy vinyl in black with gray mottling plus a large diagonal tile pattern with triple cabochons, all outlined in white to imitate grout lines. The vinyl wall covering is copied from a wall hanging in an Italian palazzo, and the design is repeated in the lavatory bowl.

Another arrangement using the pewter-plated finish is 209, which features an enclosed lavatory cabinet having pewter handles plus trompe-l'oeil designs in color in the panels. This has a white-marble top and a basin decorated with a Greek-key pattern to match that of the medicine cabinet frame and the tissue holder. The bath fittings are a French lotus design, including a shell-shaped soap dish. Although the pattern is indistinct in the picture, the vinyl wall covering has a damask pattern which is well suited to the gray pebble vinyl flooring and its interlacing charcoal stripes.

The small interior of 210 actually represents a remodeling which might better be called a transformation since the original fixtures are thoroughly disguised, the bath with its new sliding enclosure in gold-anodized aluminum and rippled glass, the replacement wash-basin top in black marble, and its basin decorated with gold oak leaves to match those painted on the white seat.

Also gilded are the lotus-pattern basin fittings, as well as the holder for glass, soap, and toothbrush, and the medicine cabinet frame, which are modeled in a laurel wreath design. The front of the cabinet has the extra advantage of being made to slide down so that the mirror can be used from a sitting position. Other gold touches are supplied by the crystal-hung ceiling and wall lighting fixtures. Finally, the floor is covered with plain black vinyl, and the wall with vinyl simulating oriental silk, which is a triumph in itself.

The increasing use of colored fixtures in bathrooms has led to the development of completely coordinated groups, not only of the units themselves but also of matching ceramic tiles, both in solid colors and patterns, plus vinyl wall coverings in the same designs, together with shower and window curtains. Also available are ceramic accessories — towel posts, soap dishes, grab bars, tissue, tumbler and toothbrush holders, cabinet hardware, and even towels. Obviously, great restraint is necessary in the use of these things in the interest of good taste. Nevertheless, by ringing the changes on both designs and colors some attractive — and some spectacular — bathroom interiors can be created.

An excellent illustration of the benefits the decorator can glean from the introduction of this coordination of color and pattern is represented by 211, which features a lilac color without running it into the ground, so to speak. Restraint is evident in this bath recess where the lilac tiles are enlivened by very occasional touches of pattern, and the mosaic floor is more than half white. Cream-tinted wall tiles likewise reduce the area of the decorated wall fabric to bearable proportions, while the lavatory has a creamy-white marbleized top that sets off the china faucets.

In the next photograph (212), a bathroom of the same style is shown with a corner lavatory fixture which can be an important space-saver even with a wall-high mirror above it. This short-circuited corner, it will be noticed, is made to look continuous with the walls by a scalloped, pink-bordered valance that takes the place of a cornice. This picks up the color of the darker mosaic tiles and repeats the tints of the flowers in the wall covering. The white toilet also sports an occasional flower, but a stronger accent is supplied by the deep green of the towels and chair cushion, the seat itself being of maple.

Where space is a problem, the corner lavatory may not be the only solution, so that the foregoing is worth comparing with 213, which displays a triangular corner toilet in a room five by six feet. With the tank shaped to fit into the corner, it is possible to put shelves over the fixture for towels, etc., or even a small cupboard.

The colors here are particularly interesting because of the unusual, and quite effective, contrasts. The three pieces are in a colonial yellow which is quite creamy. Two of them — the water closet and washbowl — however, are set against a plank wall which is painted an emphatic orange, while the tub, hiding behind its white curtain, has walls of white with vertical black stripes, except for a low cabinet at the head end which has a white top and orange front.

The floor is covered with varicolored tiles ranging from dark orange to a gray violet, with wide grouting

210.

stripes in white. Accents are provided by the deep yellow towels and the violet of soap and tissue, while the black of the stripes is duplicated by the Victorian light brackets which are of black iron with white frosted globes.

Still another note is struck by the bathroom in 214, which introduces wood tones paired with the bright yellow of the shower curtain, a darker yellow being used for the white dotted wall covering, with the floor and bath towels of an intermediate shade. The exterior wall tiles

211

211.

213.

212.

214.

213

215.

214

are almost pinky by comparison. Insets in the bath tiles are white with a tulip red.

The design for the bathroom shown in 215 (dubbed Victorian Garden because of the multicolored posies on the walls, curtain, and towels) has a somewhat classical look due, in part, to the restriction of decorated insets to the bath and mirror borders. In actuality, these are mostly blue, pink, and yellow. The other tiles are all-white, and the walls above the tiling are a dark orange which the floor mosaic almost matches. The fixtures are white, and touches of gold are supplied by the embossed metal legs of the lavatory, the decoration of the antique-white lamps, and the frames of picture and mirror. An even more individual touch would probably have been added by using orange tiles on the floor accented with a few white cabochons.

The efficiency style bathroom of illustration 216 features twin basins which are often time savers with children in the family. If necessary, one of them could be provided with a platform step to accommodate the "shorties." Each bowl, it will be noticed, has its own cabinet. This room also should appeal to mothers and daughters who have need for a restful corner in which to relax while the hair is drying. The well-upholstered seat at the window is covered with a waterproof material and is handily close to shelves for cosmetics, towels, or even books.

The bath is set into an alcove formed by the seat and shelving, and the regular bathroom storage closet, and lined with mosaic tile of a gray-green. This color is not only compatible with the pinky-red of the tiled floor, but, along with the green of the curtain, and the yellow-green of the walls, sets off the twilight blue of the fixtures and the checked fabric of the window seat. Happily enough the bowl cabinets in dark oak combine with the brown towels to add a contrasting element that suggests careful design.

In example 217 a note of elegance has been captured through the precise arrangement of the room which looks as though it had been designed for the purpose and not merely to house a set of fixtures without regard to the total décor. The tub is not simply crowded into a tight-fitting alcove but has open space on the inner side and at one end which not only gives a feeling of roominess but can be utilized in a variety of ways.

The setting is one of rich woods, and both bath and lavatory are seen to be a part of a larger whole with a unified character. Nothing unnecessary is displayed, and the parallel lines of the blue vinyl flooring emphasize the orderly arrangement of the units and spaces and accent the pleasing curves of the fixtures. Out of the ordinary are the oval lavatory bowl with its chamfered edge, the bathtub seat which is a part of the casting, and the use that has been made of the toilet tank lid which ordinarily

216.

represents so much waste space — though the idea of a planter may be carrying things a little too far. Even the blue-tinted ceiling has been put to further use in housing the hidden lighting fixtures which complement the old-time lamps flanking the dressing-table mirror. The folding door which allows of isolating the toilet section is another admirable feature which many families find useful.

With a deep tub recess it may sometimes be possible to add both to the utility and the decorative quality by

217.

building the rear wall out to form recesses as in 218. What can be done with them depends on whether or not there is a shower. In many cases there will almost certainly be a similar setback below the ceiling, providing space for a storage cupboard. The decorative quality of this arrangement is determined by the tiles. In the photograph those tiles at the head and foot of the tub, in the small recesses, and lining the toilet space are of a crystalline cinnamon color to match the tub, as are the stripes on the floor and across the tub. The rest of the tiles are a chalk-white. The toilet fixture is a near match to the cinnamon, being a fawn beige. The size and spacing of the floor stripes of course depend upon size and shape of the room, and in some instances may be better omitted

216

218.

219.

entirely. In some bathrooms a border would be more effective as can be seen from 219.

The basic color here is horizon blue, represented in the shower and the lower walls outside it by tiles in a basket-weave pattern. The floor and the bath borders are in the regular glazed but slip-proof crystalline ceramic tile of a somewhat darker blue for contrast. These blues are emphasized by the chalk-white floor tiles, inside the tub and out, and the white of the lavatory counter, plus the background of the wall covering which is patterned in grayish-blue carnations. Sections of this same material are framed in gold to form decorative panels on the lavatory cupboard doors, and a gold-framed mirror hangs above the bowl to complete an unusually attractive bathroom interior with a light and spacious feel.

Much more conservative is 220, which has a number of interesting features besides the colors. The tub is a mere 42 inches long so that it is particularly adapted to use both as a shower base and a child's tub, as well as a second bath where space is at a premium. This particular

assembly is enclosed in a recess lined with the ceramic tiles of a basketweave pattern mentioned earlier. These have the peculiar faculty of seeming less rigid and less confining than fullsize plain tiles, and are therefore especially suited to confined spaces. Their color is a cinnamon brown which is an excellent background color for the pale-yellow tub. The shower curtain is a dark but

217

220.

of baths, lavatories, and toilets from remodeled or wrecked residences or salvage contractors. Though probably Victorian, many of these are of mahogany or other furniture woods, nicely paneled, and are readily adaptable to earlier twentieth-century fixtures. In other instances special enclosures have to be built, in which case ready accessibility to traps and supply lines may need to be considered.

Tubs that have rolled edges are usually easy to fit with wooden casings — using thin hardboard on a properly shaped frame for bent surfaces. These can be given a furniture finish, painted, or covered with adhesive plastic representations of nicely grained wood or marble. With a base innocent of curves, it may be possible to apply ceramic tiles to the exterior. In doing this, wide ledges may be added, or seats and cupboards incorporated.

It is also smart to enclose a water closet that is not quite modern, in a square, lidded seat, in which case the whole thing may have to be readily removable in case of plumbing trouble. Fixtures left "as is" are often given a decorative touch by painting the cover and seat in an attractive though highly imaginative design. A floral wreath is often both effective and in good taste, especially if the background is a satin black.

Adopting the old decorator's adage of featuring an eyesore that can't be eliminated, an old-fashioned legged tub can be transformed into an attractive if not amusing center of interest simply by featuring it — possibly in the middle of the room — and decorating it in gay color and pattern instead of trying to disguise it. Paint will work wonders, especially if details are picked out in color or gilded. Furthermore, decrepit old faucets can be replaced with new ones of pewter, silver, gold plate, or colorful ceramics.

Adequate counter space, lighting and mirrors are all important, particularly in combination dressing-room bathrooms, and offer opportunities for originality, while comfortable damp-proof flooring is essential together with sheet vinyl or vinyl-coated wallpapers in appropriate designs innocent of fishes, sea-shells, seaweed, or mermaids.

Light, receding colors are especially important in small bathrooms, preferably in restful tones and devoid of pattern. Strong colors pull in the walls, and overpowering

lively brown, well suited to this dignified grouping where inconspicuousness is a merit and gaudy treatment would have been tasteless and somewhat absurd.

In a great many bathroom decorating projects it is necessary to make changes in the appearance of the old fixtures, a matter often calling for considerable ingenuity. Sometimes it is possible to acquire wooden encasements

218

patterns induce an air of busyness and clutter in a room already rendered shapeless by the necessary but uncompromisingly inharmonious fixtures which are often far more difficult to deal with than ordinary furniture. For one thing, they cannot be moved around once connected. Harmony is therefore the first thing to aim for, making the fullest use of color and texture and treatment. It is, however, equally important not to go to extremes by introducing frippery in the form of flower-filled wire birdcages or swathing the mirror in organdy or the windows in fancy draperies, or even making a showroom display of fancy towels with oversized initials that are in questionable taste themselves.

Strikingly interesting twin-bathroom arrangements, illustrated in 221 and 222, indicate some of the basic differences that may arise in meeting His and Her requirements.

In "His" bathroom (221), the background is almost Spartan in color and texture. The wood-sheathed walls, the shutters, and the cabinet are walnut-stained; the floor, the tub, and the lavatory counter are in gray marble, while the shower is totally enclosed with a translucent rippled glass door having ventilating louvers at the top. The rug is white, and all color accents are supplied by the orange towels and terracotta accessories. In the ceiling are adjustable recessed lights arranged to project wide beams wherever needed — mostly over the tub and lavatory.

In contrast, the feminine bathroom (222), has more the air of a dressing room (minus the necessary closets), its fitted white carpet gay with pink and red flowers. The walls are gray with white panels, the cabinet white with a beautifully shaped top of gray-veined white marble matching that of the tub. The curtains, too, are white and sheer, the major accent being a slipper chair in rose-red, with a French telephone at hand on a miniature cabinet. An extra touch of luxury is supplied by the crystal chandelier which augments the adjustable ceiling spots. The combined toiletry and towel holder is of polished brass with shelves of glass, and a special feature is the three-section mirror over the lavatory which is hinged so that the outer sections can be swung wide to capture side and rear views in combination with another mirror over the tub. Behind the triple mirror leaves are glass shelves for

221.

the storage of toilet articles and medications more often needed than those kept in the large cabinets below.

A bathroom with some of the same atmosphere is the subject of 223, though this has all the earmarks of a combination bathroom and dressing room for strictly feminine use. For one thing it has a dressing table separate from the wide lavatory slab and mirror, and a number of

222.

223.

lavatory cabinets. The principal lighting is provided by sunken ceiling fixtures covered by large translucent panels giving a soft diffused glow so necessary in smaller rooms with so many highly reflecting surfaces. In addition to the wall sconces, local illumination is supplied by table lamps in front of the huge dressing-table mirror which has end sections covering the side walls of the recess.

The architectural features of this room have been given particular attention by adding such details as molded imposts below the recessed arches with low-relief decorations, building doors into the hollow side pillars (abutments), adding edge rolls (beads) to the corners and so on. Color is added by a needlepoint rug, and the striped seat of a black-enamelled chair which, along with the large gilded brass waste-basket, is one of the larger accents; minor ones consist of coal-black figurines, flower holders, etc., disposed about the room.

It will be noted that very few of these bathrooms sport a picture on the wall, which may be astonishing to some in these days of bathroom carpeting, decorated seats, up-

closets for which the space obviously was available. The floor here is of white vinyl tile with black cabochons, the woodwork is delicate gray, that of the walls relieved by large arrow-and-quiver type triple sconces in gold and black. All the hardware likewise is in gold, including the tiny gilt-bronze masks set into the miniature pilasters that are structural features of the dressing table and the

field of waterproof wall and floor coverings without paying much attention to the rumored dictum that a Picasso in the bathroom is a sine qua non of acceptance in the highest social circles. Some leave that distinction to the bidet!

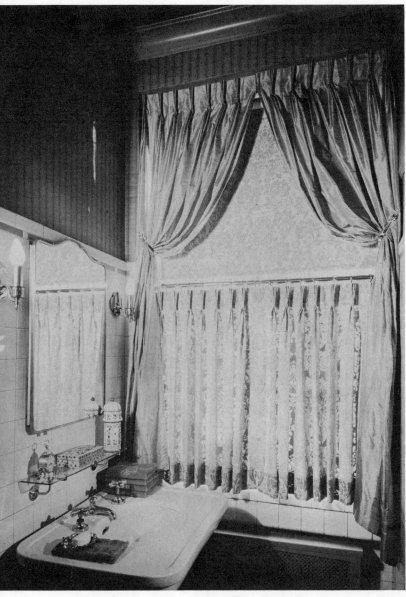

224. Many a bathroom can be transformed merely by dressing up the window. Here the draperies of iridescent silk are pulled back to reveal a brocaded patterned shade and matching café curtains, bronze-green blending with green and gold, the gleaming brass rod and tie-backs adding sparkling touches.

holstered chairs, and adequate ventilation if not air conditioning. Much of course depends upon the size of the room and the inclusion or otherwise of dressing facilities. Meanwhile the decorator has plenty of work within the

The Decoration of Kitchens

The days when maximum efficiency in a kitchen as determined by a theoretical count of steps taken are long gone. Kitchen users do not work that way. For one thing the idea was misleading, and women, who are supposed to dictate what they want in the food preparation and dishwashing departments, were rightly uninterested. Today, appearance is most important, so long as the oven is high enough to see into, and low stooping for this or anything else unnecessary. And now, when it is so easy to have a well-ventilated, odorless kitchen, the trend is toward making the room — and its associated breakfast corner, if any — as attractive as any other room in the house, though not in precisely the same manner.

The function has to be taken into consideration here as elsewhere and the appliances cannot altogether be hidden however much they are disguised. Here, that good old decorating maxim that "eyesores which cannot be eliminated should be emphasized" might well often apply. At any rate, such equipment can very often stand a little suppression of modernity, of enframing in old-time ceramic tile, or otherwise made to seem at home in flagrantly antique settings. And, like bathrooms, kitchens can often be improved by the judicious use of trompe-l'oeil decoration, painting in a window here, or a fireplace background for the stove over there, or simply a row of non-existent shining copper pans hanging from make-believe hooks, quaintnesses that will not become boring affectations in the course of time, creating distinctions based on a lively,

imaginative difference. But these things must be convincingly done.

On the other hand, if total modernity is sought, colors and textures may be the answer, alternating stainless steel with polished woods and plastic tops, the cupboard design representing any furniture period — or none. The one thing to avoid here is the use of doors and other woodwork carved or painted in a manner suited only to bedroom or drawing room furniture. Exception will of course have to be made in the case of the dyed-in-the-wool gourmet who will be satisfied with nothing less than a full-sized butcher block and a battery of steel ovens and warmers.

Missing in so many kitchens, usually to their detriment, is a variation of geometrical shapes. All the counters are rectangular even where a jog or a taper, or even an angular offset would conserve space. At other times, the rounded or bowed end is often overdone for no practical reason, and all cupboards are the same height and size so that the eye remains unsatisfied either with the everlasting symmetry or the too-obvious urge toward the easiest way out.

Apart from correcting these most evident deficiencies, then, the principal aim in decorating any kitchen, whether of the farmhouse or city apartment type, is to make the room as beautiful as it is efficient. For this purpose there is available a variety of modern materials for the walls, floors, ceilings, counters, and even curtains that are colorful, lasting, and easily cleaned. With such a wide choice of finishes, colors, patterns, and decorative details accessible, however, taste becomes more important than ever. Mere gaudiness will never suffice, and both cooking and eating areas (assuming they are together) need to be planned as a unit, with a keen eye to avoiding the deadly monotony of characterless cupboards, differentiating these and the appliances wherever possible with variations in size, proportion, and color.

Even if there is no wall space to decorate there probably is a ceiling that can be turned into a make-believe tent, or otherwise treated so as to create an illusion of things far removed from the practicalities of everyday living. If one has no feeling — or capacity — for eye-deceivers, it is still possible to run the cabinet fronts up to the ceiling or install a dummy frieze and cornice (set only slightly back to fool the collecting dust), and make them gaily decorative to catch the eye with panels of wallpaper or toile de Jouy. Failing which, each blind door may be transformed with painted posies, perhaps in a private code, to reveal their individual contents.

Color, of course, is one of the most potent decorating devices and, in kitchens, can frequently be used to smooth out unpleasant contrasts introduced by varied metallic surfaces. Oftentimes these obtrusive tones can be converted into interesting contrasts by submerging them in a sea of related shades and tints. For example if the window shutters, shades, or blinds are lime-colored, the surrounding wall areas can be painted a rich yellow, with a yellow wallpaper — figured lightly in pinks, whites, and browns — above the windows and other bare wall areas. The appliances then might be of a reddish copper color, with a vinyl floor to match, the cabinetwork in medium wood tones with bronze hardware, and the counter tops dead white. Some of the cupboards could be varied by having door panels in amber molded glass, and accents supplied by lime-colored canisters and copper utensils on the shelves. The variations are endless.

Another interesting fact often overlooked in the drive to make kitchens attractive is that possibilities may exist for the introduction of high-grade pieces of furniture, not excluding valuable antiques, both in the eating and food preparation areas if such are separate. One increasingly popular conceit is the creation of kitchens around old-time tables which can be used for bread making and food concocting as well as serving meals. In others, antique dressers and similar period storage units are both decorative and utilitarian and may well relieve those endless vistas of counters and high cupboards. As in the case of bathrooms, asepsis here is no longer the bugbear it used to be and experimentation in the field of once-repugnant combinations such as rugs and cookstoves is to be encouraged on both practical and aesthetic grounds. Just as stainless steel can consort with mahogany in the living room, so can modern appliances be made to seem at home with handsome furnishings in the home's one room where efficiency is a much overemphasized ideal.

In studying the following examples it will be noted that many of the kitchens are far larger than would be demanded by a small family, but this does not mean that they cannot be scaled to meet individual needs. A determining factor is usually the number of appliances which have to be accommodated. Here, of course, interest is centered primarily in the decorative aspects which have little to do with the amount of floor area involved.

The dining kitchen of a country cottage (illustration 225), occupies one corner of a large room which it shares with the living area (see 58 and 59), and is as compact as such things can be made, though in an emergency it can stretch its space by borrowing the dining table as counter. In keeping with the rustic atmosphere there is plenty of wood surface displayed, combined with a number of interesting refinements such as the dark copper color of the stove, refrigerator, and dishwasher, plus the little extractor hood which keeps the air uncontaminated by the cooking. An asbestos-lined rear wall has the feel of plaster, and the stainless steel counter and sink are enlivened by rows of colorful antique Goya tiles between it and the hanging cupboards and below the small window with its gay checked curtains and bamboo blind. Under the counter is the dishwasher with its satin-finished, modernistic control panel, and extending along the floor from wall to terminal refrigerator is a yard-wide strip of non-slip, greaseproof nylon carpeting.

The antique Spanish dining table is close enough to the counter to serve in the preparation of food, but, more importantly (along with the New England slatback

225.

chairs and the oil painting) adds an air of elegance while establishing the visual limits to the kitchen space.

Another type of flooring well suited to the country-style kitchen is the vinyl brick pattern of 226, which is shown with the furniture moved from in front of the fireplace so that its three-dimensional effect can be observed. This has the necessary ruggedness to match the fireplace stonework, though its surface is actually smooth and not so rough on rugs as it would appear to be.

Though this room has plain wood cabinets and a steel eye-level oven it is much less sophisticated in appearance than 227, a kitchen-breakfast room whose cupboards and drawers are actually fine pieces of furniture. Here the monotony of solid-door cabinets is broken by the intro-

224

226.

227.

228.

duction of an open shelf for cookbooks, and three screen
doors shield the better china. The shelf over these affords
an opportunity for further decoration in the shape of a
pictorial plaque, and an ultra-modern five-branch lighting fixture which supplements the general illumination
supplied by a ceiling unit.

The closed wall cabinets are given both individuality
and interest by their decorative paneling, their square
shape somehow reducing the usual monotony. Behind
them a vertically striped wall covering contrasts with the
plain tinted wall areas and the plain birch surfaces, including the hood which encloses the counter-type grill.
The floor is of vinyl in a white-marble pattern, with

229.

grill top with a square-fronted full hood against a burnished fireproof backing. In the center of this metallic
liner is a wrought-iron decorative piece in wind-vane pattern which ties in with the black-iron chairs and the
candelabrum on the opposite wall. These chairs, which
have iron filigree backs and white plastic cushions, are
grouped alongside a console table fitted to the odd angle
of the wall which is accentuated by a turned and carved
pilaster reaching to the floor.

The cabinet doors are finished in brown baked lacquer,
and fitted with tiny press knobs to match the drawer
pulls. This woodwork is combined with a yellow plastic
top and white walls, relieved by a grilled window in one
corner whose bars consist of slender wood turnings.
Where an even more decorative effect is required, various
changes could be made such as substituting flooring simulating narrow boards, adding a rounded rug in purplish
tones to fit the wall beneath the table and chairs, and
painting those chairs yellow. Another alternative would
be to complement the yellow counter tops with a floor
tiled in alternating white and yellowish-brown terrazzo
squares, as in 229. An added decorative feature in this
somewhat similar kitchen is the window pelmet and
shade patterned in Wedgwood blue with a yellow fringe.
This shade suggests what could be done with tiles of the
same hue and pattern were space available! The structural woodwork, in contrast, is finished a very dark gray.

All the counters can contribute to the decorative
scheme through a variety of finishes among which tiles
are the most lastingly beautiful if selected with due regard
for color and pattern. Some idea of the textural value of
such tiles is given by 230, which includes basket-weave
walls and mosaic-tile flooring, the latter in mottled
browns picking up the wood tones of the cabinets. Such
tiling makes waterproof joints with the porcelain sink,
and is particularly suitable for the wall oven since it is
stain-proof and scrubbable.

In modern kitchens an interesting effect can sometimes
be secured by matching the floor to the counters — or
vice versa. If red linoleum should appear old-fashioned
to some, a more lively and timeless texture may be secured
by substituting a pattern representing scagliola which
gives the effect of polished marble in a variety of colors,
as suggested in 231. This pattern repeated on the thick

sturdy curvilinear furniture of inlaid pecan and walnut,
and leather-upholstered curule-style armchairs.

Another kitchen of somewhat the same type but rather
more elaborate in a delicate fashion is represented in
illustration 228. This is adapted to a room of irregular
shape, with a terrazzo-vinyl floor, and walls covered with
an embossed waterproof white paper of a particularly
beautiful tile pattern. The focal point is a long stove and

230.

counter tops is both attractive and expensive looking, though a large floor area may call for contrasting patches of color and pattern supplied by suitably shaped rugs.

Another point to notice in this picture is that the refrigerator is matched to the cabinet wood grain, positive color being introduced by painting the counter wall sky-blue, including the areas flanking the opening to the living quarters which are also enlivened by vividly colored ornamental tiles in red and dark-blue on cream. Other accents are provided by the red-topped canisters.

A rather different arrangement is suggested by 232, with the counters forming an open square facing a wall-type oven. These hanging cabinets straddle the copper stove hood and face the breakfast area, together with the

227

231.

228

counter which incorporates a dishwasher facing outward to save steps in clearing table. The nicely molded cabinets also present their attractive side to the persons at table. For serious cooking the interior would presumably be used, with access to the sink as well as the separate desk or so-called "management center" whose wall area is faced either with ceramic tiles or a vinyl wall-covering in a tile pattern which always looks well in a kitchen. This tiling, as the picture shows, could not only be extended to the counter walls but also to the space over the suspended cabinets and around the nearby doorway, adding sparkle to the eating area in the process.

232.

PART TWO

Windows as Decorative Features

One of the most important features of any room is the window treatment. It can create or influence the mood of the interior, establish a focal point where there is none, and introduce balance; it can be the most important feature of the décor, or the least; a part of the furnishing, or merely an architectural prop, not decorative but simply functional.

With blinds or shades alone, thanks to modern materials, techniques, and equipment, not only can the quantity and distribution of the admitted light be controlled but its quality as well. Furthermore, both shades and blinds can be made to contrast with or conform to draperies, wall coverings, and furniture upholstery; they can incorporate, and emphasize, if necessary, either vertical or horizontal lines to change the apparent dimensions and proportions of a room. In short, window treatment, whether it consists of a single roller shade or a complete set of curtains and draperies, can make or mar an interior, and therefore in designing any room it should be one of the first considerations instead of being left to the last or treated as a painful necessity instead of a splendid opportunity.

All kinds of shades and blinds are now readily available — roller, Venetian, Roman, Austrian — each in an endless variety of colors and patterns; new ways have been derived to hang, control, and drape the curtain fabrics, so that any desired form of window dressing from a single colorful roller shade to a gilded pelmet with silken swags, cascades, or sheer pleatings can be adapted to any shape or size of window, to give interiors a look of austerity or the voluptuous appearance of a prima donna's boudoir, or invest it with any degree of formality in between.

One of the simplest types of window to decorate is the double-sash style shown in illustration 233. This is the sole source of light in a small study and because of the bookshelves built around it the reveal is deep and the sill high, so that nothing can be accommodated against the window but a rectangular shade without any decorative frill. Since the surrounding woodwork is of cedar, bleached and rubbed with white to give an antique effect, there is no visible color on the outer surfaces and only occasional patches on the inner ones and those partially obscured by books and the display of decorative items.

The only possible way, then, of establishing a lively focal point apart from the furnishings was to use a shade with both color and a distinctive pattern — and this in spite of the fact that the walls of the back of the shelves were painted in alternating panels of bitter green and warm beige. The shade selected, therefore, bears a handsome baroque pattern in white on a ground of the same rich sandalwood beige used on the shelves. Furthermore, the design is printed on a vinyl-impregnated percale which not only admits working light but also filters out any glare, while contributing a charming note of for-

233

233.

234.

mality. The pull, incidentally, is a copy in bronze finish of a Louis XIV design, and the shade is both washable and flame-resistant.

In the setting of a house interior furnished with seventeenth- and eighteenth-century French antiques (illustration 234), these same shades in amethyst on white, applied to two adjoining windows and a glass door, provide all the color and pattern necessary. When partially

drawn, as they would be most of the time, they eliminate the need for a fancy wallpaper in place of the off-white walls which actually form a better background for the fruitwood country pieces. They also make possible the use of sheer glass curtains, with tiebacks, in place of colorful draperies. A novel touch is the use of white-painted curtain rods with gilt pineapple finials as pure decoration, the curtains being separately attached behind them.

The next step upward in elegant sophistication is the use of an embroidered window shade, together with white tie-back curtains, set inside a white-painted window reveal so that the deep top molding covers the shade roller and curtain rod, as in 235. The pattern for the shade is set by the sofa upholstery material which is of oyster-white linen embroidered in scarlet. The same material is used on a white painted metal stool set some distance away from either.

This small figured pattern is stitched on to a window shade which has much the same texture as the linen, the shaped bottom of the shade terminating in a large white

235.

236.

celain lamp base, the whole constituting a delightful ensemble into which the provincial pieces in dark walnut interject a masculine note.

Two other methods of making a decorative feature of a window are suggested by 236 and 237. The first of these reveals the rather spartan treatment of a modern room with which the designer hoped to recapture the atmosphere of the early Southwest. Luckily, some of the ceiling timbers were exposed, and these were suitably darkened to give the effect of aging. The walls were given a rough-textured finish in white.

Unfortunately the window reveal was too shallow to take a shade, but this handicap was handsomely overcome by framing the whole, from the floor up, in wood stained to match the beams. This served to accommodate a room-darkening red-and-white striped shade with the roller reversed. The shade's only decoration is a horse brass used as a pull. Because of the need for uniformity on the exterior, the shade was made solid-white on the street side.

tassel, a replica of the smaller ones used on the curtains and tiebacks.

The walls surrounding the white-painted window trim are tinted in delicate pink, and the large ice-pink, woolly rug is backed by a floor painted geranium red. Other strong accents are provided by the cream-painted chairs with seat cushions in a gorgeous emerald green, the satiny white of a table cover, and the gold of a Chinese por-

hangs a pair of Indian cornucopias to round out the picture.

In the second of these two photographs the theme of simplicity is carried a step further with a French country kitchen where the single candy-striped shade has acquired a dignified pelmet, both with a fluffy white border. A secondary purpose of the valance is to enable the roller to be reversed and the shade hung outside the window trim which it covers. This strong accent was apparently necessary to contrast effectively with the overall patterned wallpaper which copies a toile de Jouy in a bluish gray. The checkered tablecloth in red and pink on white acts as a counterpoint to both, forming an agreeable setting in which the old wood of a miniature cabinet, a white-painted iron chair, and a wall clock in dull black set the pattern for the rest of the room.

From the foregoing it is but a short step to a style of window furnishing that is perfectly at home with a Directoire interior where simple country elegance is the goal. In illustration 238 the windows are fitted with white translucent shades made of plissé, a cotton fabric crinkled by mercerizing in stripes. These have fairly deep swagged hems of thread with a tassel for a pull. Over them hang floor-length draperies of the same material, from polished brass rods. This glistening fabric stands out vividly against walls papered in vertical stripes of brown and white, both when daylight is streaming through them and when they are illuminated by artificial light after sunset.

Alongside one window a wall-high needlework bellpull in yellow, red, brown, and blue, supplies a sharp contrast, and the cherry wood of the furniture pieces blends happily with the walls and the brown-flecked white vinyl covering of the floor.

Two problems are solved simultaneously in 239, which displays a possible treatment for an off-center window so close to an end wall that it could not be draped satisfactorily with loose-hanging fabric. The window itself accommodated a gold-colored shade in a richly textured mixture of rayon and cotton. In place of the more usual draperies is a pair of twin-paneled shutters covered with damask in red and green. Marine brasses form handles by which the shutters can be opened out to double their width and so cover the whole window.

In their folded position these panels form a stunning

237.

The simple furniture consists of a rugged Spanish four-poster in cedar, with a hand-woven coverlet in blue and white, the pattern being suggestive of Indian work. The chair is an elaborate adaptation of a Queen Anne piece with a wooden seat, carved legs, turned stretchers, and inlaid splat. To one side is an antique alligator traveling chest on a brass fireside footstool, and over the chair

236

238.

239.

frame for the shade and window, especially in contrast with the white walls and window bench. The room, actually, is furnished with Early-American and English furniture in time-darkened pine, the old spool box being an exception in walnut, and the chair is a copy of a rare English windsor. The mirror picks up the gilded sheen of the shade.

Fine fabrics in rich colors, carefully tailored, are the obvious source of the dignified window treatment which so perfectly complements the beautiful furniture and accessories in the formal dining room of illustration 240. The shades themselves are notable for the exquisite combination of form and color and texture, features accentuated by their proportions and the manner in which the cut-out hem, finished in red and gold braid, suspends the brass rod which is both decorative and serves as a pull,

237

240.

while acting as a tension device to keep the shade taut.

The shades are of the same Chinese red as the scenic wall panel's background, and the chair seats. What is not so obvious is that the shades are of cambric, hand-painted with oil colors, and washable! Equally splendid are the heavy draperies of gold fabric so beautifully accented with the yellow of the woodwork, combining with both red and yellow to form a perfect backdrop as much for the gold and green of the plant stand, the leaves of which are so closely matched by their enameled, crystal-inset counterparts in the lovely chandelier. Equally well do they emphasize the faded black and antique gold of the

238

241.

pieces. The compact lowboy doubles as a serving table and storage cabinet in this small dining room, and looks perfectly at home with the Hepplewhite shield-back dining chairs, while the floor of alternating black and white vinyl tiles, simulating marble, adds a sophisticated touch to the whole.

A novel blind and shade arrangement is suggested in 242, which shows a window wall with the upper half covered by Roman shades and the lower half by Venetian blinds. The idea here is to use the blinds to control the light and air, the shades to shut out the glare and give the upper part of the room a feeling of cool shade such as one experiences in a grove of trees at midday.

The blinds here are simply functional, with matte white slats spattered in gold, and white plastic tapes. The decorative element is supplied by the Roman shades of a heavy luxurious brocade which introduce a rich exotic note, augmented by their cut-out flaps and wooden tassels.

This arrangement also helps to solve the problem of the oddly placed small window at right-angles to the window

chairs as well as the yellows and browns of the gorgeous oval table.

An exciting alternative to the above is revealed in 241, where the windows are framed in five-inch boards painted white and decorated with a wide band of black-and-white braid. This effectively sets off the black-and-white, screen-printed shades from the bright red walls, and adds to the dignity of their Adam design.

The whole concept is quite daring, the patterns of the shades and braid accentuated by hanging the former in the reverse-roll manner within the frame. To render it possible to further increase the apparent height of the windows, when desired, the shades are made long enough to pull all the way down to the floor.

These black-and-white shades form a particularly effective background for the Queen Anne style chairs which have been lacquered red to match the walls so that they contrast intriguingly with traditional mahogany

242.

Still another idea is contained in 243, this one showing how decorative side-panels to a window can be combined with a double-fabric swag plus a cascade down each side and a pair of silken curtains beneath. In this instance the panels are of particular note since they are covered with damask to which has been applied a series of antique Spanish coats of arms. The shades, which are hung in

243.

wall. This light is enclosed within a large gold frame attached to the side wall above the end table. Inside the frame hangs a small white Venetian blind, forming a day-light-illuminated background for a portrait in oils which is suspended at the frame's center by a vertical brass strip. With the room lights on, the blind acts as a reflecting surface, outlining the portrait with a similar result.

244.

the usual manner, are made of a translucent cloth to which a textured off-white casement fabric has been laminated. This, as can be seen, blends nicely into the rather formal window treatment, providing filtered light for reading by day, and privacy after dark. The valance, made from olive-green damask to match that of the panels, is draped over an antique brass tieback rosette well above the window head, lending both height and softness to the whole window treatment.

The extra-tall windows of some high-ceilinged Victorian houses may occasionally offer problems of their own. In the example represented by illustration 244, the impression of height was not particularly important since the furniture was in good proportion. In fact, as will be observed from the illustration, the tall windows are emphasized as a dramatic feature by bordering them with a fabric considerably darker than the walls, and topping them off with fringed valances of a lighter color so that they would not unduly accent the horizontal line.

The draperies are of linen in an overall traditional pattern, the colors rose and wine. These hang in straight folds to the floor. Two sets of shades are used to each window, those next to the glass being of the room-darkening type which completely shut out the light when lowered. Normally, they are rolled all the way to the top. Covering each of these is a dainty white embroidered shade with a scalloped and fringed hem.

The walls are painted a champagne beige, and the rug is just a shade darker so that together they provide a sympathetic, receding background for the dark mahogany of the heirloom furniture and well-designed reproductions

Bay windows introduce a variety of problems, one of which very often is that of unifying the projecting area with the room. This is the case with 245, where a three-sided bay is part of a dining alcove. The two areas have been drawn together by extending the wallpaper to cover both the bay ceiling and the shaped valance that extends across the three windows.

Although a valance is used, draperies are omitted. Instead, delicately shirred café curtains of net cover the bottom areas of the windows, with translucent shades in sheer textured shantung above them. These shades have wide panels outlined on them in two tones of blue paint

picked up from the wallpaper. The deeper tone emphasizes the outer edges of the panels giving them a three-dimensional effect. A blue vinyl floor and a white area rug echo the background tones, and a painted chest and chairs add a touch of sunshine yellow.

An outstanding feature of the lavishly adorned windows in 246 is the reproduction of a 1795 English chintz with its garlands of roses in soft red with touches of topaz

245.

and olive-green on a ground of taupe. This material is laminated to the shades, and is also used for the arm-chair slip-cover.

In the windows the shades are framed by tie-back curtains and an artfully draped valance of pin-striped moiré in topaz and beige. The tasseled fringes pick up the colors of the stripes, and matching, tassel-style shade pulls add a further fillip to a scheme which combines an eighteenth-century Aubusson rug with the eighteenth-and nineteenth-century furniture pieces and fabric designs.

A lovely three-dimensional cotton print of traditional

flavor was the basis of the window decoration in illustration 247, the same material being used on the walls and some of the upholstered furniture pieces. In spite of this lavish use of the same pattern, the design is not at all oppressive. For one thing, its colors are a cool citron-yellow and cream, and the pattern is broken up into areas of various shapes and sizes. This floral design climbs the walls where it is broken up into panels, and the draperies are tied back to reveal conical areas of cream-colored window shade, topped by swags which are bordered with the same fringe as the draperies and the bottoms of the shades.

247.

A citron-yellow area rug ties together the conversation group composed of a loveseat and a pair of bergères, one of which is upholstered in a cotton velvet introducing the welcome accent of hunter's green. The rug itself stands out boldly against a dark parquet floor. The total result is a certain formal elegance which one does not normally expect from cotton fabrics.

246.

242

Even the smallest and most insignificant of rooms can be endowed with both character and interest by proper window dressing, as 248 shows. In this sitting-dining-bedroom, an extremely important feature is the tremendous impact of the wallpaper with its large, widely-spaced pineapples in black. This serves as a dramatic background for the draperies.

Normally, one would use a small-patterned paper in such a tiny room because large patterns tend to make any room seem smaller. Here, however, the very boldness of this combination far outweighs any other consideration, besides eliminating the need for a series of fussy little pictures as eye-resting punctuations.

This window is quite deep, with a storage cupboard beneath. For this reason the vinyl-impregnated bouclé shade, fringed to match the draperies, is set forward, leaving space behind it for a birdcage whose colorful silhouette looks for all the world like a fascinating design on the translucent material.

The floor-length curtains with their deep swag and its cascading ends are of a rich blue fabric with a black, tasseled fringe, the blue almost matching that of a patterned rug and the upholstery of a sofa-bed. With the white painted cabinets and their fabric panels in gold, plus the black counter top, this window ensemble and wallpaper complete an interior so rich as to justify the fine antique tables and chair which in any other setting would have seemed wholly out of place.

A long, narrow room with a 15-foot ceiling, and a spectacular pier-glass between two tall windows, all three topped by matching gilt cornices as in 249, would hardly constitute the simplest type of Victorian interior to bring up to date. Nevertheless this was handsomely done, first by adding deep valances under the window cornices to help reduce the apparent ceiling height. Behind these was hung a single pair of curtains, one against each wall. To these were added shades of the same matching fabric, the only difference being that the valances and shades were printed in vinyl ink on vinyl-impregnated shade cloth.

The pattern of this material is a large-scaled but subtle contemporary interpretation of a traditional design in golden-ochre and white. This material naturally lends itself very well to use for the upholstery of a pair of easy chairs, the old-new pattern helping to fit them more readily into the sophisticated décor established by a variety of antique pieces ranging from Italian to Biedermeier. These are grouped on an area rug in bronze-green which only partially covers an old parquet floor. Over all hangs a six-foot-tall crystal chandelier, dated 1860, which helps to draw the interest from the pier glass toward the center of the room.

248.

243

250.

249.

The wide bay pictured in 250 has three windows in a row, an arrangement that not only simplifies the placement of furniture but gives the designer more scope for variety. These floor-to-ceiling windows (one large, two small) are separated by wide painted panels set off by molding in a deeper color, with a cornice carried across the top. These serve to frame each window so that there is no confusion between the adjoining set of draperies, shades, and curtains, and each represents a definite individual unit.

The drapery fabric, which is also used on the walls and the sofa, is of Chinese inspiration involving what someone has dubbed "birds on a chinoiserie bough." This represents a wide range of colors on a pale yellow background. The tie-backs are of the same material, but the valances are formed of voluminous swags in a deep red, this color being picked up by the Spanish-footed wing chair.

The shades are screen-painted to match both the colors and design of the drapery material, and behind them are stretched glass-curtains to the height of the lower sash. On the parquet floor is a light-beige rug with a leaf and pineapple border. Against this total background the rich mahogany eighteenth-century pieces appear to gain added warmth and charm.

The ten-foot-high screens made from venetian blinds eliminate the need for any other kind of treatment on the window-wall of 251. The room itself combines Chinese, Moorish, and Italian influences, a touch of sheer comfort being supplied by a pure-American armchair.

244

The screen panels, it will be noted, incorporate the Moorish arch. Both the panels and the blinds are lacquered in a Chinese red, and since the latter can be adjusted to control the admission of both light and air they are actually functional as well as ornamental.

Of the furniture pieces, the bench is covered in gray damask and lacquered in black, the details being picked out in gold. The low table, on the other hand, is lacquered red, with decorative touches in black. The rug picks up most of these shades and some others, in contrast to the natural linen of the modern chair. The total result is an elegant little interior combining the practical with the exotic, and constituting a novel idea that could well be adapted to a town or country house as well as a city apartment.

Shades which are raised instead of lowered to shut out the view are useful in a variety of situations when the usual pull-down style would be impractical. With a large window, for example, especially one that extends to the floor, it may often be desirable to ensure privacy by covering the lower part while leaving the top section open to view. Under similar conditions, where the window is located beneath a porch roof, or is otherwise shaded, it may be more advantageous to filter the light coming in at the bottom, thereby eliminating glare. The decorator's principal problem here, of course, is to incorporate a large expanse of shade into the general decorating scheme.

In illustration 252 the example is somewhat extreme

251.

252.

245

because much less of the shade is ordinarily visible at any time, nevertheless it demonstrates one way of adding a touch of flavor by attaching a colorful fringe to the upper edge of the shade and adding a fringe valance that looks like the bottom of an Austrian shade. In this photograph the shade and rug are white while the tassel fringe adds a touch of deep red, raspberry, and white — the same

254.

colors as found in the rug fringe also. This makes an interesting contrast with the light red walls and the red and white of the print covering the chair. The accessories are relied upon to add accents of Bristol blue. Naturally, there is no reason why the shade itself cannot be of any color or pattern, not only to suit the mood of the interior but also to eliminate the need for any other window adornment.

Quite different circumstances are represented by 253, which shows the "bottom-up" shades used to accommodate the slant of ceiling timbers, while regular shades installed beolw the principal cross-member keep that window-wall entirely uncluttered in the shoji manner as befits a room fitted out in the oriental style, with reed chairs in black lacquer and red cushions, a Chinese rug in gold and blue, with scrolls and pottery as accents, and walls and floor finished in natural tones of wood.

Still another method applying the bottom-up shades as part of the interior décor is demonstrated by 254. This suggests the effect to be secured by covering the shades

253.

246

255.

256.

in the same colorful floral design as the wallpaper. Plain, sheer glass curtains can be used between windows and shades or the glass left bare.

In the illustration, the two windows and the bookcase between them are arched by lambrequins of plywood covered with the shade fabric which is in tones of blue and raspberry on white. Much of the time the shades (in this case operated by a central cord) would naturally be lowered far enough to admit the necessary amount of daylight without sacrifice of privacy. After dark, the added warmth of pattern due to the raised shades would increase the air of cosy comfort supplied by the shaggy pale blue rug, and the midnight blue of the armchairs whose squared cushion trim in raspberry and white adds a dramatic touch.

Two final illustrations show how one fabric can be used for two related purposes in the same area. Although both views pertain to dining rooms, the same principles can be applied to any other interior.

The first photograph (255), is of a dining area in a

window bay at one end of a living room, the whole carpeted in white nylon. The bay windows are curtained in a blue and white toile de Jouy print on dacron, forming a logical setting for a French provincial dining table and chairs under a wrought-iron chandelier. Whenever desirable, the small area can be closed off by a tall, handsome screen whose upper panels are formed of the same fabric, creating the illusion of draped windows.

In the second picture (256), a small country dining room is equipped with a corner cupboard having twin folding doors. This serves as a storage area for desk equipment (and also as a desk when a flap is let down), so that the glass doors need to be obscured. This is accomplished by fitting into the glass panels strips of the same translucent red and white dacron fabric used for the window draperies. Obviously, this adds at the same time a touch of both color and pattern in an area where painted wood panels would normally be found, in a tint compatible with the brick-red carpeting that stops short of the walls.

247

257. Rich fabrics, textures, and colors can turn a room into a jewel box. In this one Thai silk, cane, and a velvety carpet serve as a setting for checked and plain upholstery fabrics and cushions, emphasizing brilliant tones of gold, red, orange and green with the lamp as a smashing white accent.

248

Furnishing the Walls

Silks, velvets, toiles de Jouy, rich colors and textures can turn a room into a jewel box, while stone and whitewash may be used to establish a mood of austere simplicity. In designing any interior, therefore, whether according to eclectic principles or not, the walls can be used either as one of the most decorative features or merely as a neutral background serving to bring out the character and beauty of the furniture pieces. Very often they serve to synthesize disparate types of furniture, since the background can not only modify the apparent quality of any piece but reduce or enhance its impact and therefore its importance in the room. In other instances wall coverings may be used to introduce areas of subtly provocative color, or accent some corner that unbalances an interior through its lack of character. This is often seen in rooms that are paneled, or given occasional emphasis by isolated areas of wall covering framed in simple molding.

Wall coverings, therefore, constitute an important and useful decorative tool that can be used not only to adorn a room but also, in a sense, to furnish it. All good and well-chosen furniture should of course do both, but it is usually necessary to enhance any furniture at all by enveloping it in a background suited to the mood it is desired to establish.

When deciding upon any style or type of wall covering it is helpful to remember that the appearance of most good antique pieces may be improved by a contemporary background often with interesting and novel effects. On the other hand, a faded or otherwise shabby wallpaper can rob old pieces of their color and apparently dull their patina. Equally interesting is the fact that with a mixture of styles and periods a plain, untextured white wall can act as a catalyst though the overall result may give the room a modern feel.

One important use of certain wall coverings is to counteract the visual effects of architectural deficiencies, such as raising or lowering the ceiling. Printed materials are available to represent moldings and panels; others imitating fancy borders can be used to frame panels or whole walls where such emphasis is needed, while similar paste-on panels often have to suffice in rooms with curved walls that make it impossible to hang pictures.

In some instances the most satisfactory wall covering may be a simple coat of paint. Where some special effect is desired, the painting can take the form of a mural design, or be confined to the representation of panels (often with a central motif), cornices, or dados, or even elaborate architectural and landscape paintings such as that in illustration 259.

In this dining room the mural extending right around the room is a tremendous work of art embodying some highly imaginative details. A creation of the late James Reynolds, it encompasses the room with a stone balustrade, tall classical columns, and wide archways opening

258. Here the apparent wall height is reduced by ornamenting the ceiling and painting a deep border in similar colors below the cornice, leaving the walls a pale solid tint.

on to gardens, distant skies and mountains. The total effect is to open up the walls to the outdoors so that the room seems far bigger than it actually is, and to fill it with light and air besides endowing it with an exotic atmosphere.

The architectural features are rendered in grays and blacks, the Italian landscapes, the houses, flowers, and fruits being shown in their natural colors, with the addition of draperies in a deep green. In happy counterpoint, the floor covering is in a neutral tan, the eighteenth-century Florentine furniture in white and gold, with the chair seats as accents in watermelon-pink brocade.

The value of such a wall treatment lies in the oppor-

250

259.

tunity afforded the artist to make use of the entire wall space, and take advantage of any architectural quirks that may exist, including the ceiling if desired.

Special panoramic wallpapers are an interestng and vaulable alternative, and they are usually much less costly. These are of particular value in halls which need

to be made to appear wider and lighter than they actually are, besides being endowed with interest. (A number of these are shown in the chapter on Halls.) Such panoramic papers were made in France and England in the nineteenth-century, and among the most famous today are the highly popular French Zuber papers which are

251

260. Traditional decoration in the classic Chinese style such as this is equally at home in a contemporary interior.

forming a picture up to 18 feet long or more. To cover a long wall or an entire room these sets have to be repeated. In other instances several strips form a scenic panel which is separated from a similar panel by special background paper, an alternative being separate design-strips used as panels.

Where complete wall-size or room-size murals are used, producing a continuous trompe-l'oeil effect, it is as well not to obscure too much of the design either by furniture or pictures, or the end result will be disappointing if not totally absurd. It is largely because of this that such wall decorations are reserved for very large rooms where major pieces of furniture can be arranged away from the wall, or having most of them low enough to avoid serious interference with a view of the design. This, incidentally, is the value of including in the mural some representation of a physical division between the room and the picture, as was done with a balustrade in the mural illustrated in 259.

Apart from some scenic wall coverings, the size of the pattern design to be used is normally gauged by the size of the room, and the design should bear some relation to the predominant period of the furnishings, if there is one. Ordinarily, in a room furnished with pieces representing a variety of periods, historical dating is of little importance, and choice is made on the basis of general suitability to the mood it is desired to capture. In the ball-room represented by 263, for example, a seventeenth-century painting accompanies a nineteenth-century mirror, Louis XVI-style seating, and a modern piano. Here it was hoped to recapture some of the quiet elegance of the late eighteenth century, and since the room height has been visually reduced by a white-painted dado it was possible to use a pattern with both horizontal and vertical movements. In this paper the major emphasis is on the horizontal, and it has the further merit of an evenly flowing wave pattern of urns, swags, and shells in gold with touches of pink on a white ground. There is also plenty of open space so that the large design can express a rhythmic dignity without becoming oppressive. The room colors are quite compatible — the draperies in a rose velvet and the white-painted chairs covered in a pale yellow striped silk. The mirror and console are painted tan with touches of cream and black.

produced in period styles going back to the eighteenth century.

An acceptable alternative in the majority of cases is the scenic wallpaper, many of which emphasize the third dimension. Usually there are mural designs divided into vertical sections something less than a yard wide, each set

252

261. Individual designs of this type can be used separately as accents or grouped to produce a garden effect so that they are equally adaptable to either a small or large space.

Chinese papers have been popular since the eighteenth century and those representing bamboos and tall sinuous trees with slender, vine-like trunks — many of them illustrating folk tales — can cover large areas without repeating the pattern. These, therefore, come nearest to our hand-painted landscape murals, though the perspec-

tive is quite limited. Very many more, however, are painted in repeat patterns with attractive colors, and these may be perfect for panels, for wall recesses, tiny foyers, and other isolated areas. The reason for this adaptability is that each section of the design is the equivalent of a separate and complete representation of a natural grouping sufficient to form a decorative unit in the manner of a framed picture. On the other hand, the

253

pattern may be so open and irregular that a whole room can be covered with delightful results. Such a pattern is shown in illustration 265 which represents a type used in Queen Anne times from which sprang the rage for chinoiserie that carried over into early Georgian days. This pattern, with its colorful flowers and birds, goes well with both formal eighteenth-century walnut and mahogany pieces, as well as Directoire, Regency, Victorian, or even Modern where the interior is given over to art objects from the East.

Also indebted to the eighteenth-century chinoiseries is the original French design from which 266 has been adapted, and simplified in the early nineteenth-century manner. Slightly more formal than the all-over pattern, it is produced in a variety of color combinations without sacrificing the natural appearance of the birds and the flowers. Being rather dainty and feminine, it is quite adaptable to Louis XV interiors, and other situations

262. A scenic wallpaper that gives the effect of a hand-painted mural represents a flowering bough which can be hung with equal effectiveness either down from the ceiling or vertically as shown.

where delicate scrollwork is ordinarily used, and in certain halls where it will not have to compete with heavy Victorian mahogany pieces. It would be perfect with Chinese Chippendale!

Since New England has long been associated with the Orient through its early China trade, it is no surprise to find the decoration of a peach-blow vase found in Massachusetts being transferred to wallpaper as in 267. These chrysanthemums represent timeless classicism at its best, guaranteed to endow any room with an air of elegant simplicity. The strong contrast between the flowers whose petals are heavily flocked and the almost translucent quality of the foliage gives it both strength and delicacy. Furthermore, presenting the two patterns on separate planes emphasizes their differences while magnifying the impact of the flowers.

Another overall design which has a peculiar secondary effect is that of 268, an overall pattern of English roses which seems innocently enough to have acquired a vertical axis. As the photograph shows, the leaves are darker than the flowers with the result that certain clusters of them repeat perpendicularly to produce the illusion of an upright pattern duplicated by the roses in a lighter key. This is a contemporary design in the manner of an English chintz of the eighteenth century when fabric design began to assume a fresh, vibrant look in contrast to the heavy opulence of the earlier periods. It should therefore have many applications in interiors that are romantic in tone.

Belonging to the same period is the lovely French provincial pattern revealed in 269, which was adapted from a typical late eighteenth-century fabric. The delicate flowers, the rustic costumes, and the classic ruins are reminiscent of Petit Trianon days, and suggest the paper's use with Louis XVI furniture or modern adaptations thereof, or even the present-day small-scale reproductions of Louis XIII's majestic designs.

Turning to colonial days, few symbols are as well known as the pineapple, token of hospitality which graced New England furniture and doorways for so long. This same pineapple is now featured in a design based on that of an antique resist-printed fabric. This traditional motif is invested with a certain dramatic elegance in the pattern of 270, which, printed in black on white, may well be

254

263.

264. The delicately classical wallpaper with its colorful birds and leafy swags, and ample areas of white "air space" is particularly suitable for a bedroom furnished with beautiful fabrics in pastel shades, regardless of the style of furniture, providing it is not wholly rustic. As with this adaptation of early American pieces, the quality must suggest a certain amount of refinement and sophistication.

265.

266.

267.

268.

269.

270.

259

271.   272.

used for either contemporary eclectic or period interiors, or even as a nostalgic accent with modern furniture.

For those more interested in a slightly post-Revolutionary period, 271 pictures a wallpaper design copied from a hand-blocked original discovered in a New Hampshire inn. This has something of the air of an old-time stencil combined with the vee-grooves of chisel carving, and is therefore one of the most authentic designs of its type. It is especially attractive in a delicate gray-blue, and constituting a definite stripe it should be of particular value in low-ceilinged rooms of an early vintage or tall ones with dadoes and deep friezes in wood.

The next example (272) has the distinction of representing a contemporary version of a style originated by Robert Adam in the late 1700's for the interiors he designed. Inspired by the ancient relics of Greece and Rome, he utilized classical themes and personages for his designs which his contemporary, Josiah Wedgwood, adapted for use in decorating his pottery. The contemporary interpretation of the style centers upon Eros, the Greek god of love, in developing a traditional design flavored with today's expressionism, a feature that adapts it to a wide variety of interiors, old and new.

Design 273 is a world apart from the foregoing in both origin and style. This is an elegant interpretation in gold on white of a type of design much admired by members of the eighteenth-century French court who became so enamoured of Rousseau's return-to-nature philosophy that they built themselves expensive and elaborate rural "pavillons" where they retired on occasion to enjoy the rustic life and bucolic pleasures of the common herd.

Unfortunately they were unable to resist decorating these retreats in the highly sophisticated manner suggested by this and similar wallpapers. Today a design such as this can find application in many formal rooms and dignified entrance halls.

The spindling vines and oversize roses of 274 — a "large-scale floral" to the trade — is introduced to show that some wallpaper designs of this type can be used to cover the entire wall area of a room, from baseboard to ceiling, without inducing a feeling of oppression.

Furthermore, this particular design is nicely scaled to

261

274.

the room, since with its strong vertical feeling the interior still seems in perfect proportion. The design is reminiscent of some fine eighteenth-century French fabric, and the room itself is mostly French in spite of a Victorian marble fireplace, and the stunning sculptured rug that might be mistaken at first glance for an Aubusson on the parquet floor.

In illustration 275 still another suggestion is embodied, creating a background with a fairly neutral mottled paper, or one with a plain textured appearance, to give

262

275.

tremendous impact to a pictorial unit at its center. In this instance the design area resembles a small but magnificent Beauvais tapestry with a border that suggests a frame for the huge flower-filled jardiniere. The balance of tones between background and design is responsible for the appeal of this colorful trompe-l'oeil effect which complements so graciously the French provincial piece beneath it. The unusual piece of furniture stealing the spotlight is a Basque wing chair.

Vinyl Finishes and Fabrics

One of the most interesting of modern materials for use in the home is a polyvinyl plastic commonly known as vinyl. This material which is now used as a wall covering has long been utilized on floors, a fact which speaks well for its durability and wearing qualities. The requirements of wall covering, however, are somewhat different than those of flooring, one of the most important being that the wall-covering type is comparatively thin, and is acquired by designers in a solid color. The designs are silk-screened on to that surface, after which a coating of clear vinyl is added to protect the pattern. Special paste adhesives are used for attaching the material to the walls. Some of these vinyls are made so that they are porous and therefore able to "breathe" in the manner of leather, and this is often an advantage in preventing dampness. This type is built-up on a knitted-fabric base which allows of stretching that is often an important addition to the normal characteristics of vinyl. It cannot stiffen or crack, is color-fast, easily cleaned with soap and water, and is scuff-resistant.

In addition to the vinyl wall coverings there are a number of wallpapers which are given a coating of vinyl to make them scrubbable, and must be differentiated accordingly. All those shown in this section are on solid vinyl backings. Another interesting factor is that the same vinyl material, usually in heavier weights, is used

276. A simple design for a simple bedroom — roses, butterflies, and falling petals widely spaced on a pale blue ground, fill a corner between windows with light and air. The sheer draperies over Venetian blinds, capped with tasseled pelmets repeating the color of the roses, add the slightest touch of formality to match that of the crystal lighting fixture.

263

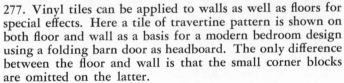
277. Vinyl tiles can be applied to walls as well as floors for special effects. Here a tile of travertine pattern is shown on both floor and wall as a basis for a modern bedroom design using a folding barn door as headboard. The only difference between the floor and wall is that the small corner blocks are omitted on the latter.

278.

for upholstering furniture. This has made it possible for decorators to design some fascinating interiors covering the furniture, walls, and sometimes the ceilings, in the same or contrasting patterns. An exceptionally intriguing example of this technique is illustrated in 278 and 279, which cover two sections of a room designed for the famous comedian Bert Lahr. This room, obviously a catchall for mementoes, was impossible to decorate in the usual formal manner. The problem was therefore solved on the principle of overpowering the inevit-

279.

able clutter with an overall indeterminate pattern of low color contrast.

The greater part of two walls was covered by bookshelves which introduced plenty of wood tones with which the walls obviously should not contrast too strongly. This no doubt helped influence the decision to use the vinyl in a wood-toned tortoise-shell pattern in autumn accent colors not only on all available wall space but also on the ceiling and for the furniture upholstery. A surprising air of richness and sophistication has resulted. The varied tones of brown, which include an oriental rug, are accented by chair seats in red and pillows in orange and white, and the Victorian white-marble mantel is established as a focal point in a room in which almost every detail is a conversation piece.

Another interior which demonstrates the versatility of

280.

vinyl coverings, but in a much more sedate mood, is 280. This is a room overwhelmingly Grecian classical in atmosphere, and also extraordinarily attractive, thanks largely to the disposition of straight lines and curves, of the contrast between patterned and plain, and the evident quality of the pieces including the strange smoothness of the upholstery vinyl in black which seems to have an almost sensuous feel.

Practically the whole room is encased in vinyl — the floor, walls, including the Greek-key border in black and red-orange, and the draw-up shades which share that decorative touch. The walls are light, smooth, and almost textureless, producing the cool effect of marble without its rigidity; the blinds fold accordion-pattern, a tribute to the vinyl's flexibility, and the wing chair displaying the tortoise-shell pattern printed on white, gives an antique form a modern touch.

In 281 the vinyl wall covering whose rust on white pat-

281.

tern is duplicated in the sofa upholstery again demonstrates the versatility of this medium which both the room decorators and fabric designers are exploiting to the full. The honeycomb floor in black and brown is an excellent foil for this pattern, and both work together to make the most of the yellows, pinks and touches of black that continually draw the eye in a new direction.

Of particular interest is the refreshment serving area with its white formica-topped table and the suspended cupboards overhead, each with its own lighting fixture designed to obviate any shadows below them. This area is further psychologically separated from the rest of the room by the short section of returned wall, the difference being emphasized by covering the wall behind the table with vinyl of a contrasting pattern to that of the main area. This consists of small fern-motif designs in rows

across a white ground, one below another like a shower of falling darts. This room, it will be noticed, has walls of a sufficiently high reflective capacity to eliminate the need for any high-intensity lighting with its concomitant of glare.

A number of things are demonstrated by 282, among which is a notable color compatibility in an interior which is exquisite by any standards. The lilac (technically a red-purple tint) patterned vinyl on the chaise is repeated on the wall panels. Spanning the entrance to the alcove are pelmets and draperies of the red-purple itself braided with the same color on white. Irregular spots of this color adorn the white-carpeted steps to the adjoining room where vertical panels and pillars are covered in the patterned vinyl. In that same area are two other sets of the draperies marking the limits of a circular ceiling

267

282.

hung with folds of white fabric centering on a crystal and gold chandelier. In this area the floor is covered with the same dotted white carpeting as the steps. From either level, however, it is the wall panels that catch the eye, their sweeping curves forming wavelike horizontal bands in steps from top to bottom suggesting a lively checkerboard of curlicues from whose reflections even the gold-framed mirror gains in glamour.

One of the loveliest — and liveliest — apartment rooms to which to retire for a conference, refreshments, or the study of one's hobby or specialty is depicted in 283. This owes much of its charm to the inspired employment of fabric designs in vinyl calculated to capture a mood, adding distinction without pomposity.

The basis of this decorative scheme is, as might be suspected, the framed Vatican Library prints hanging

268

283.

on the walls. This is seen in the pair of Directoire high-backed, bergères flanking the porcelain stove which oc-cupies a niche in the center where it serves as provocative conversation piece. The sofa is covered in the same material as the chairs, complete with the pattern in white on mottled green. The stove, too, is green with white accents standing out boldly against the white wall.

The tub chairs alongside the coffee table are uphol-stered in a heavy vinyl leopard-skin print in a yellowish brown, green, and slate gray. All of these pieces are either antiques or first-class reproductions. Certainly antique is the fine Aubusson rug in beiges and muted pinks, as are the small commodes with their bronze-doré sabots. The coffee table is a Directoire model of steel and brass with a plate-glass top.

Altogether this constitutes a stunning interior with far

284, 285. Vinyl wall coverings such as these are a pair of stock patterns available in a variety of color combinations in the manner of wallpaper. The first of them is an impressive design adapted from an early Italian damask, hand-printed on a textured ground, the second an unusual stripe with a contemporary flavor forming an interesting background for traditional furnishings in different periods.

286. This classical design of riders and horses from a Parthenon frieze is made up of four vinyl panels totalling nine feet in length.

PANEL 1   PANEL 2   PANEL 3   PANEL 4

287.

more élan, thanks largely to the colors, patterns, and textures, than the monochrome picture can reveal.

Antique prints reproduced on vinyl fabric in monochrome are an excellent substitute for trompe-l'oeil drawings of an outdoor scene, preferably applied above a colorful dado, or used in a series of panoramic panels.

Such a series of ruins by Piranesi would be particularly attractive in the large room needing architectural character, providing the sizes were properly related to the wall areas, and uniform. The example in illustration 287 is composed of four panels.

271

288.

Textile Fabrics

Ever since medieval times, the most important wall coverings were a woven cloth fabric, the most famous in the Western world being tapestries. With the advent of smooth dependable dry walls, lighter fabrics were at first hung, and later attached directly to the surfaces, stretched between moldings. Todays fabrics are pasted to walls, or mounted on frames as a matter of convenience in keeping them clean, to preserve the fabric or to space it out to hide pipes, ducts, and imperfections in the surface. Regardless of the method of application, however, the fabric performs the same functions as wallpaper (usually at a higher cost), but offers certain advantages, particularly where formed of man-made fibers and subjected to modern treatments to assure longer life and ease of cleaning.

A prime example of the adaptability of such fabrics to the decoration of a small room is illustrated by 288. This shows a beautiful paisley pattern rayon fabric whose basic color is blackberry, though it actually blends mink brown and russet red with azure. It is used not only as a wall covering but also to line the royal-blue window draperies, and to form the floor-length table cover. It is the richness of the coloring plus the depth of texture displayed by this fabric, whose pattern might be mistaken for needlepoint, that gives the whole room an air of affluence commonly associated with period design, investing the reproduction furniture pieces with a look of authenticity. As a matter of interest, the chairs are a fiery red, and the rug the same blue as the draperies so that there is plenty of life and vivacity in a room that otherwise might have been left with no more than a mood of quiet distinction.

The paisley pattern, incidentally, is adaptable to a wide variety of interiors depending upon the major colors it is desired to introduce. This has led fabric designers to vary the pattern details in an effort to produce wall coverings that have both the paisley appeal and utility yet escape the penalty of monotony when applied to large areas. Several of these are pictured (unfortunately not in color!) to show how the impression of authenticity has been retained while the details are changed. In one instance (289), a much more open pattern is created which would form a perfect background for a modern Victorian interior which is less crowded with furniture and bric-a-brac than the originals. In another pattern (290), a suggestion of chinoiserie has been captured in a riot of colors, shapes, and intensities, while a third (291), introduces the sinuosities of vines that tie the floral units together, and make room for a leafy background that adds a more naturalistic note by which its adaptability is widened.

272

289.

291.

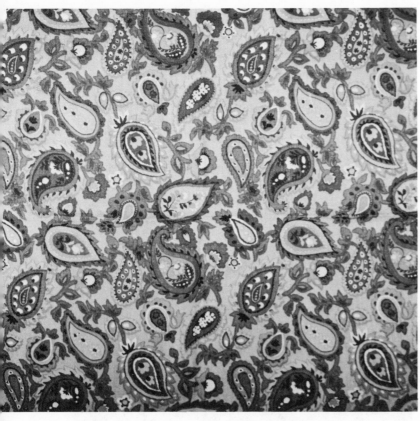

290.

292.

273

293.

295.

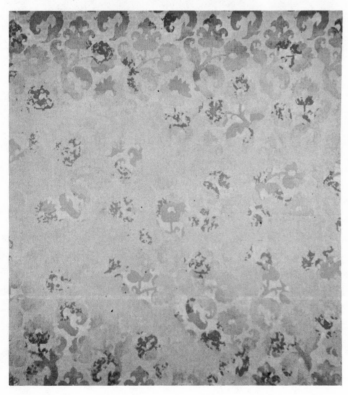

294.

296.

All of these actually are provincial type patterns, somewhat less formal than the pure paisley, happy in living rooms, dens, bedrooms, and even some kitchens of country houses in France, England, and America. The first is in dramatic blues on white; the second has a gold ground, with reds, pink, pale green, and mauve; the third is content with indigo and brown on a vivid red ground.

Far removed from the paisley pattern yet peculiarly suggestive of it is 292, which combines peacocks with wheels, flowers, and fruiting vines in broad vertical bands, with pink, reds, and browns on a dark blue ground between red stripes. Deeply dramatic, it still belongs to the provincial group, though guaranteed to rescue any room at all from mediocrity.

Much more in the romantic vein is the hedge-rose pattern of 293 in a blazing yellow, well accented with other roses in red and white, and a scattering of deep-green leaves. This all-over pattern is a gay, informal print, useful in town or country dwellings providing it is not used in too-great areas. For panels it would be ideal, using the same fabric to cover sofa pillows.

Even more elegant, each in its own way, are the two overall patterns 294 and 295, definitely different yet equally tasteful, and suggestive of Williamsburg, though one can picture them as pleasing backgrounds for English, French, or Italian fine furniture whether in the drawing room, the library, or living room. Though 294 has a free-hand air, it retains the same soft golden-brown touches that give character to 295, and reflect the dappled appearance of some vinyl fabrics. In 294 the background is blue, the figures in kelly green; in 295 the pattern is the color of unbleached linen (though the material has no linen in it), and the ground a lovely soft gray-green.

Spring seems to burst out all over in two cotton prints (296 and 297), both of which are somewhat impressionistic, though lively in color and pattern. The spring flowers in 296 are a wild mélange of brick-red, yellow, green, blue-gray, and brown on white (though the summer version switches over to purple, lilac, several blues, and bright green!), which is a sheer puzzle when reduced to monochrome, but actually gaily informal, suggesting painted furniture in a variety of compatible styles. The pattern of 297 is somewhat more decisive (and discoverable), comprising bunches of posies in various blues,

from Prussian to sky, plus amethyst and pink, with fat stems in deep green, all on white — a summery design, mostly as covering for wicker, rattan, or metal furniture in a solarium, or patio, or places equally informal and warm.

Artificial ruins in an eighteenth-century garden are portrayed in 298, which might easily be mistaken for an excellent French toile de Jouy in the classic blue on off-white. An amazing feature of this pattern is the amount of delicate detail that appears, investing each item with a three-dimensional air that stamps it as a product of the first quality, fit to consort with the best of furniture, antique or new, or a mixture of both, from Louis XV to Chippendale, to Directoire, or even painted Italian pieces in the barochetto style.

Where doubts exist about the possibilities of eclectic furnishing, there is need to analyze today's wall coverings which are adaptable to so many styles of furnishing and endow with new life and interest interiors that rely on nothing more than antiquity for their charm — nostalgic rooms that need a "lift!" Simply stated, this means that if the proper choice of wall covering is made, any piece that looks well with the rest of the furniture will look well with the wall covering — a trite saying perhaps, but one with connotations that lie at the roots of the eclectic theory.

The importance of such a wall covering in brightening and unifying an interior is demonstrated by the history of 299, which was first printed in 1948. This proved popular for a number of years but was finally retired in the usual process of making way for new designs, only to be revived at the insistence of interior designers who found the original colors and lively pattern well suited to eclectic furnishing schemes.

This design features the jack-in-the-pulpit plant, among ferns and smaller wildflowers wholly reminiscent of spring in the country and the burgeoning of nature everywhere.

Quite similar in spirit, though slightly more formal, is 300, based on beach grasses and other seaside flora, and intended primarily for both contemporary and traditional interiors. In this design the vertical is accentuated and a third dimension suggested by the contrasting lights and darks. The beauties of nature are likewise

297.

298.

276

299.

300.

301.

recaptured in 301, which is a happily natural representation of a plum-tree orchard, faintly stylized, that also bridges the gap between the new and the old in an intriguing manner.

Striking still another note, the sandpipers in 302 are amusingly absurd in a print which might find welcome application in a sportsman's den, or the room of an older child, a games room, or indeed any interior where a lighter touch would not come amiss, with perhaps a special appeal to the modernist with reservations about being taken too seriously.

Turning from this to 303, there is little cause for levity inherent in the dramatic mood expressed by the pattern of chains which actually was inspired by the black iron gates of Ireland's Dromoland Castle — a symbol both of protection and captivity depending on whether one is looking out or in. At least it has the merit of being unusual, tied to history yet modern as tomorrow. These of course are the things one has to learn to see in analyzing the possibilities of any wall-covering design at all.

302.

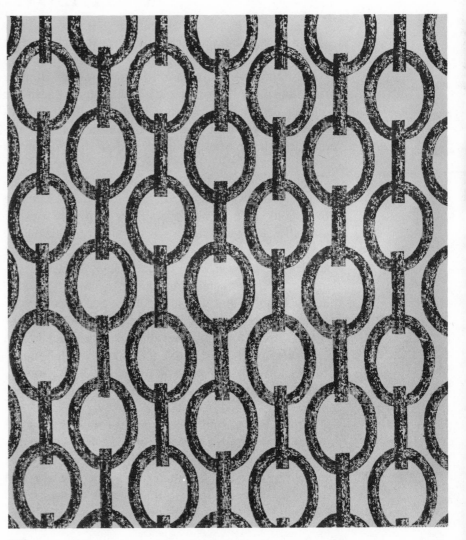

303.

Furnishing the Floors

Almost every interior that stimulates the imagination owes no small part of its appeal to the floor, floorings and floor covering being basic to interior design in more senses than one. This is a subject that has engaged the minds of designers for a very long time, their dreams fulfilled during recent years by reason of the new materials that have been invented and fresh applications of old ideas that have been devised.

There are many rules about the decoration of floors, and today most of them are best forgotten. Looking through old pictures one encounters lavishly furnished rooms all color and pattern — as much of both on the floor as elsewhere — rooms that enfold one like a soft and pleasant cocoon, and others where the floor is a thing forgotten or treated like a painful necessity — something to stand on but which is not allowed to contribute anything to the general air of comfort or aesthetic satisfaction. Others form vast negative expanses that beg to be broken up by the luxury of a rug, areas of monochrome short-pile carpeting that look just as frustrating, and the more vivid the color the more repellent they can be.

To do its best for any room, the floor must make some positive contribution to the general décor. A bare expanse offers only monotony unless it is in perfect rapport with the furniture it is supposed to enhance, just as a wall covering is expected to do. It is a part of the room's background and can make or mar any furnishing scheme.

It is therefore not to be treated as an afterthought, the last thing to receive consideration after all else has been decided upon.

One thing that may need careful study is the material to be used. Some floorings are more or less permanently applied and are therefore difficult or costly to replace. That aristocrat of floorings, hardwood parquet, may be noisy to walk on unless well supplied with rugs. A third point concerns pattern. Those that are too boldly geometric, such as black and white squares of marble, and some parquet designs, whether in the original material or copied in vinyl, may be unsuited to certain décors and spoil the desired mood. Apart from these considerations, there is no reason, practical or aesthetic, why such floors cannot be used with both modern interiors and period furniture, much less in rooms that are wholly eclectic in style.

Among the oldest of floorings are those of stone, slate, marble, terracotta and ceramic tile, as well as dependable wood which made possible the ever-popular parquet. This type of wooden flooring luckily is due for a revival, in one form or another, since new methods of reproducing the patterns, and simulating them in new materials have been developed, with some of their drawbacks overcome in the process. Meanwhile the quarried materials, once used only in palaces, have found favor in modern interiors together with wood parquet combined with stone or brick. In all types of houses, terracotta

tiles in a dozen shapes, antique and new, have become popular, together with new patterns of ceramic tiles, glazed but made safe to walk upon.

Practically all of these patterns and materials are reproduced in thermoplastic vinyl, or any kind of pattern or material covered with the transparent vinyl which is neither cold, nor rough, nor unyielding. Similar advances have been made in the fields of fabrics and fibers, so that marble slabs can be duplicated as to appearance in wool, and carpets laid in small squares like tile. Waterproof and dirt-proof rugs and carpets of nylon now make it possible for even bathrooms to share the underfoot luxury of warmth, color, and pattern once reserved for bedrooms, transforming their potentialities for total decoration.

With furnishing in the eclectic style (that intermarriage of cousins, as it has been called) most of these floor treatments can be adapted to a wider range of interiors than ever before, as some of the pictures to follow should make clear.

Parquet Flooring

Theoretically, floors composed of square blocks of wood — in these days rarely more than ⅝-inch thick, and often less — are not parquet (which is inlay), but from a practical standpoint the two may be grouped together, particularly since blocks or tiles with decorative grains produce a somewhat similar effect.

The hardwoods most commonly used for parquet — principally oak, maple, beech, walnut, and teak — provide an interesting variety of colors and grains, and some vary greatly in themselves. Ordinarily, walnut will be the darkest and maple the lightest in color. Usually it is not advisable to mix the woods because of the variations in wearing quality and shrinkage, but one very successful combination of light woods and dark, used in certain

304. The use of vinyl as a base for an applied design makes possible such enchantment as afforded by this assembly of field and pattern units to any desired size and in any variety of colors. The small rectangles are 7¼ inches square, and the background suggests large monochrome tiles laid diagonally. With this system the floor covering can be made to fit any shape or size of room.

281

305.

Louis XV interiors, encloses squares of maple framed in strips or "pickets" of oak.

Turning to actual examples of parquet flooring, illustration 305 employs solid squares of teak, relying for its decorative qualities on the delicate feathery grain and the variations in tone which give the whole surface the appearance of watered silk. In this view the teak-block flooring is shown with contemporary furniture also made of teak, together with modern upholstered furniture and a variety of antiques. A French desk, country chair and chest, English armchairs, and a number of porcelain, brass, and pewter accessories, plus some modern art and a fine Italian rug — the whole thing representing the peak of eclecticism.

306.

A quite different mood is secured through the use of teak parquet in which each square block is composed of five finger-like strips, some dark, some light. This is seen in a definitely modern setting (306), in which the only antiques are Chinese and Thai accessories. The wood pattern is particularly compatible with the upholstery fabric which simulates, to some degree, a Hungarian point tapestry.

Another parquet design (307) is developed by constructing the teak squares from these wide strips to form what is sometimes known as the foursquare pattern. Because of the area devoted to each strip, more definite and complete grain is shown by each one so that a stronger pattern is achieved. This goes very well with a fireplace wall composed of used brick which presents an equally vivid contrast between the black rectangles and

283

307.

the pink ones among which they are scattered at random. This theme is emphasized by the contrasting colors in the hearthrug, the whole set against a background of white walls and natural linen upholstery.

A much more unified pattern than any of the foregoing is achieved in 308, where the teak parquet unit is built up of three strips enclosed in a frame. Dark and light woods are mixed at random so that no two pieces of wood are alike though the squares are, for the most part, clearly defined. The effect, therefore, is more like that of a geometrically patterned rug in its total impact, and both old and new furniture pieces seem perfectly at home with it as they do with the multifaceted lantern and the carved panels of the door, two items that introduce an exotic note which the flooring does nothing to diminish.

In this picture the room is divided into two separate

284

areas by covering one with a rug which also has a rather definite, though different, pattern. Fortunately, the wall to one side of the door is in monochrome while that at the other side has but a faint indication of a woodsy landscape so that there is no conflict with either the pattern of the bare flooring or that of the rug.

The herringbone pattern of parquet flooring has a long and honorable history, even though it may not always have been composed of teak as is the floor of a contemporary living room (309) with its oriental décor. The short teak planks, set at 90 degrees to one another, seem to constitute an ideal pattern with which to finish off the edges of the "conversation pit" where parallel borders or square blocks would have looked contrived. The whole area is extremely colorful and exotic, taking its theme from the painting mounted on the wall whose tones are repeated in the sofa pillows and shaggy rug, and the translucent curtains that line the glass wall.

Most of the parquet patterns are available in vinyl which is obtainable either in wide rolls or as single tiles. These are usually made from photographic reproductions of wooden parquet, printed on vinyl that is then covered by a heavier coating of clear vinyl which protects the design without obscuring it or affecting the color. This "sandwich" forms a lasting, resilient material that neither chemicals nor stiletto heels can damage.

An especially interesting example of such a parquet design is the subject of 310, in which the pattern is laid diagonally, a scheme usually calculated to increase the apparent size of the area. An unusual feature is the manner in which slabs of the same vinyl in a straight wood grain are carried up the wall to ceiling height. These slabs are chamfered along their vertical edges to give the effect of vee-jointed wood sheathing.

The room itself is a study with gaily painted metal furniture and adjustable shelves whose modernity is counteracted somewhat by the antique mantel set against whitewashed bricks, by the iron sconces and chandelier, and an old-time barometer, porcelains and miniature figures in bronze, stone, and terracotta. The simulated woods, the fabrics and furniture supply a variety of effective tones — orange, white, terracotta, tobacco-brown, and black — to complete an unmannered but bright décor distinctly different, with pleasant wood grains the

308.

predominant background feature.

Vinyl herringbone parquet comes with the pattern in a variety of sizes to suit the largest or smallest rooms, and also to make possible special effects. In a larger size, as in 311, it has the appearance of planking and therefore shows make-believe pegs by which it is assumed

285

309.

to be fastened to an underflooring. In this particular example the planks are supposedly chamfered to form edge grooves. This gives them a look of three-dimensional strips, in which pegs are simulated in lighter end-grain.

In this setting of antiques and modern pieces, or nubby and sheer fabrics, it seems especially effective, taking into account the large area of moderately light wood tones as background for the yellow, oranges, and reds of the fabrics, and the huge wall-hung screen with its white birches and colorful birds, and varying tints of the painted pieces.

It will be noted that this flooring is laid with the planks parallel to the walls, producing an entirely different effect than when laid diagonally to imitate herringbone parquet.

Some idea of the effect secured by laying vinyl parquet blocks as a setting for furniture inlaid with a somewhat similar convoluted grain structure is made evident by 312. This actually seems to identify the flooring with the panels of the china cabinet and the top of the oval table, both of which are highly decorative, as are the smaller areas displayed by the woodwork of the tall vitrine and the pedestal desk. With so much pattern, the plain walls and draperies are needed as foils, even the sofa decora-

286

310.

smooth, light-colored stones in random shapes are set off by a grouting of crisp chips, each group of four tiles held together by heavy bands of walnut vinyl, the alternating light and dark strips adding a three-dimensional effect to the oversized grating.

The grain of plywood walls, coated with clear vinyl,

311.

tion being confined to a modest tufted border on the back cushions, and the armchair limited to a damask of a modest classical design.

When a floor of a more definite, different, and highly geometric pattern is required, the double-textured vinyl tiles of illustration 313 might well serve, especially where the atmosphere of an outdoor terrace is required or plantings are featured. In this outdoorsy looking room, the

287

312.

313.

314.

produces an overall effect of watered silk which reconciles the sturdy flooring with the rich pattern and variegated coloring of the sofa, and the golden gleam of the thin bamboo-style metal table. Like the walls, the molded pillars contrast effectively with the dark oak of the French provincial cabinets housing the television set, recorder, etcetera, all topped by planters and offering space below for an array of blooming African violets. In the

foreground another grouping — this time of ferns and flowers — emphasizes the fact that this type of flooring is unaffected by either a warm, damp atmosphere or the spilling of water.

The enormous difference that the absence of walnut framing of the tiles makes to the character of this flooring is obvious from a glance at 314. This is the same basic tile pattern as the foregoing, minus the walnut strips, a

the counter and the entrancing canework of the fanciful chairs.

Another pattern of wood-encased stone flooring in vinyl is represented by the elongated hexagons of black travertine outlined by strips of a pale yellowish hue, as in 315. This shape tends to add length to a floor and invest it with a positive character and masculine air, heightened

315.

change that adapts it perfectly to a small room such as this breakfast alcove. Since it is so reminiscent of a country courtyard or patio, the pseudo-stone flooring is perfectly at home with the black-iron furniture, and the stark simplicity of the shelving, endowing the corner with an air of the outdoors despite the scarlet walls, red-and-white striped window shade, the white formica of

316.

290

in this case by the damask pattern, printed in brick-pink on antiqued white vinyl which covers both the walls and the sleeping sofa. The bookcase room divider provides storage space for china in the high cabinets, and a deep counter in white formica provides for dining in case one does not care to use the mosaic-topped Italian table.

A world away from this in both concept and coloring is 316 with its vinyl tile design in scarlet and black, the pattern dividing the floor into a multitude of squares, quadrants, and ellipses, the black figures like double-pointed arrows guiding the eye diagonally across the floor. In this room the warmth of the red floor has been somewhat subdued by covering one wall in fabric of a cooler red, patterned in black and cream, and tinting the other walls and the ceiling a very pale pink. The woodwork, too, is a purplish pink, this tint repeated in a mixture with tan in the sofa fabric.

A red-lacquer chest, upended, is used as a table in the center of the floor to serve both the sofa and a chaise, the latter enveloped in a purplish silk. An antique carved lion on the chaise, and a tiger's portrait on the wall, accent the exotic, while an oriental chair in black lacquer and white silk contemplates a Victorian iron coal scuttle which seems to be a distant relation of the sofa despite the latter's bamboo-patterned trim.

The intriguing cloudiness and amber-veined translucence of white onyx is recaptured in the wall-to-wall vinyl sheet in 317, which is divided into large squares by amber strips matching the color of the veins, with squares of green set in the corners to complete the illusion that the stripes actually cross. This is a formal and impressive pattern which could well adorn a dignified classical salon, yet is just as much at home with a modern interior as with Louis Treize. The room shown, however, has little of either, yet is extremely effective with its pale amber walls that reflect the stripes, investing the room with a golden glow. Touches of scarlet are found in the pillows, and in the portrait's pigment. The bookshelves are modern, but a cane-backed chair and a pair of stools speak of the eighteenth-century France, while a half-moon, iron-based table and a tall-backed, scroll-footed chair add a distinctly Iberian air, completing an interior that is practically timeless.

Some indication as to how far a designer can go in

317.

devising ways of using vinyl products is revealed in 318, which not only brings the outdoors indoors but constructs an open-air dining room (complete with kitchen) under its own roof. Facing the ocean or a lake, this hot-weather retreat is proof against both water and perspiration. The floors are pebbled vinyl, and the banquettes sheathed in the same material disguised as marble, the backs decorated with an etched scroll design.

291

Wood vinyl sheathes the kitchen cabinets in alternating dark and light vertical stripes in startling contrast to the counter of white formica. All cushions are of a waterproof plastic, while the tray tables are lacquered a pale blue, and wallpaper is a vinyl-protected replica of woven cane.

Delineating the common boundary of the cooking and eating areas is a hanging screen of crystal and cork beads. Its purpose is practical as well as psychological since it is decorative without interfering with the light distribution. After sunset the kitchen's translucent ceiling diffuses the artificial light throughout the area. One huge painting of

318.

319.

Here the mosaic is used to indicate the curving junction between the living and dining areas of an apartment, which happens to follow the sweep of an overhead track from the ends of which fishnet curtains are hung. The dining area floor is paved in white mosaic tiles; in the living area they are black, so that there is a definite psychological transition involved in stepping from one to the other without any physical obstacle. The curtains, in addition to their decorative value, help to establish the changeover from the ceiling down so that the difference between the two contrastingly decorated areas will seem more natural.

A more unusual arrangement is that of 320, but even here advantage is taken of the versatility of the tiny cubes to establish lanes and areas by confining them between heavy, solid lines. These particular strips are of a dark brown to complement the décor, and by their use not only are areas established but patterns created which give order to irregular floors as in this instance.

The actual dining table grouping is tied together with an octagonal rug, with the after-dinner coffees on separate small tables alongside their own settee by the window. This is a cheerful though odd-shaped room, with the accessories, including the Roman shades, in yellow and orange against a background of pinkish off-white. The lighting is supplied by copper wall-lanterns and a tôle chandelier is finished a flat brown with accents of red. The chair seats and backs are in white silk damask which contrasts boldly with the dark furniture woods, emphasizing the difference between them and the walls.

Still another application of mosaic-tile vinyl is represented by 321, which is quite formal, with a wide border that robs it of that bathroom feel in the areas where it joins the walls. In addition, the squares are set diagonally, a detail emphasized by black cabochons in the corners. This gives extra apparent width to the narrow room, plus a modicum of distinction.

For situations where simulated wood is preferable to imitation stone, foot-wide planks of vinyl in Nubian brown, innocent of grain, may be a practical substitute. The short planks in 322 are defined by white joints, their ends suitably "pegged" to some theoretical sub-floor (joists would necessarily be very closely spaced.) Laid at a 45-degree angle, they soften the rigidity of the setting

320.

gorgeous tropical birds in vivid, lifelike colors, provides both a focal point for the interior and its decorative highlight affirming the source of its inspiration.

Mosaic tile has for long been a favorite pattern with the designers of vinyl flooring, and some interesting and useful ideas have been evolved. One of these concerns the adaptability of mosaic tile to the formation of odd shapes, a good example of which is represented by 319.

only pleasurable to walk on but practically indestructible. The blue-gray pattern is particularly adaptable to an antique interior, such as that shown, with dark-blue walls and plain white draperies, touches of French and Spanish in the furnishing and Italy in the painting. Gold upholstery and red cushions matched by a lampshade, provide lively accents, the window wall enlivened by tiled, square columns and architrave in black on white which

321.

which, though interesting, suggests plenty of space to spare.

For a variety of decorating purposes there is nothing more delightful than delft tiles, and it is fortunate that in their reproduction as vinyl flooring, as in 323, nothing of either color or character is lost. Most important of all, of course, is the fact that in this medium they are not

322.

294

extends the architectural theme into the third dimension.

Undoubtedly one of the loveliest of all vinyl tiles is that pictured in 324. In two tones of blue on white it suggests blue delft but seems to have more of a Spanish character than Dutch, which is amplified in the gold and black version, rich and exotic, and quite geometrical in the manner of parquet. As shown, it is arranged in squares of 16 tiles, one square framed in light yellow stripes, the surrounding squares framed in dark yellow, with a black strip separating the two. An altogether splendid piece of design, it should endow any room with an air of unusual elegance, both because of its pattern and the selected colors, with or without the framing strips. Actually, it is hard to think of any style of interior that it would not improve — traditional, contemporary, or modern.

323.

Another exceedingly pleasant design is that of the Moroccan rustic terra-cotta tile illustrated in 325, which shows the vinyl version in which it achieves a certain air of refinement despite its provincial simplicity, a feeling that renders it usable in a variety of rooms from kitchen to foyer. Classically simple, it retains the earthy redness of the originals, grouted in white, its wavy pattern escaping the limitations of the geometrical without destroying altogether its directional characteristic. It does, in fact, combine tone and pattern in a manner that has romantic connotations suggestive of its Mediterranean origins.

Apparently Dutch, though popular in several other countries, the hexagonal red tile of view 326 also has been transformed into vinyl with commendable results.

324.

296

325.

326.

Changing the color to green in addition to the red, as has been done, should extend its application, especially in view of the fact that this also changes its apparent character.

The regular terra-cotta colored tile goes very well with brick, as might be expected, and seems perfectly at home with either unfinished or painted wood. It is especially suited to roofed terraces, rumpus rooms, and enclosed porches, as well as the kitchen, though much of course depends upon the style and quality of the furnishings. It is obviously best adapted to country furniture, and the outdoor styles used in summer dining rooms whether of wicker, wood, or metal, and where potted plants are grown — and watered!

327.

328.

Square terra-cotta tiles that have all the unevennesss of common bricks produce an interesting pattern solely by reason of those irregularities which result in a wavy mortar line, as in 327. This effect actually makes the material appear all the more naturally rustic, if that were possible. In any event such a pattern is notably suited to country furniture, bare wood, and stoneware pottery as

the picture should make clear. It would, however, suit the same alternative purposes as 326.

In most instances where rugs are not to be used, the tiled flooring may often need to be inlaid to form localized patterns or special designs. This applies especially to those of, or representing, marble, as in 328. In addition to the plain vinyl tiles which look like white marble, other

298

tiles can be had which bear etched designs in the surfaces having the appearance of intaglio decoration.

Such tiles can be used to form a room border or even create an eye-catching area accommodating a special furniture unit, as in the picture. Alternately spaced they can even provide an all-over checkerboard pattern to fill an otherwise arid expanse. A somewhat similar effect is provided by the decorated tile in illustration 329, which is shown there made up into squares of four, spaced between strips arranged to form a gridiron pattern. Regardless of the color used, each has a somewhat Spanish air.

329.

Carpet and Rugs

Whatever kind of flooring is used, from stone to carpeting, rugs are usually desirable as providing areas of color or pattern, and the added luxury of a thicker, softer material underfoot, to emphasize special areas such as a fireplace hearth, or tie together visually various furniture groupings, as well as to protect more or less permanent carpeting in much-used areas. Apart from these considerations they form definitely decorative units in the same manner as a picture or tapestry; they can be placed in the most suitable position on a floor, moved around in rearranging furniture, or replaced without effort.

The colors and patterns are, needless to say, of first importance, and consideration needs to be given to the use of plain or monochrome sculptured or shaggy rugs over carpeting whether the latter is patterned or not. Obviously, long, loose textures are not advisable in traffic lanes, where inattentive walking can result in accidents. Each rug type contributes its own effect, and the texture can make all the difference to the mood just as much as the coloring or design. These and other basic points are brought out in the examples which follow.

To clarify understanding of the subject it should perhaps be stated that the term "rug" refers to any fabric floor covering woven as a unit, usually less than room size and with or without a fringe. A carpet, on the other hand, is considered to be a section of loomed carpeting cut to fit an area or a complete room, not necessarily wall-to-wall, without regard to pattern, and obviously with no border.

In the first picture of this series (330), the interior is floored with parquet from a French chateau. In the absence of bulky pieces of furniture such as the usually heavily upholstered sofas and armchairs, massive cabinets or tall secretaries, etcetera, which would have hidden much of the prized tapestries and pictures, it was decided to decorate the floor center with the large rug shown. This is a copy of a Savonnerie dating from 1790, woven especially for this room at the Royal Tapestry Factory in Madrid. The colors are blues and yellows on white, and, with its paneled centers and borders, the floor needs no other decoration. Furthermore, the Louis Seize painted pieces look just as much at home with this rug as they do

330.

real focal point to attract attention beyond a general casual appraisal. In this instance the floor is of antique parquet and the wall furniture needs nothing more to add to its richness. On the other hand, the dining table and chairs should obviously not be left to float aimlessly in the middle of the floor as five independent units.

As can be seen in the photograph, a circular rug of a quality equal to that of the furniture can be the life-raft that saves the situation. It not only ties the pieces together but makes a seat at table more comfortable under foot, while hiding very little of the floor itself. In this way a collection of pieces becomes a gracious grouping, especially if the rug has some color association with either draperies or upholstery fabrics so that in turn it becomes a part of the total décor.

The same principle could be applied to a pseudo-Early American room where the rug can be of the braided type just large enough to accommodate the table and chairs, as in 332. Normally, the rest of the floor would be bare to show the primitive planking, as suggested here. The dining group, however, could be farther away from the fireplace, leaving room for a handsome country-style hearthrug in compatible colors, one little added amenity that can provide a touch of cosy comfort on a cold winter's eve.

Such rugs, and such rooms, are of course special cases — two ends of the spectrum. Most rooms have ordinary flooring, however smooth and polished, that calls for something thick, soft, and resilient, of a suitable overall color, as in 333, where a luscious golden carpet ties in with the mottled gold of the little dining room's walls and the yellow paint of the kitchen. The varied blues of the settle and chair cushions, door trim, and china, are perfect as accents, the gold setting off the rich, honey-colored mahogany of the furniture. The carpet, it will be noticed, defines the limits of the dining area, the floor imitating the faded tones of the table.

Fitted nylon, loop-piled carpet with the appearance of a colorful nubby tweed, as in 334, is often specific for hard wear and cleanability in rooms that are both busy and informal. In this games room it also represents the largest single area of color, a mixture of bright orange, soft brown, gold, rust, and white, that sets the overall tone, investing the interior with a warm

331.

with the splendid mantel mirror from Versailles where its mate still resides.

Turning to the other extreme, even a small rug can, on occasion, be an important part of a grouping, particularly in cases like 331, where the floor is an especially beautiful one of its type and so much of it is exposed that it has no

332.

302

glow. Red-related colors were used elsewhere in the room, covering the long window with a translucent fabric, shadow-striped in yellow, gold, and orange — colors repeated in the stained glass panels of the sky-light — which gives the room an autumnal glow when the sun is high.

The most intense color was reserved for the two sofas covered in orange, accented with red thread, which is reinforced by the ruby-red velvet of the antique wing chair. In this setting the rugged Spanish furniture and the brass English Regency table and accessories combine to emphasize a brilliant example of the eclectic style.

Another setting, shown in illustration 335, which represents a modern living room, is arranged around a wall-to-wall nylon rug in a bright emerald green which extends into a stepped bay arranged for plantings, and forming the upholstery of built-in benches both sides of the fireplace.

An interesting feature is the legless chair in brilliant gold nylon. The sofa and two armchairs are covered in off-white nylon tweed, and the draperies, white and semi-sheer in a willow-leaf pattern, are of dacron. In spite of the old Spanish iron-bound coffer serving as an end table between the armchairs, the whole room has an air of bold and bright sophistication, augmented by wall sculptures in paper and gold and a pair of molded platypuses on the hearth.

The value of the overall carpeting here is that it unifies the principal area with the bay and the hearth. This not only makes the room seem much larger, but ties together the scattered elements, adding to its air of comfortable attractiveness, despite the bright color which the brown wood tones of the walls and the tones of white contrast with so rewardingly.

Even a converted sun porch (336), adapted for year-round living, can absorb its quota of intense color as represented by a small square of brilliant blue nylon carpeting. The room itself is white-tiled for coolness, and the carpet adds texture, color, and walking comfort (along with sound deadening) without diminishing that effect. A certain warmth is added by the long, pleated dacron curtains which are vividly striped to warm the daylight. An unusual feature is that these can be drawn

333.

out of sight behind plywood panels to expose the whole of the tall casement windows. The choice of blue for the carpet is especially felicitous in view of the tropical atmosphere created by the oriental reed furniture and its warm tones with which the blue is quite compatible.

The adaptability to almost any style of furnishing, modern or traditional, is a feature of most oriental rugs. As a rule those with a geometrical pattern go best with

334.

304

335.

336.

337.

338. In floor coverings, design is often as important as a pattern or color, and there is something stately about a carved rug in light beige with end fringes whose design suggests that it would look its lovely best on a polished parquet floor of dark woods.

339. Almost any formal room would welcome a black and gold rug such as this modern reproduction of a Savonnerie design which looks like an antique. It was given its appearance of age by the use of a special antiqued yarn and should withstand a century of use.

340. A modern multilevel rug of this type has a universal appeal because of its intriguing pattern which makes it suitable for almost any room, period or modern, whether in the diminutive size shown or as overall carpeting. With the proper choice of colors it can be made to dominate a room or subdued to a point where it serves as an agreeable background for the liveliest of decorating schemes.

308

341. This custom-designed rug in orange, red, blue, and green on a white ground would be perfect with an interior having an oriental flavor. It would also serve as a keynote to a brilliant modern room design.

342. The Point de Lys rug is eminently suited to a period bedroom with a feminine air such as this, or any other interior that would welcome a floor covering in the Aubusson style.

modern interiors to which they introduce color and motion without quarreling with starkness of detail, outline, or background, as in 337. Almost in the same category are the monochrome wool rugs whether the pattern is sculptured or clipped, so that in many instances choice is simplified by its reduction to a mere matter of color — and class — an observation that applies to other forms of floor coverings as well.

Lighting the Interiors

Artificial lighting is one of the most important factors in successful interior design because it affects the appearance of everything in the room. Too much light, too little, the wrong kind or a badly placed source can not only spoil the effect of a well thought-out décor designed only by daylight, but make the room unpleasant to have to endure.

Too much light is often worse than too little, and lighting every part of each wall equally tends to suppress the third dimension — to flatten things out. Likewise, a room with too much shadow can be quickly fatiguing to the eye. Unluckily there is no rule of thumb method of determining which of these things prevails; conditions change not only with the furnishing but also with the activity to which a room is devoted at the moment. Lively affairs with many people usually call for a higher light intensity than the same room used for quiet family diversions, so that the same interior may demand some method of controlling this.

The first requirement, then, is not only for the proper total amount of light but also for its correct distribution so that an approximation of natural daylight is secured, without the slightest glare or unpleasant reflection. In arranging for these things the reflective qualities of the various sections of the walls need to be taken into account. Furthermore, the light source must be localized, as it is when it comes through the windows, so that

variations in intensity add to interest. There must be sufficient total light to make all things clear, but the sources must not be equally distributed or there will be no gradations of light and shadow to emphasize the shapes of objects. Another point that needs to be remembered is that beautiful lighting fixtures, including the movable variety, should themselves be visible when in use so that they can contribute their share of charm and interest just as they do in the daylight.

Normally most rooms not carefully planned in these respects call for a lesser quantity but better quality of illumination, not far removed from a pleasant degree of sunlight. It is also desirable that the quality of the light be such that the color values of the elements of the interior are not distorted, and contrasts are maintained. With ordinary incandescent lamps there is always some apparent change in the colors, an effect that may be either worsened or improved by changes induced through the use of a colored shade or globe, or by reflection from some other colored surface. Fluorescent lamps normally will not improve matters because the so-called white light is likely to contain an excessive amount of blue, while incandescents lean toward the red end of the spectrum. This suggests that a combination of the two might yield satisfactory results (one cancelling out the other), but the problem then is not only to attain the correct balance but to devise some means of incorporat-

344. Still popular in private houses today are the smaller period-style chandeliers such as this, made of bronze and crystal. This particular design is adapted from a Spanish piece of the Charles IV type made sometime between 1788 and 1808.

343. An exquisite living room setting, its crystal chandelier with emerald drops complementing the delicately beautiful printed floral wall panels whose colors are picked up by the furniture upholstery and cushions and the mottled rug in this eclectically styled interior. General lighting is augmented by large-size wall fixtures, with table candles for reading, and interior lighting for the cabinet displays.

345. Other popular period-style chandeliers are those of the Georgian era in gleaming antique brass, the body and bobêches faceted to add to the reflective surfaces. Even the arms are of diamond section. Such a fixture is appropriate for the more formal rooms furnished in the Queen Anne, Chippendale, or Sheraton styles.

346. A contemporary chandelier of this type does its work by providing ample light to the dining table from eight shaded candle-type lamps open top and bottom and supplying reflected light from the ceiling for general illumination. The chandelier itself constitutes a decorative feature whose antiqued wood body ties it in with the old-time furniture. Its shades are in cherry-red silk shantung, its arms a satin black contrasting with polished brass to give it a sense of countrified luxury.

347. Modern chandeliers in black iron with gold details are eminently suitable for use with country-style interiors showing a Mediterranean influence, whether Spanish, French, or Italian, as well as with indoor metal furniture.

348. Some current designs of chandeliers for use in rustic interiors capture the nineteenth-century flavor as the above example shows. The tinted globes with the look of brandy inhalers are particularly effective while arms finished to look like wrought iron with brass collars and finial are quite at home with the shapely wooden turnings.

ing both types of lamps in one fixture. Fortunately this is no longer necessary since there is commercially available a system employing two fluorescent tubes to secure the same effect.

In this system, called Vi-Plex, the lamps are used in pairs, one member of which gives off light predominantly from the blue end of the spectrum, the other from the red end. These rays mix to produce a light that is almost pure white so that it has comparatively little effect on the colors of fabrics, oil paintings, and other surfaces. It really constitutes a "standard" light that can be used for color comparisons, instead of the less accurate daylight which changes in quality according to the time of day, the season, and the weather. The only practical objection to such lighting is that the fixtures must be designed to accommodate fluorescent tubes or rings in pairs or multiples thereof, resulting in a lamp somewhat bulky for home use. Meanwhile the general practice is to use concealed, color-matching fluorescent lamps for general lighting, and incandescents for local illumination.

Apart from the question of color, the illuminating device should provide soft, diffused light, either by reflecting it from the ceiling or similar surface above the line of sight, or enclosing it in a translucent globe or shade or using frosted bulbs. In the employment of table or floor lamps as an aid to even distribution, the proportion of light reflected down to that projected upward is of considerable significance. It will depend largely on the reflective qualities of the walls, ceiling, and furnishings, and also the provisions made for background lighting or general level of illumination throughout the interior. Whether ceiling, wall, floor, or table lighting devices are used, and in what proportions, will of course depend upon the particular circumstances and style of interior.

Bright lighting may be necessary in rooms that are being used for large gatherings, otherwise it is psychologically bad. Private rooms, such as bedrooms, boudoirs, or dens, too, are usually the most pleasing with soft lights from a number of sources. In dining rooms the reverse is ordinarily the case, with a principal light over the table, except for banquets where the table lights consist of adequate candelabra properly placed, and the serving areas are illuminated from the walls.

The drawing room ordinarily will call for distributed group lighting among various conversation centers, and in all instances lighting dimmers can be an advantage, permitting variations of light intensity to meet the conditions of the moment, which will vary with the time of day as well as the weather.

Despite their importance, all these things are of course generalizations, the principal point being that illumination needs as careful a study as any other factor in interior design, and that the lighting fixtures themselves can be an important part of any décor, and actually need to be styled and placed according to the type of interior and the mood to be established. Insofar as the general illumination is concerned, these factors will be governed by the reflectance of the walls, floors, and ceiling, and the furniture finish.

As for the color of the light, where that of the incandescent lamp is too cold it is sometimes possible to use amber globes or lamps of low intensity reminiscent of the old carbon-filament type. Ordinary fluorescent lamps are often unusable because of the stark quality of the light, though this can vary considerably. Hidden behind cornices they can provide an acceptable diffused glow whose color is softened through the use of tinted glass or copper reflectors, perhaps combined with a slight coloring of the nearby ceiling.

Another pertinent factor in lighting is the use of illuminated display cabinets which add to the total room lighting. Different kinds of displays, however, call for different arrangements of fixtures and colors of lights, their tone, and intensity. Where flat porcelains are concerned, a fairly even lighting all over their surfaces may best suffice to illuminate the pattern, but for statuary pieces and other three-dimensional objects slanting light rays will usually be required to accent their form.

Types of Fixtures

Nowadays chandeliers are considered more ornamental than practical, and therefore need to be emphasized as decorative features in themselves — the emphasis being supplied by their own light which obviously must be glare-free. A chandelier of the carved and gilded type often can be equipped with candle shades, using

349. In contemporary designs the modern look may be combined with antique iron for informal interiors ranging all the way from Mediterranean to Early American where a rugged masculine character is essential, as in this multi-tiered spidery candle cluster with its intriguing silhouette.

350. Wall and ceiling lighting fixtures can be more important as decorative features than as sources of general illumination though multiple candles, well separated, contribute a pleasantly diffused glow. In this view the table lamps are the principal sources of light for reading and other activities in a living-room fireside grouping.

351. Present-day styles of hanging lanterns are as decorative — and romantic — as ever, whether fitted with translucent light-diffusing panels or clear glass for area lighting. Available in a wide variety of shapes and sizes they still can be used in traditional, contemporary, or eclectic halls, though their use has been extended to bedrooms and other odd locations either singly or in pairs, and sometimes in clusters, a development arising out of the latter day dictum that hall lanterns which have become collectors' items can be displayed anywhere — including the bathroom!

352. In locations where the chandelier is too large or too fussy, an excellent substitute is the pendant fixture with three "candles" under a single opaque shade. Finished in antique brass, with iron scrolls and a fruitwood spindle it should be quite compatible with the highly-finished modern version of early American, as the picture suggests, and actually would not look amiss in certain Victorian and even contemporary surroundings.

317

353. A single bedside lighting fixture can be confined to a droplight over the side table as shown, another one of a somewhat Moorish pattern hanging over the covered table to the right where the easy chair offers comfort to the insomniac.

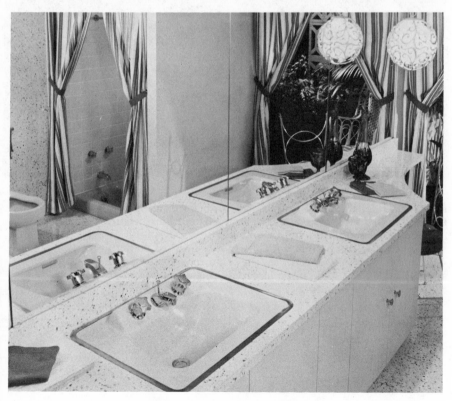

354. Even in a bathroom the lighting can be distinctive, as the filigree globe-style hanging fixture, reflected in the mirror, suggests. A second one at the opposite end of the lavatory counter is not visible though contributing its quota of illumination.

355, 356, 357. Torchères and sconces are brothers under the skin, both are attached to the wall and either may be used singly or in pairs. As with all lighting devices their suitability to any décor depends upon their design. Historically the torchère is the older, and is undoubtedly the more pretentious. The black-iron three-light sconce also is highly decorative with its gold accents and sweeping curves. Since it is not electrified it is most suited to public rooms where the candles will be lit only on formal occasions, as is the twin two-light pair handcrafted in wood in the Baroque style and finished in gold leaf.

bright bulbs to make up for any light loss through diffusion. Some crystal chandeliers have small light bulbs hidden around the stem so that the prisms and drops seem to glow apart from any light they reflect from the small-bulb electric candles. In other instances high-intensity lights can be used so long as they are rendered glare-free by frosting the candle-shaped bulb.

An important development in the field of overhead lighting is the modern practice of using hanging lanterns in rooms other than halls and foyers. These sometimes can be substituted for chandeliers where the latter would represent over-emphasis on elegance. This practice, apparently launched by collectors of antique types who wished to give them due display, has led to the production of period and modern designs for use in any room.

To the interior designer, next in importance are the wall fixtures or sconces and torchères which, for obvious reasons, cannot be expected to provide much illumination, even for local purposes. As a rule they need to be at least seven feet above the floor, and if they are spaced far apart the illumination will be too localized both on the wall and on nearby furniture. Care also needs to be taken in the selection of a background, avoiding strongly patterned wall coverings. Painted panels in light colors are usually the most satisfactory.

Floor lamps are often a necessity in providing good reading light, the more recent type eliminating the shade in favor of a translucent globe shaped to conform to the overall design. These however do not provide a downward directional beam and therefore are more useful in contributing to the general room lighting. Of perpetual interest, on the other hand, are the table lamps which can either diffuse light by the use of translucent shades, or make it wholly directional with opaque ones, often with the cooperation of interior reflectors that project all of the light downward. The principal parts of such a lamp, from the decorating standpoint, are firstly the base which can be anything from a fire-hose nozzle to a Ming vase, and, secondly, the shade which may or may not contribute a colorful surface or pattern either lighted or dark, but usually offers something in the way of texture. The overall designs are limited only by the imagination, and cater to every period or style.

Though table lamps have the advantage of being

358. One of the loveliest of table lamps ever designed is the French bouillotte style with its deep hollow base and adjustable shade height to suit the burning candles of which it may have possessed but two instead of the three in this example. For the writing desk it cannot be excelled, neither can its decorative value.

320

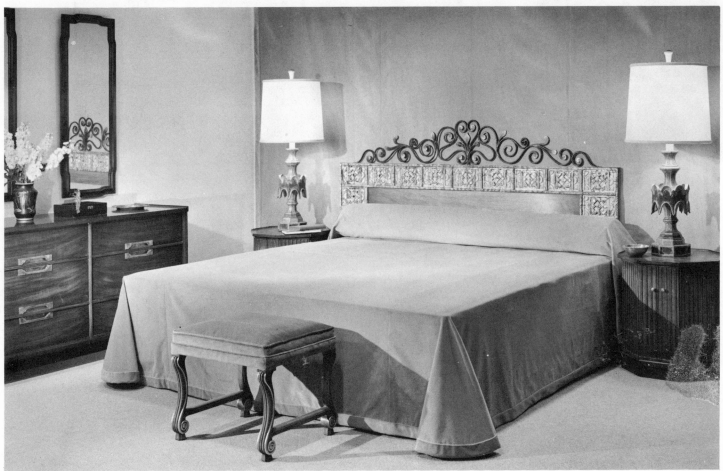

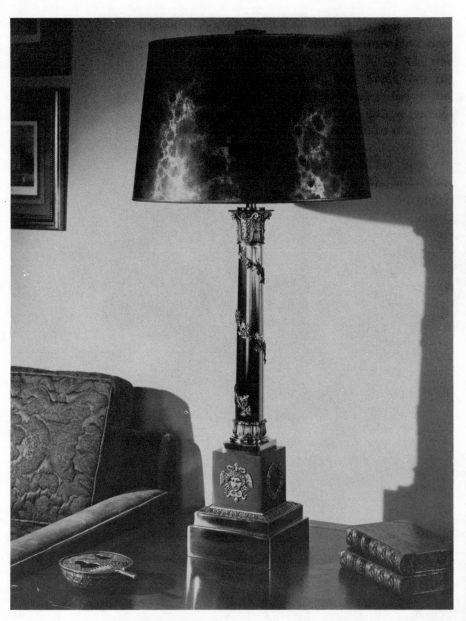

361, 362. Modern types of table lamps are available in endless variety suited to use with interiors of any period. The two shown here are variations of the same type. Though that on the left is in bronze and antique ormolu, the other has a pottery base with four slender shafts of antique brass, both have shades of gold tortoise shell over opaque parchment, and are fitted with reflector bowls to increase the light intensity below the shades. And both are full of old-world charm.

322

363, 364. Two more table lamps of equal beauty but worlds apart in design, even though both shades are white and translucent. The first of these is a chastely elegant lamp with a base of white Lenox china enhanced by antiqued soft brass, and perfectly suited to the rich Victorian interior with which it is shown. The design of the wood-based lamp, shown in a Swedish-modern setting, was actually inspired by Eastern architecture half a world away. The wood is ash rubbed with white and given a distressed finish, with applied accents in antiqued brass, all of which is perfectly attuned to the pale gold of the wall behind it.

323

movable, this is not always a necessity in which case lamps suspended from the ceiling by their own cords may be more convenient as well as eliminating trailing wires. For one thing they can be made adjustable to any height over a table — down to within a few inches of the top if desired — without interfering with a use of that surface, and constitute an important part of the décor whether lighted or not.

Since many rooms are illuminated solely by table or floor lamps or combinations thereof, there will usually be an aggregate of at least four to a room so that their influence on the décor cannot be ignored and is worthy of intensive study.

365. Table lamps rarely moved may sometimes be replaced to advantage with this type, suspended by its cord, which is adjustable as to height above the surface and eliminates trailing wires.

324

Fireplace and Mantel

However small, however plain, the fireplace as it has been known for centuries, is always an important center of interest in any room, and since its location is fixed — usually on an axis of the room — it forms a natural center around which the decorating can be planned. Actually it is an architectural feature, but also a part of the furnishing and few schemes that ignore it can be wholly successful.

In rooms that have no fireplace it is common practice to install a porcelain or faience stove, or a Dutch black and brass one large enough to be impressive. This is good practice if there is a flue available with which to connect it, otherwise there is an element of absurdity in using it for display only. The ordinary fireplace, on the other hand, whether used or not, is part of the structure, and as a strong vertical element in a room constitutes a focal center, and is therefore as important to the decorator today as it was centuries ago. Furthermore it is actually the only domestic heating device which can be fully exploited, all such equipment as radiators, air ducts and grilles being concealed or disguised as much as possible, entirely for aesthetic reasons.

In devising a decorative scheme based on these fireplaces, it is usually necessary to take note of the style and period of the mantel and overmantel sections as well as their architectural character, even in the case of the most modern interiors which may exploit them as nostalgic curiosities. The austere, massive structures of earlier days, so often copied in country dwellings, normally call for uneven plaster walls and rugged timbers. With their stones smoothed a little, and perhaps adorned with elementary carving, they may assume a more formal and imposing air, though far from sophisticated, and so on up to the definitely classical, with their monumental mirrors, allegorical carvings, and paintings and pediments.

One important characteristic of all such fireplaces is that they can be applied to curving walls which do not invite either the hanging of pictures or the attachment of built-in bookcases or cupboards. Another useful feature is that they can be made either an important feature of the total décor, or their significance reduced to any degree desired, as will be observed in studying the basic features of types most commonly used since French Renaissance times to the present. This basic unit is, of course, the simple mantel surrounding the fireplace opening (which so many modern fireplaces do without!). Its decorative qualities normally can be increased or reduced by the addition or subtraction of other components such as a mantel shelf and overmantel, the treatment of the opening which may have a narrow slate surround, or one of the colorful tiles, while the outer hearth may consist of a rough granite slab or one of polished marble, perhaps inlaid with stone of another color.

From these developed, in modern times, the plain

325

366.

square fireplace opening in a flat curtain wall, often of bare brick or stone, perhaps whitened or colored but entirely unadorned, brazen in their simplicity. A contemporaneous development was the semi-circular brick arch, the thin voussoirs their only decoration in the background of a plastered wall. Then, with the partitionless interiors, the back-to-back hearths, open front and rear, the remants of a torn-out wall — a ready-made solution of the problem of designing a central fireplace, or the open one with its suspended, funnel-shaped flue, which took advantage of the elimination of the room axis, itself often dictating the architecture and grouping of spaces around it. In any case, the fireplace remained the center of living while its constructional features and materials dictated the total atmosphere and the theme of the furnishing, as it does to this day, though the principles of eclectic furnishing are rapidly narrowing the gap between the modern, the contemporary and the period styles.

The development of the fireplace through the various furnishing periods since the 1600's can best be grasped by examining some of those that have survived the centuries and are used today, perhaps in a modified form.

The earliest of these, insofar as this inquiry is concerned, would be the French Renaissance stone mantel (366) which is beautifully carved in a somewhat primitive manner as would befit the sixteenth century, and not without a sense of humor revealed in the anguished heads trapped between the columns and the entablature. This mantel is not quite so large as it may seem, being but five feet wide, and probably accommodated a stone surround or facing, reducing the opening somewhat, incidentally initiating a practice that became extremely useful in saving the old structures as the succeeding periods called for even smaller hearths.

In the Louis XIV period (1643-1715), the marble mantel (367), supported by caryatids, and carved with horns of plenty flanking the Roman Bacchus and his grapes, apparently was popular in mid-seventeenth-century France, though probably retaining a carved marble overmantel of equal height, and possibly colored. This it may have lost in the late seventeenth century when pictures and mirrors in this position presaged a change in the mantel itself. At any rate, such a mantel today would prove an exquisite addition to a period or even eclectic interior with a certain amount of dignity and free of curvilinear furniture. Even some geometric modern pieces would not look amiss in its company.

Shown in a present-day interior, the small modern adaptation of a Spanish mantelpiece (illustration 368), contributes an air of dignified solidity, plain but graceful in its curving pillars, square panels, and beautifully proportioned cyma-recta molding of the mantel shelf. This is particularly suited to a room with a cathedral-type ceiling with heavy black beams, and the quietly beautiful European style furniture which displays plenty of wood and a touch of iron. One can imagine it in a masculine den.

A far cry from any of the foregoing is the Louis XV fireplace mantel of 369, with its sweeping curves and deep carving, its paneling and reeded fluting, its Granite-Belge black-marble facing, and its front hearth. This is an early example of a type that was to become more refined and lovely as time went on; the details smoother, and a flat shelf prepared for the tall pier glass that would carry it up to the ceiling.

This was not the first break with the flat-topped opening of the Louis XIV style. A little earlier this had been foreshadowed by another Louis XIV mantel with scrolled ends turned sideways under the shelf, the ends of the opening rounded into the pillars. Its round-topped mirror was built into the chimney breast, facing another mirror in the opposite wall to create added perspective.

In this Louis XV-type mantel the outer edges of the posts were rounded slightly to reduce the apparent projection from the wall. In later ones, such as 370, this angle was increased, usually separating the pillars from the inner molding by a deep V-shaped groove. This made the posts heavily three-dimensional so that the scrolling was complete on both sides, together with the separate carving above it. The sweeping curves of the mantel apron were now even more pronounced, making room for a larger central motif, requiring the shelf to be bowed out at the center to form a protective cap.

Mantels such as this were well suited to the Louis Quinze furniture style with its elegant curves, its painted and gilded details, and today they endow a room with a delicately gracious (though slightly feminine) air to

367.

368.

369.

371.

370.

372.

which a variety of less-rigid furniture styles — some Chippendale and painted French Queen Anne, and rococo Italian, and certain chinoiseries — are well suited.

During this same period, the country carpenter was busy making these mantels of wood, reducing the carving to gouge grooving except for a simple central decoration, as in 371, done in relief by cutting away the background in a heart-shaped central plaque. Such a mantel is ideally suited to French provincial furniture that is not too highly finished, and for rooms with rustic pieces, plank walls, random stonework, or a rough plaster surface. Preferably there should be a paneled overmantel or an old-time painting in place of a mirror. Nothing here should appear fragile.

This style came to a sudden end with the Louis XVI heavy, rigid, straight-lined mantels (372), though many were elaborately carved with fruits, flowers and masks. Others, all in the same colorful marbles, were scroll-bracketed, the single carved ornamentation being a row of rosettes or medallions, or guilloche band along the architraves. Some of the more formal of these mantels betrayed their origin by using the same quatrefoil ornament above the stiles as that appearing on the Renaissance designs 200 years before (see 366). These mantels, obviously, have a more formal air, suggesting straight-legged furniture, including modern, and some American Empire, and English Regency pieces.

Of a somewhat similar geometric style is 373, an English pattern mantel in white marble with green inlays and front hearth panels. The tooled decoration is confined to fluting of both the pilasters and architraves, and the carving to three oval medallions with nicely detailed draped figures. The whole thing has a classical air which suits it to a drawing room or formal master-bedroom, or perhaps some Federal interior by McIntire or Seymour, and early Phyfe pieces, or even the modified classicism of English Sheraton.

Another English mantel, this time an eared type of hard pine, with composition carvings in great detail, is 374. The molding around the T-shaped opening is carved in a rococo pattern, the central unit a ribbon-bound bolster of oak leaves and acorns, with dentils and egg-and-dart molding, plus a finely detailed cornice. This exposes a lintel which seems to overhang the stiles at each end.

373.

374.

375.

Such a type of mantel, either plain or painted, should be compatible with a Greek Revival interior, thanks to its architectural character and classical decoration, as well as the many styles far removed, including a number of Victorian types, baroque and otherwise, though it actually belongs to the early Georgian period.

In illustration 375 is shown another carved pine mantel of a far different type which has all the earmarks of an Adam design though somewhat more elaborate than usual with the flanking scrolls. Here are the familiar urns and the bell husks, but the rest is reminiscent of French taste to which Robert Adam catered after he had acquired from the Swiss, Liardet, the formula for the composition from which the ornaments were molded.

Thousands of molds were made of English and French designs between 1770 and 1790, during which time Josiah Wedgwood was creating jasper-ware plaques and medallions for use on the same fireplace mantels. Both firms are reproducing these decorative units today so that the Adam mantels are still available. Those shown here are of recent production. The first of these (376), is called "Dancing Hours," the second (377), "The Judgment of Hercules," from the themes of the central plaques.

The two designs illustrated are totally different in detail (though the coal grates are the same). That illustrated in 378 incorporates small portrait medallions

376. Detail of Wedgwood plaque: "Dancing Hours."
Modeled in 1775 by John Flaxman, R.A.

330

377. **Detail of Wedgwood plaque: "The Judgment of Hercules"** — choosing between a life of pleasure or of fame. Modeled in 1773 by William Hackwood, Wedgwood's chief modeler, 1769-1832.

of Lord Nelson and King Charles XII of Sweden in the pilasters. In the other mantelpiece (379), these pilasters are simply fluted. Both patterns are used with a wide variety of furniture styles, and the plaques are produced with a choice of two ground colors — pale Wedgwood blue, and sage green.

Some of the mantels designed and carved by Samuel McIntire (1757-1811) are similar in general style to those of Robert Adam made between 1782 and 1792. Illustration 380 is a representative example, and a rather popular one, made of whitewood with composition ornaments. This might also be compared with 381, which has the same deep marble surround without the Adam inside metal trim.

The somewhat smaller wooden mantel of 382 relies for its interest both on its proportions and the delicate quality of the facing tiles which are quite large, with a multicolored design on white. This style is particularly suited for small personal rooms such as bedrooms or dens, and old-fashioned ones in particular.

Some of the large eighteenth-century New England mansions furnished in the Queen Anne and Chippendale styles were partial to well-developed architectural features including wide fireplaces and tall mantels, usually with shallow but heavily molded shelves, scaled to make the most of the decorated overmantels which carry the eye up to the massive cornices. Two mantels of this type in the Governor Langdon House at Portsmouth, New

378.

331

379.

381.

380.

Hampshire, are worthy of study. The first one (383), apart from its great projection, is more formal than the second because of the greater restraint of its decoration. The overmantel is framed in a Greek key border, and is flanked by entirely separate leafy pendants. The swags and clusters below the shelf are likewise independent of the decorative pilasters. In the smaller room (384), the overmantel border features an irregular procession of leaves that escape from confinement at each end and riot over the background surface. The same thing happens on the mantelpiece where the whole space around the fireplace molding is filled with a tortuous writhing procession of leafy vines reaching down to the baseboards — all in keeping with the naturalistic scenic panels that fill the walls in place of the graceful wallpaper pattern of the other room. The plan, of course, is deliberate, and fulfills its purpose in establishing a proper background for the respective furnishings.

In the small country house of this period, the local carpenter was usually called upon to design the mantel,

382.

333

383.

384.

385.

386.

387.

388.

often adapting ideas encountered elsewhere. Such appears to be the history of 385, which is actually quite successful, and an improvement on some of the same basic design. The turned pillars and their moldings are nicely proportioned, as are the four panels and the stacked ogee moldings that are topped by elementary chisel carving simulating a row of gentle swags beneath cornice and shelf. Such a mantel would grace any Early American interior, and today would be a charming conversation piece in almost any unpretentious room dating from 1830 on.

This ushers in the mid-Victorian days when castiron fire grates with arched marble mantels were all the rage. But a white mantel such as 386, with its beautiful, romantic design and high-relief carving was not for everyone. This is an exceptional piece belonging to the romantic Burne-Jones era. Any present-day interior designer would carry it off with enthusiasm, even if only to house a Franklin stove.

A much older fireplace (387), serves to illustrate this point. The mantelpiece itself dates from 1840 and may have originated in Tennessee where it now is, or New Orleans where its first owner lived, though the design has been observed in Greek Revival homes as far afield

389.

hearth, but the chimney breast was left a smooth white undecorated expanse.

This is a small room, but the ceiling, as can be seen, is exquisitely decorated with a huge stucco medallion having a strapwork border plus a raised ring decorated with floral swags and cluster. From its center hangs a splendid crystal chandelier — all in tremendous contrast with the flat white expanse between mantel and high ceiling. To tie ceiling and mantel together, and break this uncomfortable hiatus, the artist-wife of the owner had the stucco wreath applied to its center, where it seems held by a stucco replica of her own hand. The effect was magical, and the stark whiteness of the surfaces came to life while the central space acquired character and interest.

Two types of modern fireplaces that lend themselves to eclectic furnishing remain to be discussed. The first of these (388), is a roughly plastered white wall whose bareness gives tremendous impact to a ceiling-high panel that houses the modern hearth, raised to provide wood storage as well as increase the effectiveness of the heat radiation. Vertical posts cover the brick side walls of the fireplace, and help support the metal lintel. Above this the flat wood panel, painted a vividly contrasting color, is decorated with three vertical columns formed of square, carved wooden blocks, tinted copper to provide colorful accents.

Equally modern but far from similar is example 389, which carries out a comparable idea with a fireplace wall covered in white enamel squares. Certain of these "tiles," bearing a sunray design in gold and black, are arranged to form the desired pattern. The result is a bright and cosy corner whether the fire is lit or not, a perfect background for the bright vermillion, geranium pink, and mustard yellow of the rich upholstery fabrics, vivid draperies, and textured area rugs that form a setting with a Moorish air for the snow-white red and gold flecked sofa, scarlet armchair, and the small tables whose tops repeat the wall design. Both background and foreground offer opportunities for the introduction of antique items as accents, preferably Spanish or Eastern, perhaps with a more convincing moucharabieh screen.

as New England. Its chief merit is that though of white-painted wood, it is so chaste in design, so simple yet so lovely. Its sweeping curves were copied in the window architraves, and it was given a white-marble front

338

Antiques, Reproductions
and Modern Furniture

Roots of the Eclectic Style

Eclecticism or the mixing of styles in furnishing, as pointed out earlier, is based upon compatibilty or otherwise between certain units of various furniture periods, and a great deal of effort has been expended over the years in attempts to classify the mutual features that determine whether one piece is likely to look well alongside certain others or not. In other words, experts have sought to reduce to a formula the characteristics that make for mutual compatibility by analyzing each design to see if there are not certain aspects common to both that would ensure one augmenting the other. Quite often, in making these comparisons chairs are used as examples in analyzing the styles because of their limited basic elements — legs, seat, back — and their comparative simplicity. Normally they are quite sufficient because they can be used to illustrate the principal characteristics by which all furniture pieces from stools to wardrobes can be compared in such attributes as outline (geometrical, curved, or complex), posture (rigid or resilient), character (ponderous or mobile in appearance), and scale as applied to two or more pieces of the same general form. In practice, however, these bases of judgment are not wholly sufficient because of the differences due to the variation in degree to which the criteria can apply. For example, some curves are exaggerated, some restrained, and certain stiff and sturdy pieces have flowing lines, which work to counteract that impression, while other designs may incorporate equally contradictory elements, so that it is practically impossible to decide whether a certain design must be considered as expressing (for example) dynamic energy or mere static strength. This can perhaps best be understood by examining a few pieces of different period styles, in an effort to appraise the underlying bases of compatibility or otherwise, that they suggest.

Beginning with furniture made in this country, photographs 390, 391, and 392 show the sturdy, standpat look of a Philadelphia Queen Anne style armchair and a Chippendale side chair which have much in common, compared with the prancing sinuosities of a Belter piece whose primary function seems to be to look pretty at all costs. In like manner, the restrained curves of the windsor-type chair (393), with its gentle flowing back and seat contours and swelling spindles, are the equal of those of the highly decorated Hitchcock type (394), yet visually the two have little in common except that both are suited to country kitchens and plank-tabled dining rooms, though the windsor would also have a certain

390. Queen Anne

391. Chippendale

340

392. Belter

393. Windsor

394. Hitchcock

395. Hepplewhite

342

396. Sheraton

affinity for a modern interior thanks to its purity and simplicity of line and truly functional design.

Another interesting comparison is implicit in 395 and 396, the Hepplewhite chair having the solidity of a straight-legged Chippendale chair, the beautiful curves of its shield-back belying the heavy rigidity of the uncompromising slip-cushioned seat and squared stretchers. Though the Sheraton piece is lighter and has more detail in its back, it has the same innate stiffness and formality, suggestive of Adam, lessened somewhat by the slender reeded and carved front legs, and the fact that the seat frame is hidden by the upholstery fabric. On the whole it displays a certain femininity compared with the masculine air of its more rugged companion.

Much more in keeping with the latter is 397, a Phyfe creation reminiscent of certain late Sheraton designs, with a carved crest rail and fluted legs, and possessing the same dainty air to which the silk seat fabric adds so much.

Of the same period, though far different in style, is 398, the more deliberately Empire side chair with its saber legs, sweeping, curved back, and elaborate carving. This is a pleasantly genteel piece which should be compared with 399, made about five years later, with all its painting and gilded ornament and hairy paws, a far lesser work of art and craftsmanship, so that used alongside the other it would appear somewhat contrived.

The American taste for French furniture is reflected in 400, which is a typical Louis XVI chair made in Philadelphia in 1790. It should be compared with another fauteuil of the same period pictured in 409.

All of the foregoing pieces were made here between 1750 and 1850, some of them sufficiently like their English prototypes to be considered the same period style. Two English chairs of rather radical design that occasionally inspired copyists this side the Atlantic in the late eighteenth and early nineteenth centuries are shown in 401 and 402.

The first of these is an Adam design which has a look of a transitional Louis XV–XVI piece with some important differences, including the straight, square and heavy legs (the rear ones set at an angle), with an oval back, and a long downward sweep of the arms. The sturdiness of construction, the curves of seat, back, and

397. Phyfe

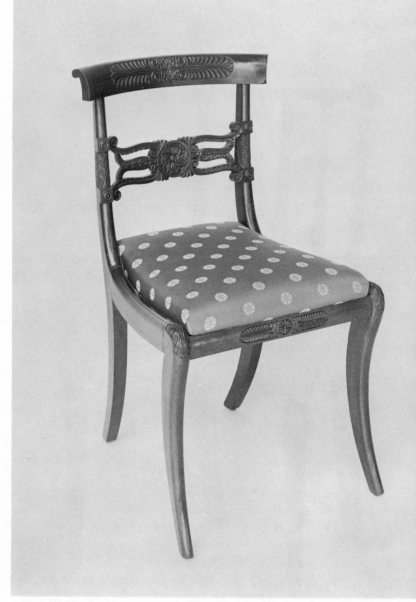

398. Empire, early

344

399. Empire, late

400. Louis XVI

401. Adam

346

402. Regency

arms, plus the turned and carved feet betray its kinship with both the curvaceous and stolid types. The other chair is an elaborate English piece produced during the Regency period when our relations with the Old Country were not such as to encourage the import of frivolities. Nevertheless the trend left its mark upon both the American and Second French Empire designs which added Greek to Egyptian motifs. These impressive monumental structures are best used as desk chairs (because they need to be moved about very little), even at the risk of hiding their most decorative features. One such chair would be sufficient to establish a focal point in any room.

French prototypes of this latter chair include one dating around 1805 which has a pleasantly sloping back adding to its comfort (403). This is painted and gilded with sturdy tapered and fluted front legs and curved rear ones set at an angle to the front ones into the rounded back, its principal decoration a pair of swans, carved in the round, which formed the arms. This same theme was revived during the Second Empire period under Napoleon III in the somewhat clumsy pattern of 404, which had a higher but no more comfortable back, its flowing lines offset by its massive construction. This however was the decadent Victorian period, when, even in France, the smaller and less pretentious pieces were likely to exhibit finer qualities of design. The Restoration (or Charles X) side chair in illustration 405 is an example of this, neat and workmanlike and no doubt a close relative of the Seignouret chairs made in New Orleans (despite difference in backs), a neat and practical design that calls for no-nonsense types of furniture to accompany it. Incidentally, it is quite surprising how well these pieces look in an elegant gray and white Louis XV interior.

Going back to the seventeenth century, the French designers made Louis XIII period armchairs very much like England's Cromwellian style, with spiral turnings, handsome but barely comfortable since the padded back was no more than ten inches high (illustration 406). Finished in stamped leather with brass nails, this was a highly presentable design which seems to call for an Elizabethan interior, or the English country-style room with a gateleg table and Jacobean molded dresser. This style was popular here in the early twentieth century, and curiously enough it mixes well with a variety of modern pieces.

347

403. French Empire

404. French 2nd Empire

348

405. Charles X

406. Cromwellian

349

407. Louis XIV

408. Louis XV

350

409. Louis XVI

Of greater general esteem in the United States for almost a century for the more formal interiors have been the French furniture styles of the Louis XIV, XV, and XVI periods. Even that of the Louis Treize era has grown in appeal during the past few years, largely because of the availability of reproductions of these massive pieces being made to a smaller scale, for use in present-day rooms, alongside less unwieldy types.

One of the great Louis XIV fauteuils is the subject of 407, from which it will be observed that the style owes little comfort to its multiple curves, and its 18- to 20-inch-high seat. Much better proportioned for the average person is the Louis XV fauteuil of 408, which is roomy without being particularly massive, and a seat lower by at least two inches. This piece, which is upholstered in Beauvais tapestry, is in the style of Juste-Aurèle Meissonier (1695–1750), carved out of walnut and gilded. The accession of Louis XVI to the throne in 1774 coincided with the influx of German cabinet makers and a growing interest in neo-classic designs so that by 1780 a typical fauteuil was something like that shown in 409, though many had spiral turnings on the straight, tapered legs. The one shown is of beechwood, carved and gilded.

Up to this point all the chairs shown have been actual antiques, though some of them were copies made in one country from a style originating in another. The latter specimens are, in other words, not originals but copies, though made long enough ago to be classed as antique today. Their value therefore lies to a great degree in their age and this will, in turn, be reflected in their patina, providing they have been properly cared for over the century or more since they were made. In any event the good ones, whether originals or early copies, are likely to be extremely valuable, particularly if rare and even unobtainable on the market. This gives rise to a further question that needs to be considered by both the owner of the residence and the decorator regarding the status of copies (i.e. authentic reproductions) of the old pieces, made at the present time. Such are not only available but are so well made by hand in the early manner from aged material that even experts would find it difficult to detect the slightest difference.

All the carvings are in the solid wood where in cheap

410. Régence fauteuil reproduction. Original by Menier (1715-1723).

411. Régence bergère reproduction. Original by Michel Cresson (1715-23).

352

412. Louis XV side chair reproduction. Original 1740; scroll *pieds-de-biche*.

413. Louis XV, Genovese fauteuil reproduction. Original 1715-74.

415. Louis XVI bergère. Original by Georges Jacob (1774-92).

414. Louis XVI side chair reproduction. Original about 1784.

354

416. Louis XVI fauteuil reproduction. Original 1774-92.

417. Directoire high-back bergère reproduction. Original 1795.

355

418. Gothic fauteuil reproduction. Original 1830-33.

imitations they would be applied, and neither glued-up stock or facing woods are used so that the new should last as long as the antique. Each of the chair styles presented here has certain definite characteristics which distinguish it from any other among those shown. For the most part these differences can govern their degree of compatibility so that they need to be studied with this in view. It will also be helpful if the outline, posture, character, and scale criteria are applied.

Modern Designs in Wood and Fiber

In the 1860's and 70's some interesting and practical furniture was devised by Michael Thonet using round-section beechwood bent into fantastic shapes. Widely acclaimed was his rocking chair of "bentwood" which is once again becoming a popular piece, even to the point of being refashioned in aluminum. Other designers meanwhile have developed wooden chairs in which the parts are not only bent after pressure-steaming but shaped (sculpturing is the preferred term) as well. Hans Wegner's 1949 creation in oak and cane (illustration 419), is a good example. More recently the combination of bending and shaping (without the use of laminated materials) has been applied to comfortably upholstered pieces as in the "Curvelle" chair of 420. Here the back supports are sculptured into wide flat arms that add to the graceful appearance, while the seat and back provide large areas for decorative fabrics.

Notable advances also have been made in the application of that historic — and exotic — furniture material rattan, both in forming joints and in bending, as 421 shows. The joints here are locked together by rawhide thongs shrunk to secure permanent tightness. An equally spectacular development in the application of rattan to furniture design is the use of larger-diameter pieces which can be squared and otherwise treated as ordinary lumber while taking advantage of the density of the material and its high tensile strength. Pieces whose frames are made in this fashion are shown in 422. The hand-carved, pierced panels with brass inlays are made in India, and the furniture designs, as usual with rattan, are inescapably oriental.

An outdoor group in quite an exotic style but owing

419. The Hans Wegner sculptured chair of oak (1949) has a cane seat wound through the bent and slotted frame. Sometimes the steamed-and-bent back also is cane-wrapped.

357

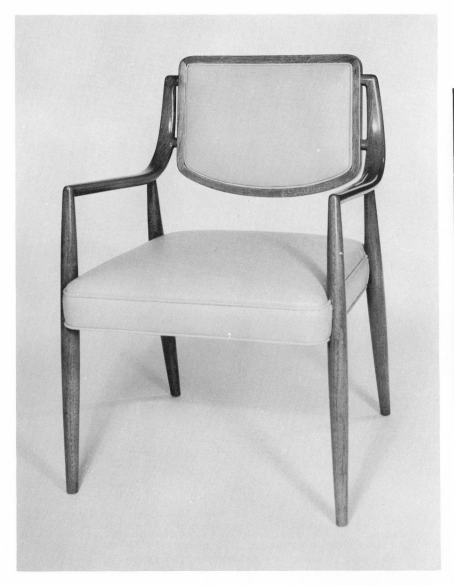

420. The "Curvelle" combines wide bent and sculptured arms with an upholstered seat and back to form a strong and rigid side chair of considerable grace. Given the proper upholstery material it should be compatible with several period styles.

421. Thong-lashed joints add strength to beautifully designed rattan pieces such as these, waterproofed, for use indoors or out.

358

nothing to rattan is that of 423, which is all redwood except for the plastic table top and the brass-shafted canvas shade. Though extremely sturdy in appearance, it is actually quite light in weight and beautifully made, with a mandarin-style umbrella.

Some of the most attractive indoor-outdoor furniture is made of wicker, and photographs 424 and 425 show two of the most delightfully practical designs ever made. These are calculated to associate amiably with sunroom pieces in iron, bamboo, or redwood, or even Chinese shapes in teak or rosewood, particularly against a background of things growing. Equally amenable are the smaller but highly comfortable pieces in raffia, 426, shown in a suitable environment though ready to lend their charm to someone's bedroom if required.

Metal Furniture, indoor and out

There are a number of modern furniture pieces which can be introduced into certain period or contemporary rooms because of their compatibility with a variety of earlier styles, regardless of the materials from which they are made, or even their finishes. This fact is vividly exemplified by the widespread use of such well-known designs as the Barcelona chair of Ludwig Mies van der Rohe; the molded, pedestal-type armchair of Eero Saarinen; and the wire armchair of Harry Bertoia. Although made largely of metal, these are found associated with widely differing furnishing schemes, old and new.

Metal furniture for indoor use is, of course, no new thing. It was extremely popular during the Napoleonic era, and some of the most beautiful tables and guèridons were made of bronze during the Louis XV period, many seemingly adapted from designs unearthed in Herculaneum. Iron furniture of the throne or heavy armchair type, some of which probably could be traced back to ancient Egypt, was made in the ninth century, and rustic iron rocking chairs were popular in the nineteenth century. Nevertheless, wood has always been the most favored material, thanks to its availability, ease of working, and decorative qualities. However, from time to time much of it has been adorned with metallic substances, often gilded, suggesting that there is no inherent objection to the use of metals for furniture construction (as

422. Heavy rattan can be squared and otherwise shaped in making furniture combining the utmost comfort and convenience with exotic beauty as these pieces demonstrate.

423. "Bamboo"-legged pieces made wholly of redwood —
except for plastic covered cushions and formica top — is not
only durable but far more portable than it looks!

360

424.

witness the return to popularity of iron and brass beds!) once the problems of manufacture have been solved, as they have in recent years. A number of such furniture items in iron or steel or aluminum which have stood the test of time are illustrated. These have all proved their adaptability to interiors furnished largely with wooden pieces, and others equally good are rapidly becoming available.

For many years outdoor furniture has been made of metal. In Victorian times most of it was of cast iron; today is may be of wrought-iron, steel, or aluminum, and some of the designs are not only quite at home in the patio or garden room, but look exceedingly well in the closed porch or even a living room with the usual rugs and draperies, and case furniture. Particularly delightful, and far from unwieldy, is the metal furniture in 427. Though delicately patterned, it is as well suited to the modern roofed patio as the potted plants themselves. Two other types (428 and 429) are shown, which are equally versatile.

Distinctive Groupings

Almost all interiors are made up of individual furniture groupings — the exceptions being rooms too small to accommodate more than one assembly of units — and in any such interior there is customarily one major grouping which sets the tone of the whole room. This latter rule, however, is not so utterly rigid that in eclectic furnishing it must consist of more than one style or period of pieces. Neither is there any reason why, in a room using antiques, these should set the pace, regardless of the setting although this is one of the most important factors in determining the mood.

Normally the setting or background will have been designed to do the best for the entire furnished room and not for any particular style of furniture, new or old. Furthermore this background may have several aspects — differing textures, colors, and shapes — since it includes the floors and walls and ceiling together with such architectural features as doors and windows, fireplace, arches, recesses, and so on. As a rule all need to be unified to some degree which, in simple terms, means "planned."

Equally important is the scale of the furniture which

361

425.

426.

363

427. Metal furniture such as this is often used indoors as well as in the patio or garden, the cushions offering opportunities for variation in color and pattern.

must be arranged to produce a sense of balance between related units, not forgetting that color (lightness or darkness) and the degree of solidity (all legs or all body) need to be taken into account as well as overall size. This affects the relative placing of the individual items, that is, the composition of the group which must be balanced within itself as well as with its background including the size of the wallpaper pattern, if any. The remaining groups are then related to the principal one as regards quality and general style though they need not be of the same design or pattern or even of the same finish. As a matter of fact, in some contemporary interiors the décor may be designed deliberately to emphasize the unconventional, stressing the unexpected by associating the most disparate objects. Cleverly done, this can be not only amusing but useful in establishing a theme or introducing a note of novelty into what would otherwise be trite and uninteresting. Such a gambit however should never be attempted by the inexperienced tyro.

In the principal group of any interior there is usually one dominating piece, but this is not always essential. On the contrary, many such pace-setting groupings may occupy a corner of a room, dividing the pieces into two sections of approximately equal weight, one against each wall, instead of centering them against the principal wall or straddling a fireplace. A good example of this is represented by 437, in which the furniture is definitely traditional in pattern even though the pieces are actually either reproductions or adaptations from antiques. In this arrangement attention is divided between the sofa under a large ancestral portrait, and the tall curio cabinet against the adjacent wall — once the eye can be lured away from the magnificent tray of cast brass, gleaming like gold, that serves as a cocktail table in the foreground.

The Philadelphia-style sofa in its cherry-pattern chintz needs the oil painting to help it counterbalance the height of the cabinet, just as the cabinet needs the velvet-upholstered wing chair to lend it weight. The picture is completed by a tub chair which faces the sofa across the cocktail table, though the hexagonal table in the corner and the heavy lamp upon it, plus the two smaller canvases are needed to tie the divided group together.

Another corner grouping which involves quite a different problem is presented in 438. Although this picture

leaves part of the grouping to the imagination it shows enough to indicate that even a corner doorway need not involve a waste of space. Quite properly this door and its surround are given the same finish as the wall in order to diminish its importance so that attention can be concentrated on the furnishings. A certain amount of traffic space is preserved in the door area by placing a boldly

428. This modern outdoor dining group combines square metal tubing with plastic webbing of chair backs and seats and a formica table top. This, too, may be used indoors.

patterned, light colored oriental prayer rug parallel to the door wall but separated from it by a small bamboo bench. In the corner beyond the door, and between it and the window, is placed a striking piece of tall furniture, definitely oriental in feel, which not only emphasizes natural materials — bamboo and teak — but is topped by a fascinating and unusual objet d'art behind glass, a colorful detail visible across the room.

This tall cabinet is not, of course, the centerpiece of this grouping. It is, however, an important factor in

365

429. Bertoia chairs, minus upholstery, shown as a dining group with a petal-type table, will withstand the weather outdoors.

430. The famed "Barcelona" chair, designed in 1929, is of chrome-plated steel with seat and back cushions of leather, supported on leather slings. Thanks to its innately springy construction it is extremely comfortable in use while its clean lines render it adaptable to many period interiors.

431. The Saarinen pedestal-type armchair (1957) is of molded plastic reinforced with fiber glass on aluminum and enameled. It has a fabric cushion. The table, having the same type base, is shown with a marble top though a slender wooden one is often substituted.

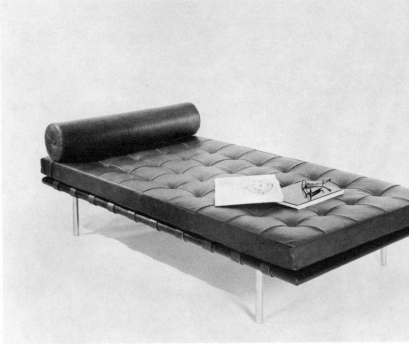

432. This is the Bertoia chair (1952) made of chrome-plated steel wire mesh on a frame of black-iron rod, the seat section padded and covered in fabric. Sometimes the back is left exposed, using only a seat cushion.

434. A daybed designed by Mies consists of a tubular rectangular frame on stainless-steel cylindrical legs, with the bolster-type pillow strapped in place and therefore adjustable.

435. The modern coffee table, also designed by Mies, supports a heavy plate-glass top on a cross-base made of rectangular steel tubing — the acme of simplicity and stability.

433. A modern descendant of the Louis XV ormolu pedestal table or guéridon is this stainless steel modern creation with a glass top, which is compatible with furniture of many periods.

436. Modern sofas tend to be massive, with extra-thick cushions and padding which not only adds to comfort but results in an imposing piece of furniture which would add dignity to any room. Such designs, many of which are of Italian origin, are well suited to coverings of the new materials among which simulated black leather, heavily button-tufted, is a decorator's delight. For use with period pieces, however, a decorative fabric, treated in the manner shown, may often be preferable.

369

437.

438.

439.

establishing its location as an area of prime interest. The completed group actually takes in the tall window with its nubby, woven hangings, a rich yellow in color. Centered in front of this is the major furniture piece — a sofa in heavily brocaded material, behind which a long sofa-table supports a tall lamp whose massive and highly decorative Chinese porcelain base is gay with chrysanthemums and birds.

In the matter of style, the foregoing has little in common with another type of grouping shown in 439, which gives the effect of greater formality because of its symmetrical arrangement. The three principal pieces here are two tall cabinets balancing one another across the Chippendale-style loveseat between them. To counteract the discrepancy between the height of the sofa-back and that of the cabinets, a large four-light applique is mounted

371

440.

441.

442.

on the wall, flanked by a pair of oval gilt frames displaying antique coins. To complete the ensemble a window at each end of the wall is draped with ceiling-high draw-curtains, while a butler's tray type cocktail table in front of the sofa leaves space on either side for an easy chair. Whenever necessary, other chairs can be drawn up from a separate grouping beyond the center of the room.

An equally interesting but more austere and modern-looking group is 440, which mixes the old and the new while leaving large expanses of plain wall free of decoration. The focal point of this group is an oversize trumeau on the wall over the sofa — a splendid creation elaborated with a rococo molding and a floral painting in the upper panel which occupies only one third of the frame. This mirror has a twin-candle carved and gilded sconce on either side of it, the three pieces centered over a large sofa which is slightly curved.

The trumeau extends upward within a foot of the ceiling, quite overshadowing the bookcase-cabinet which rises a mere five feet seven inches against the nearby wall. In the corner between the two is a French Empire guèridon, or round table, supporting a lamp whose shade top is level with the top of the nearer sconce, though both are lower than the cabinet's cornice molding. The rest of the group consists of a coffee table, and two round-backed chairs, and all are tied together by a geometrically carved rug which runs the length of this side of the room.

It should be noted that the cabinet, though comparatively small, is extremely attractive, largely because of the grain pattern in the walnut and cherry woods of which it is made. To have surmounted it with any wall piece would have made it seem smaller than it is and thereby reduced its significance in the setting.

At the opposite end of this room there is another and quite different grouping (441), which serves to establish a longitudinal axis for the furnishing. This second grouping is confined to the end wall, and is tied in with the sofa-wall of (442) by a duplicate pair of swan-design wall sconces. The basic piece of furniture here, however, is not a sofa but a low chest whose importance is increased by a group of three unequally sized pictures which ascend between, and slightly above, the sconces. The chest is unlike the cabinet but has the same flat front and a decorative grain.

373

The accompanying pieces in this group are an Empire style armchair and an adjustable wing chair, with a late eighteenth-century bouillotte lamp so that the same atmosphere is preserved, and both room ends are tied together by the light-colored sculptured rug.

Still another method of grouping is the subject of 442, which has a fireplace as the central feature, with a marble-topped, painted chest on one side and a slightly taller chest of cherry on the other. Each is surmounted by a pewter, vase-based lamp. On the wall over the cherry chest is a pair of framed montages, one above the other, and below them a number of books occupying the same linear space. Centered on the other chest is a growing plant which keeps the balance about even.

Between these two chests is the fireplace of plain, white-painted plaster with a bronze-mounted architectural mirror over it, and a French mantel clock centered on the shelf. In line with the paneled chest, and at right-angles to it, is a six-foot sofa with a five-foot cocktail table separating it from a round-backed armchair at the opposite side of the fireplace. The heavy sofa is therefore in line with the seemingly lighter painted chest, the armchair being opposite the darker chest which has a heavier visual load, thus somewhat evening the score.

The sofa also has a two-foot diameter French guèridon at its outer end, but the armchair allows space for its twin within reach of the end of the cocktail table to which it can be drawn in the more convivial moments, despite the fact that the rug is barely wide enough to include it.

Turning to the next picture, the balance of furniture arrangement in 443 has obviously little to do with conversational grouping as such but it does illustrate the advantage of having an important fixed center for any formal setting.

That setting here is a room-high french window which serves as a light source for a study desk. Also centered on the window, some distance away, is a Chinese table used in studying books under artificial light when the window is sealed off by the silk-covered folding screens. Between desk and table are a couple of light but sturdy reed chairs of the rawhide-bound type which are normally placed one each side the window. The tidy instincts of the owner are revealed by a tall Chinese beaker and the pair of Indian sculptured heads placed so as to balance

443.

one another on the desk top. On the floor an Oriental rug sets the limits to the chair and table location in relation to the window.

The group in 444 is a simple study in balance and design which incidentally draws attention to this example of a modern substitute for the old-fashioned dining-room suite. The quietly elegant rectangular sideboard is paired

374

444.

445.

with a round table whose base has the same architectural character though the two pieces have interestingly different colors and finishes. The sideboard is stained malachite green and antiqued, but the table is finished a light honey brown. A third form is introduced by the tall, slender chairs which add a note of lightness and grace to the ensemble. These match the table in the color of their woodwork, but they are upholstered in a green and gold mixture designed to reflect the green of the sideboard, the whole assembly constituting a lesson in tying together three otherwise disparate pieces into a pleasing whole.

Finally, in 445 is an example of perfect balance in an architectural setting, beginning with a beautifully pedimented and carved double doorway leading from a parquet-floored hallway down shallow, handrailed steps which could have no higher function than that of enabling guests to make a regal entry into the drawing room below.

This room has been described on another page, but here the emphasis is on its axis which extends from this doorway between two crystal chandeliers to the floor-length window opposite. At the window side of the room mahogany consoles flank the triple sash, leaving space between them for a writing table with a cane-back armchair on either side of it.

The window matches the doorway in dignity with its double-swagged valance, its straight-hanging draperies whose shoulders are squared off by dark and narrow cascades. On either side the window, from console to cornice, chinoiserie panels of colorful birds and exotic flowers occupy short sections of the curving wall whose graceful contour is matched by that of the great oval rug which occupies most of the floor.

On the mahogany consoles are six-branch candelabra and carved Chinese figurines, on the table a porcelain flower bowl on a stand of lacquered bronze, completing a picture of perfect symmetry and expressing perfect taste — the crowning glory of skilled and knowledgeable interior design.

Glossary

Amphora

Beaker

Amphora: Greek clay wine vessel with bottom pointed to stand in soft earth. Sometimes footed.

Atrium: Center court, or square hall in modern house, usable as sitting room, giving access to other rooms.

Aubusson: Tapestry factories at Aubusson, France, began making Savonnerie type carpets without knots in 1789 to cartoons by Beauvais. Closed down 1819.

Barochetto: A gay Italian style of flower-painted furniture.

Beaker: A tall cylindrical vessel of ceramic, glass, etc., with swelled lip for pouring; also footed type with beak.

Beauvais: Tapestry factory founded 1664 near Paris. In Louis XV period made furniture coverings also.

Bergère: A chair with closed arms.

Biedermeier: German style of furniture, 1815–48.

Boiserie: Interior woodwork, wainscot, etc.

Bombé: Bulging sides and front of case furniture. Bulbous or kettle base.

Bouillotte lamp: Lamp with adjustable shade used on bouillotte card-game table.

Boulard chair: Chair designed by Jean-Baptiste Boulard (1725–89), Parisian menuisier to Louis XV and XVI — pieces of generous proportions.

Bouillotte Lamp

Chaise percée: Night commode in form of armchair.

Chimére: A chimera; a she-monster having a lion's head, goat's body, and dragon's tail.

Chinoiserie: Chinese-style art and decorative items produced elsewhere than in China.

Coromandel: A reddish-yellow color, colcothar; also a Chinese lacquer, sap of the tree *rhus vernicifera*; also a folding screen painted with the lacquer in several layers, the outer ones cut into to form designs in a layer of the desired color.

Bureau-plat: Flat-topped writing table, usually with single row of drawers.

Cabochon: Originally an uncut jewel, or oval convex ornament, now also applied to decorative inserts of other shapes.

Canapé: Sofa.

Canapé à Corbeille: Sofa with ends curved in, basket-like.

Canterbury: A low stand, sometimes on pedestal, with divisions to hold sheet music, newspaper, etc., often on casters.

Caryatid: A draped female figure supporting an entablature.

Celadon: A color, grassy green to sea-green (yellowish green), also a Chinese porcelain of that color.

Caryatid

Curule: Any seat having crossed ogee-curved legs like two half-circles one above the other.

Cycladic idol: Any idol carved or sculptured by the pre-Mycaenian civilization (1600–1400 B.C.) of the Cyclades islands, now Greek.

Dentil: A tooth-like rectangular block, one of a series forming a decorative border.

Directoire: French Directory period (1795–99).

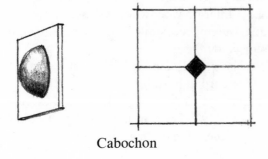

Cabochon

378

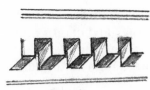
Dentils

Dufour, Joseph: Famed French painter of scenic wallpapers — Monuments of Paris, Bay of Naples, Cupid and Psyche, and Telemachus series (1825) most popular.

Églomisé: Painting and gilding on reverse side of glass, devised by French framer named Glomi.

Etagère: A what-not, or set of shelves on legs.

Fauteuil: Armchair.

Fauteuil de bureau: Desk chair.

Faux bois: Any surface painted to imitate some special wood grain.

Faux marbre: Any surface painted to imitate marble.

Gadrooning

Gadrooning: Fluting or reeding of a rounded edge.

Genre painting: Depiction of realistic scenes from everyday life.

Guéridon: Round table to support a candlestick, or any circular table, sometimes with shelves.

Guilloche: Ornamental band of interlacing curved lines.

Guilloche

Han Dynasty: Early–206 B.C. Late–A.D. 25–220.

Koa: Hawaiian fine-grained acacia wood.

Lavabo: Wash basin.

Lit de repos: Day-bed.

Menuisier: Cabinetmaker in solid wood (not veneers).

Ming Dynasty: A.D. 1365–1654.

Mutule: A block on the underside of a Doric cornice above a triglyph.

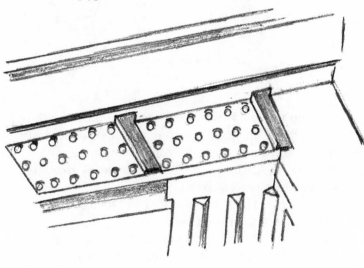
Mutules

Pecky cypress: Cypress wood rotted during growth so that pockets of powdered wood form interesting markings when sawn.

Pembroke table: A small rectangular table with a drop-leaf at either side.

Pied-de-biche: Doe-foot; form of foot much used on Louis XIV furniture legs; during Louis XV period deteriorated into a volute on a block.

Saracenic hardware: Decoration, hand-styled by Saracens whose Moslem faith excluded representation of anything in nature.

Savonnerie: The first French workshop to produce tapestry, carpets, and furniture coverings in foliage, flower, and bird designs. Name derived from soap factory originally occupied.

Scagliola: Artificial marble.

Secrétaire-à-abattant: Drop-front desk.

Serviteur fidèle: Tripod table with revolving round shelves on central post (also Servante).

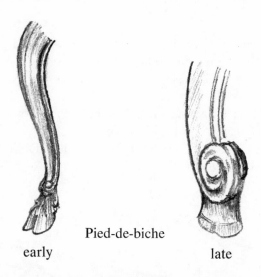

Pied-de-biche

early   late

Sgraffito ware: Pottery decorated by scratching through a layer of opaque glaze to reveal color underneath.

Shoji: Japanese paper screen serving as partition.

Spandrel: A triangular space enclosed by the curve of an arch and an enclosing right angle.

Spider-leg: Thin, round legs of small tables, etc., often turned to represent bamboo.

Strapwork: Narrow, decorative band or fillet folded, crossed, or interlaced forming part of a design.

T'ang Dynasty: Chinese, A.D. 618–907.

Egg (or Tongue) and Dart Molding

Tongue and dart molding: Alternating partial ovals and arrows (also egg-and-dart).

Tric-trac table: Backgammon.

Trifid: Three-toed; a form of furniture foot.

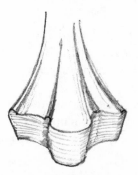

Trifid

Trompe-l'oeil: Literally eye-breaker; paintings representing three-dimensional objects.

Trumeau: Looking-glass incorporating a painting.

Verde antico: Green Italian marble.

Vermeil: Silver gilt.

Vitrine: Glass case for displaying objects.

Voussoir: Wedge-shaped brick or stone used to construct an arch.

Zebra wood: A brown wood from Guiana with vivid dark-brown stripes, used as a veneer in eighteenth century.

Zuber (Jean):   French producer of scenic wallpapers, 1804.

Acknowledgments

*Designers and Decorators**

Ethyl G. Alper, New York: 242
Altman-Dwork, New York: 251
Bachstein & Lawrence, A.I.D., New York: 281, 313, 314, 315
Mrs. Thomas H. Berry, White Pine, Tennessee: 1, 69, 108, 111, 259, 263, 387
Bloomingdale's, New York: 86, 87, 103, 278
Ronnie Brahms, New York: 322
John and Earline Brice, A.I.D., New York: 67, 156, 389
Rhoda Bright, New York: 317
Arthur Brill, New York: 283
George Clark Associates, Inc., Boston: 92, 93, 94
I. W. Colburn & Associates, Inc., Chicago: 41, 42, 139
George Doan, A.I.D., Philadelphia: 12, 97, 98, 101, 133, 180, 181, 182
Harry Dunn Associates, West Chester, Pennsylvania: 91
Audre Fiber, New York: 342
Eleanor Forbes, San Francisco: 71
Milton Glaser, F.A.I.D.: 282
Michael Greer, F.N.S.I.D., A.I.D., New York: 30, 31, 137, 138, 142, 143, 165, 195
Richard Himmel, A.I.D., Chicago: 280
Phyllis Horton, New York: 168
* Numbers refer to photographs.

Gerald I. Jerome, A.I.D.: 309
Carroll A. Johnson, Houston: 254
Barbara Joseloff, New York: 183
Melanie Kahane, A.I.D., New York: 151, 158
Paul Krauss, New York: 153, 235, 237, 239, 241, 245
Arthur Leaman, Shrewsbury, New Jersey: 233, 236, 238
Dorothy Liebes, New York: 341
Emily Malino, Inc., New York: 335
Ellen Lehman McClusky, A.I.D., New York: 102, 318
Mallory-Tillis, Inc., New York: 155, 159
Lois P. Monroe: 244
James Childs Morse, A.I.D.: 175, 247, 250
Muller-Bachich, Ltd, New York: 152
Paul Associates, Inc., New York: 205, 206, 207, 208, 209, 210
Bette Sanford Roby: 248
Renny B. Salzman: 334
Henry Sheehan, Inc., New York: 249
St. John Simpson, New York: 246
Stark & Ranes, Ltd, A.I.D., Philadelphia: 4, 5, 29, 33, 34, 35, 39, 40, 65, 83, 128, 134, 137, 141, 144, 173, 200
Jack Steinberg, Shrewsbury, New Jersey: 233, 236, 238
Virginia & Archibald Taylor: 368
Thedlow, Inc., New York: 13, 14, 15, 46, 47, 48, 49,

Photographers

Manufacturers, Institutes and Associations

Miscellaneous

Index

Numbers in *italics* refer to illustrations.